The Maravillas District

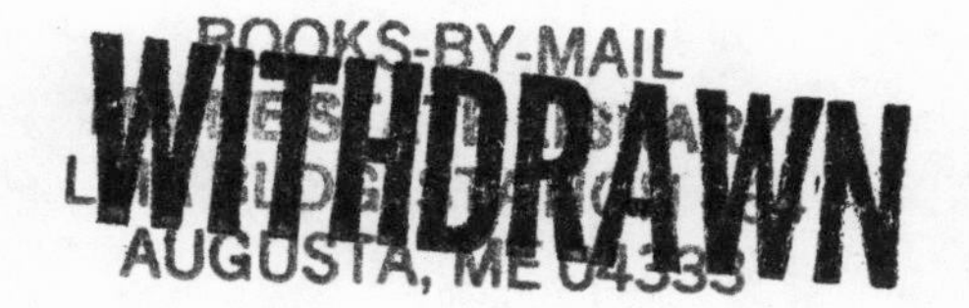

by Rosa Chacel

The Maravillas District

(Barrio de Maravillas)

Translated by d. a. démers : Introduction by Susan Kirkpatrick

The University of Nebraska Press : Lincoln and London : 1992

Originally published
as *Barrio de Maravillas*,

Manufactured in the
United States of America
The paper in this
book meets the minimum
requirements of
American National Standard for Information
Sciences – Permanence
of Paper for Printed
Library Materials,
ANSI Z39.48-1984
Library of Congress
Cataloging in Publication Data
Chacel, Rosa, 1898-
[Barrio de Maravillas.
English]
The Maravillas district /
by Rosa Chacel;
translated by d.a. démers
p. cm. – (European
women writers series)
Translation of:
Barrio de Maravillas.
ISBN 0-8032-1449-9
(cloth: alk. paper). –
ISBN 0-8032-6353-8
(pbk.: alk. paper)
I. Title. II. Series.
PQ7797.C412B313
1992 863-dc20
92-8098 CIP

Introduction

SUSAN KIRKPATRICK

Rosa Chacel belongs to the brilliant generation of Spanish artists that were born at the beginning of the twentieth century and moved into the cultural vanguard in the 1920s and 1930s – Federico García Lorca, Luis Buñuel, Salvador Dalí, José Alberti, Vicente Aleixandre. As a young artist, a sculptor and a writer, she participated in the ferment of Madrid's cultural and political life during those decades. But the flowering of her generation, and of Spanish culture in general, was cut short by the historical rupture produced by the Civil War: when that bitter conflict ended, the generation of artists and intellectuals to which Chacel belongs was either dead or scattered in an exile that lasted, for those who survived so long, until 1975. Whereas after the disruption of the German Occupation Marguerite Duras – to take the example of a Frenchwoman of Chacel's generation – was able to continue writing in the context of the fellow writers and reading public with whom she had shared the experience, Chacel was forced into an exile's precarious existence, first in Brazil and then Argentina. The events that destabilized Chacel's career have also affected the cultural history of twentieth-century Spain, obscuring among other things the place of the woman artist.

Since Franco's death in 1975, the recuperation of lost bits of

Spain's cultural history has begun. Not only is attention now being directed to the writing of women in the early decades of this century, but the women writers themselves are also giving us their own accounts of their experience in that period. Of the several autobiographical works recently published by women born at the beginning of the century, Chacel's accounts of the early part of her life have aroused the most critical attention in Spain. These works include *Desde el amanecer* (*Since Dawn*, 1972), an autobiography recording her childhood, and a trilogy of autobiographical novels, *The Maravillas District* (1976), *Acrópolis* (1988), and *Ciencias naturales* (*Natural Sciences*, 1988). Her project – recreating through memory the quality of earlier experience and at the same time subjecting the remembered experience to scrupulous analysis – can best be compared to that of Proust; yet Chacel's style, her theory of memory and of the word, are uniquely her own. The peculiar 'time warp' that gives much of modern Spanish literature its distinctive quality can be observed very clearly in Chacel's work: because of the rupture in Spanish cultural continuity, she is bringing to fruition in the 1970s and 1980s a project conceived in the artistic climate of the 1920s and 1930s. The result is striking – something of that earlier moment lives and breathes in texts that also show themselves to be fully aware of our contemporary preoccupations with the relationship of language and subjectivity.

It would be tempting to say that Chacel rewrites Joyce by offering a portrait of the artist as a young woman, except that the latter term would have to be plural, since Chacel focuses not on the alienated individual but on dialogue, on interactive discovery. *The Maravillas District* recreates the daily life of two girls and their families who live in a small apartment house in a slightly seedy district of Madrid during the second decade of this century. The narrative traces the two girls' growing consciousness of their artistic and intellectual vocations, emphasizing both the invincible impulses of imagination and intellect through which they encounter the world, and the enabling power of their mutual support.

The narrative present of the novel begins in the early spring of 1912 with the developing friendship between thirteen-year-old Elena, the daughter of a singing teacher and the granddaughter of an opera composer (the maestro), and eleven-year-old Isabel, whose unmarried mother earns her living as a seamstress. Near the attic, an unused room which the girls call their studio serves as a retreat where they can practice drawing, all the while discussing and subjecting to mutually fascinating analysis their perceptions of the other inhabitants of the building and the neighborhood. In the course of the novel, the girls are engrossed in the affairs of another family that lives in the building: Doña Laura, who runs a small school for girls, and her beautiful but rather vacuous younger sister, Piedita. The death of Doña Laura's sister-in-law; the visit of her widowed brother, a professor and scholar, with his son Ramón and his brilliant young disciple, Montero; Piedita's marriage to rich Mrs. Smith's widowed brother: these are capital events in the lives of the two friends, the intimate context in which Elena and Isabel begin their transition from childhood to adulthood, exploring questions of existence, identity, vocation, and sexuality as integral aspects of daily life. The novel ends in the hot dusty days of September 1914, as the two girls anticipate their matriculation in the Academy of San Fernando – the most prestigious academy of fine arts in Madrid – and wonder about the new world that will open for them as they commit themselves to vocations in painting and sculpture.

Readers familiar with *Desde el amanecer* (*Since Dawn*), Chacel's account of her childhood, can identify the situation narrated in *The Maravillas District* as closely corresponding to that of the young Rosa during the period when she and her mother lived with her grandmother in that same district of Madrid. According to the autobiography, it was during this time that the author, reveling in the relative freedom she found in this heterogeneous and colorful urban neighborhood after a childhood in a provincial city, began to choose a path in life, a vocation in art, for herself. Thus much of the material in this novel and the adolescent working-out of identity that it recounts are drawn from Chacel's own life. But it would be misleading to suggest that *Barrio de Maravillas* is essentially an intellectual autobiography. It has the multidimensionality, the dialogical quality, of a novel.

Art is a central theme in the novel's exploration of the relations among psychic reality, identity, and social interaction. Indeed, the narrative begins with the series of events that leads to Isabel's first trip to the Prado Museum: a visitor at Elena's house has remarked that Isabel looks like a 'Carreño,' and Elena organizes an excursion to the Prado to show her friend that the remark, far from being an insult, refers to the portraits of the royal Hapsburg family painted by the seventeenth-century Spanish artist Juan Carreño. Although Isabel concludes that the Carreños are really rather unattractive, this discovery opens the realm of art to her and allows her to identify with its values, with an 'elegance' denied her by the mothers of her schoolmates who will not let their daughters associate with her. It is also through her identification with these seventeenth-century portraits that Isabel first expresses her budding feminine sexuality by copying the hairstyle of the Infanta Margarita of Austria as a way of teasing and enticing Luis, the pharmacist's son across the street.

The connections Chacel draws among art, identity, and sexuality crystallize around a key motif: Ariadne, which is the name of Elena's mother, of the opera composed by the maestro –

Elena's grandfather – and of a statue in the Prado that inspires Elena's sense of her artistic calling. The mythical associations of the name are explored early in the novel in the special meaning this myth has for the maestro. Ariadne supplied the thread that led Theseus through the maze to light, life, and love, and the maestro associates her with the beauty that inspires both erotic pleasure and transcendent longing. The conception and gestation of his daughter coincide with his decision to devote himself to creation rather than performance; Ariadne is the name he gives both to his first composition and to his daughter. But there is another side to Ariadne: she was loved by Dionysus, and it is this darker aspect of the myth that obsesses the maestro as he struggles to compose his masterpiece, the opera *Ariadne*, while raising and training the lovely, talented human Ariadne. The coincidence of creation and procreation culminates in Ariadne's marriage to a young poet in whom her father has found not only a son-in-law but the ideal librettist for his opera. This fruitful interaction between the musical arts and the literary arts is echoed stylistically in the recurring fragments of sixteenth- and seventeenth-century Spanish poems around which the maestro's reflections on artistic transcendence crystallize. The most important allusions are to Fray Luis de Leon's ode to the sixteenth-century composer Francisco Salinas, which celebrates Neoplatonic notions of music's correspondence to the ideal, and to a baroque sonnet by Francisco de Quevedo in which the poet compares his passion for an unresponsive lady to the magnet's eternal attraction to the cold North.

In the legacy that Elena receives from her grandfather, then, 'Ariadne' is a term that unites human love and artistic endeavor under the sign of eros. At the Prado, she has created a ritual that acknowledges this filiation in her own calling to the art of sculpture: she circles round and round a statue of the sleeping Ariadne, chanting Ariadne's lament, an aria composed by her grandfather and set to words by her father. Isabel is introduced to this cult when Elena explains the significance of the small statue of Ariadne that stands on the piano at which her grandfather had composed the opera. Ariadne, concludes Isabel, 'is something very much ours . . . as if it were our saint or our Virgin on the altar of music' (33). Indeed, Ariadne is the presiding icon in the girls' relationship to art.

Elena's erotic relation to the mythical figure is somewhat different than that of her grandfather or her father, however; for her, Ariadne is both mother and art. The connections are explored in Elena's reflections as she listens to her mother working with a singing pupil on the *habanera* from *Carmen*:

> *Elena sees the agility of that pudgy hand – pudgy, sedentary – which dominates the keys as though Ariadne were making them sound by a direct command of her thought. The keys* say 'io t'amo' *because the hand thinks it, the dimpled hand that she, Elena, kissed and nibbled when she was a baby, the hand that knows how to say* io t'amo. *So she, Ariadne, has said it because, if not, she, Elena, would never have existed.* (148)

For the adolescent girl, the eroticism of mother-daughter love, the shaping power of the artistic idea, and the sexual mystery of her own origin are all profoundly intermingled in the figure of Ariadne, mother-opera-statue.

As the cluster of associations around the Ariadne motif suggests, the girls awaken almost simultaneously to their artistic vocation and to their sexuality. At a key moment of the narrative, for example, Elena – having recognized the other girl's talent in her ability to correct an embroidery pattern – proposes that Isabel begin to practice drawing just as the two begin their first conversation about boys. Art and sexual fantasy are inseparably tangled in the infatuation of the girls' friend, Felisa, with a young man whom she calls 'the Bohemian' and whom she watches pass by every evening while she buys milk: he's a poet, she assures her friends, and is undoubtedly on his way to some well-known café to drink wine, or even absinthe, with other visionaries. But Felisa's greatest exploit along these lines is her use of a Schubert violin sonata as an intermediary in her flirtation with a handsome young German in the apartment house opposite hers.

The connection goes deeper, however, than the aesthetic coloring of romantic daydreams. Chacel insists on the erotic roots of the aesthetic impulse. As Elena and Isabel sit sketching sculptures in the Prado, the narrator's voice suggests the erotic sources of their commitment to the forms they see:

As if you'd closed your eyes and could hear only what they ordered, the obedience they demanded, feeling the compensatory mystical pleasure . . . a response, a corroborating echo rising from the depths, the final depth. Because it was as though your feet and hands, the pulsing in your chest, the stab of hunger, the soft, tense bellow or the incalculably extended stretching of limbs, came from . . . not exactly from the sexual organs, but from the rootage – that immensity which can be estimated well when looking at an elm: innumerable buried branches, tender little rootlets advancing, penetrating hard earth – and the awakening of Eros spreads out . . . through the veins? Yes, through the veins too, but it penetrates, moves and shakes the diamantine realms of thought. (259–60)

This erotic awakening – most explicitly described in Isabel's account of what Elena helps her to recognize as her first dream of sexual arousal – characterizes the girls' relationship to the world as a whole at this time in their lives. The narrator, in fact, identifies the sexual crisis of puberty as a crisis concerning vocation and identity: 'To understand the drama, the irrefutable fact of vocation is the crisis of puberty, because eros begins with life but advances silently, at life's own pace toward the season of genesis, the spring' (135). This idea is reiterated later in the reflections of Manolo, who views the girls from a teacher's perspective:

You can see it in their eyes, in the way they blink in admiration before an image, before a name. You can see they're in heat, in rut, because they've reached the season of genesis. They swallow everything – I don't know what elemental creature is fecundated via the mouth, as the mind is: fertile in direct proportion to hunger – but they would reject any theoretical drug that would counteract their appetite. And their appetite inspires respect. (269)

The calls to which Elena and Isabel must respond in working out their identity and their calling include more than the calls of myth and artistic heritage, more than the calls of their own flesh and inner being, of their immediate familial context. History both positions and incites them through all the concrete forms it takes in daily life. The girls are conscious of their modernity, for example, in their unreserved response to the experiences new technologies make available to them. The tram that carries them to the Prado or to Piedita's new house in the ritzy Salamanca district had been around for at least twenty years and is treated affectionately as an old friend. But the cinema and the phonograph are new marvels that occasion rhapsodic interior monologues on the realms of pleasure and imaginative life opened up by these inventions.

As the two girls discover their artistic vocations, their pursuit of their calling is inevitably channeled along lines prescribed by history. Elena develops a passion for the modernist poetry she hears recited at the Atheneum, a venerable Madrid cultural and literary institution. She and Isabel perceive a correspondence between *modernista* poetry – a Hispanic movement that should not be confused with the broader term "modernism" – and the English Pre-Raphaelite painters, reproductions of whose works are brought back by Piedita on her return from her honeymoon. In the house of Mrs. Smith, Piedita's sister-in-law, they also discover works by Maeterlinck and Mallarmé. True daughters of the fin-de-siècle era, they are drawn to the aestheticizing, antirealist tendencies of such works, and feel in them the expression of impulses at work in the maturation of their own generation.

Social and political history is at work, too, in the daily reality in which the two young women are growing toward adulthood. Dramatic events, such as the assassination of Prime Minister Canalejas in 1912, break through their obliviousness to larger public issues, though Elena can only apprehend this event in its concrete impact on her personally: its coincidence with the death of Doña Laura's sister-in-law in Zamora, its reflection in the arguments between her grandmother and her father, and in her father's letter of condolence to his former boss in the Ministry of Public Education. Concern with the collective destiny of Spaniards, however, is a significant element in the familiar matrix in which Elena breathes and thinks. Her father's thoughts reveal the perspective of a liberal intellectual on the deepening crisis of the Spanish state at the beginning of this century. Canalejas was seen as a leader who could restore the credibility of a corrupt system; his assassination was attributed to the machinations of a traditional oligarchy that – as events were to demonstrate conclusively twenty-four years later – was willing to resort to any level of violence to preserve its rule. The most elaborated meditations on the state of Spanish society come from Manolo, Laura's professor brother, in a diatribe to his disciple, Montero (223–26), and in a long internal monologue on the threat of war near the very end of the novel. In these monologues, Chacel offers a remarkable reconstruction or interpretation of the consciousness of the famous dissident generation of intellectuals and writers, the generation of 1898, which opposed the values of the oligarchy and sought new ways to rouse the Spanish people from what these intellectuals regarded as its apathy and ignorance. Manolo rails against the failure of his own kind, the intellectuals, to reach the people and at the same time reveals his own paralysis, his sense that the pursuit of knowledge precludes action. In defining the historical consciousness of Elena's parents' and teachers' generation, these monologues, fraught with anxiety and self-doubt, establish a ground on which the narrative can pose the question that concerns it: what about the new generation that was reaching its season of genesis in 1914?

If the first half of the novel focuses on the myth-shrouded enigmas of origin, creation, and procreation that preoccupy the adolescent girls, the last half – particularly, the last third – brings to the foreground the enigmas of history, posed for Elena and Isabel in the mystery of Montero, Manolo's disciple. He becomes their mentor, their guardian angel, but he belongs to another world they cannot fathom. Unlike any of the other major characters, the narrative voice never identifies with his consciousness and he remains as much a mystery to the reader as he does to the girls. Hints are dropped in the reading he suggests for Elena – Dostoevsky's *The Insulted and Injured* – and the plays he encourages them to see – *Juan José*, a socially conscious naturalist drama about the plight of the Spanish lower classes. While the girls go to the Prado to sketch, Montero goes there for brief, whispered meetings with other young men. It is through Montero, who teasingly calls their taste in art 'decadent,' that the girls learn that the realm of aesthetics is neither autonomous nor exempt from conflict, but consists rather of 'condensations of the mind' that 'rush to battle with one another with the violence of ocean currents' (271).

Only with the assassination of the Archduke of Austria in Sarajevo, the precipitating event of World War I, do Elena and

Isabel begin to glimpse what Montero is up to. The narrator describes the news of impending war as ominous storm clouds that accumulate on the horizon of all members of the network of family and neighbors, most of whom sense only vaguely and inarticulately that their lives are going to change. Manolo is the most lucid about the war's significance – 'We are beginning a chapter of History' (262) – but he confesses himself unable to convert his lucidity into action, even in relation to his pedagogical vocation. It is his student, Montero, who makes the decision to act, breaking with his mentor, with the bemused intellectualism of the preceding generation:

In the end, what had to happen carries the day. It's not a good-bye; it's a conclusion. The person who is true to himself goes by himself. The professor stays, defeated not by ideas, but by events. The disciple departs, emerging from the clouds, leaving them behind as though the only way to challenge the storm were to take it upon himself: to become a storm, to fill himself with storm. For the first time, his gaze was not empty: the decision that filled it made it seem blind, blind with decision. (275)

The specific form of Montero's commitment to participate in and shape history is never made explicit. The professor's sarcastic references to his student's asceticism suggest that he had submitted himself to the discipline of a party such as the marxist Socialist Workers party (PSOE), which was organizing a powerful mass movement in Spain at this time. The significance to the girls of Montero's parting hug as he calls them for the first time 'comrades,' is the realization that they have other options, choices to make that go beyond the personal, as they face a future that is determined by collective life as well as individual vocation.

The question of their relation to history is posed for Isabel and Elena in the query left them by Montero. His confidant and proxy, young Ramón, Manolo's son, passes it on:

Sometimes we would talk about the two of you, and we would suppose one thing or the other. If such and such a thing were to happen, what part would the aesthetes play? . . . What good are those aes-teatlets? *Do you get it?* (279–80)

One part of this question refers to the relation between art and history, of course. Early on in the novel, the narrator had stated that art and history cannot be separated, that the pursuit of art's truths has a positive impact on collective life. Elena and Isabel, poised to begin their training as artists while Europe crosses into a new chapter in its history, must work out their own answers to that question. They cannot do so, however, without taking into account their gender, a factor playfully – and condescendingly – indicated by Ramón and Montero in their derivation of *aes-teatlets* from aesthetes (the phonetics work better in the Spanish: *estetas* becomes *es-tetas*). Ramón suggests that to play any part, to be any good or of any use, the two might, like the Amazon they were sketching the day the Germans invaded Belgium, have to cut off those parts of their anatomy, or more accurately, of their mentality, that identify them with their sex.

The novel makes it clear that the two girls live in a social world in which femininity has been identified with neither artistic achievement nor political activity. Piedita offers the most conventional model of femininity, and at the beginning of the novel Elena is totally absorbed in Piedita's emerging destiny, fascinated by her passive, unreflecting identification with the role of being beautiful, of being the object of desire. Yet, once Piedita is married and off on her honeymoon, the girls reject this form of femininity, realizing that they do not miss her because she was never a person, a someone who could be missed. But what are the other options they see in the women about them? Eulalia, Elena's grandmother, seems to have shared none of the aesthetic passion of her husband and represents to the adolescent girls the domineering power of conventional and petty concerns. In the next generation, the mothers of Felisa and Isabel are as passive and as uncomprehending of what lies beyond the domestic sphere as the traditional stereotype of the Hispanic woman. Doña Laura, the freethinking schoolteacher, offers a model of a woman committed to intellectual life, but she defers to the authority of her brother, the professor, and cannot entirely free herself of nostalgia for comforting religious certainties. Ariadne, loving mother and talented pianist, comes closest to combining femininity and vocation. Yet instead of enjoying the brilliant career as performer and composer that her father did, she spends her life in the daily drudgery of voice and piano lessons for uninspired pupils. 'She could have gone to the top!' muses her husband, 'Why didn't she?' (168–69). No doubt she did not because Ariadne encountered much the same attitudes that Elena and Isabel must deal with when they announce their intention to study at the Academy of San Fernando: 'To aspire to that purity, that loftiness. To make it [their] profession, to take it so seriously as to . . . It was too much!' (258).

The girls do persist in aspiring, in taking their creative powers seriously, facing the unresolved question of how that vocation can be reconciled with their gender and their sexuality. They have toyed with this issue before: Isabel has unsuccessfully attempted to deal with it by rejecting sexuality for herself altogether, while Elena has imagined a solution in a fantasized identification with the movie star Francesca Bertini, who, Felisa observes, always places herself so that her screen lover will have to rise up to her level for a kiss. But Ramón's and Montero's assumption that they must give up some aspects of their femininity to be 'good' for anything gives the question of gender new urgency. In the last pages of the novel, the dilemma is presented in visual terms by the statue the girls happen upon in Madrid's large park, the Retiro. Bare-breasted, representing 'something big,' perhaps Tragedy, the statue stands there in the posture of a person who is tearing her hair out. Faced with this icon of feminine desperation, the two girls decide they must assess the double bind Montero and Ramón have posed for them: 'It seems to me we have to settle down and think about their theory that we're going to have to cut off quite a few things,' says Elena. 'We're left with the . . . question: how much of it is true?' And Isabel replies, 'That's it – that's what we've got to figure out' (283). On this open note *The Maravillas District* ends: the question can be answered only in the concrete living of their vocation and their sexual identity, in the processes to be narrated in the sequels to the novel.

While the narration poses the relation of art and gender as a puzzle the two protagonists must solve, the text itself as a style, as a form, may suggest some answers. Many voices compose the narrative; they are heard directly in dramatic dialogue, overheard in interior first-person monologue, and often conveyed indirectly in third-person narration. Among them is also heard a distinctive narrator's voice that seems to speak from a more comprehensive and temporally distant perspective. This voice affirms without hesitation the creative power and authority of the feminine. It speaks of the productive powers of the humble Antonia's 'sacred maternal zeal; an art, or rather, a handicraft: creation. Nature – woman – abhors a vacuum; she feels, she sees – the supreme abstraction – what is lacking, what is needed, and invests herself with the power to create from nothingness' (42). The identification of woman with nature has, in the dominant Western system of gender differentiation, implied woman's relegation to the status of the material, the other, the object. In Chacel's text, however, this association implies woman's productivity, her creativity – her *conscious* creativity, because she sees. The passage just cited ties in with several other passages in which male characters – Elena's father, the poet, and the intellectual Manolo – reflect on creativity, the envisioning of that which does not yet exist, the productive flow of representational discourse, as the essential human gesture in the face of nonbeing, death, nonmeaning. The text implies that the activity of the seamstress mother belongs to the same category as the activities of the composer or philosopher that are so significant to the male characters.

In effect, Chacel refuses to differentiate reproduction and production into oppositional categories. Eros unites them. In a meditation on art as the impulse to transcend biological destiny, the narrator uses figurative language that represents creation and authorship as maternal rather than paternal:

> *[M]an leaps over [the bounds of material being], leaps to what is beyond them, desiring to procreate in a beyond that he will never reach but will possess as an inalienable signature, the sign of his contribution . . . paternal . . . maternal perhaps, because the desire is long sheltered and nourished by one's own substance and entrusted to those made of the same material . . .* (193)

Shifting uncomfortably from the universal masculine pronoun to the strictly neutral 'one' and then to the feminine adjective 'maternal,' this passage plays out the struggle between the gendered language of transcendence and the female subject. In active resistance to a language that identifies transcendence as masculine, Chacel sprinkles her text with metaphors of maternal procreation as generically human creative activity. 'The womb of human endeavor,' asserts Manolo, 'admits, takes in and shelters all semen' (270).

Analogously, the narrator represents women's relation to history as an intimate connection rather than as an exclusion. Reflecting on the sound of knitting needles that serves as a background for the apprehensive awareness of the outbreak of war, the narrator observes: 'It would be interesting to calculate just how many stitches it took to cover with breeches and stockings masculine legs marching off to fight the Turk or to conquer the American Indian' (272). The reflections that follow bring to the foreground the contribution of women's traditional work to human history:

There wouldn't have been a tricoteuse *among the hetaerae of Sappho: there they wove a many-leveled theory known as Music. There was weaving in pastoral Judea, and the loom produced taut threads. Later came the interweaving of tiny loops that link with one another in chains of hooks and eyes that go from right to left and from left to right and go on hooking up with each other until they cover whole spaces to form elastic cloths that warm and protect bodies . . . This is what the women always did, while the men . . .* (273)

Weaving has been regarded as the invention and the characteristic creative activity of women, but Chacel, while asserting that weaving stretches from the concreteness of the loom to the abstraction of theory, highlights the subcategories of knitting and crocheting, emphasizing the continuous chains of linked loops and the elasticity of the product. Women's interconnective activity, creating structures that are not rigid or fixed, but that move and breathe with life, is celebrated, while men's activity is dropped from the text, its place indicated by three dots and then the silence of ellipsis. Instead of describing what men do, the narrator goes on to a contiguous topic – the pain, the terror of historical crises marked by war.

This textual figure – the imagery of knitting and the elliptical gesture relegating men's history-making activity to the blank space of the page – can be read as a model of Chacel's writing itself, of the texture and the structure of the narrative. Composed of strands of different voices, interlinked, hooked at innumerable points to one another to form a tissue of connected experiences and subjectivities, the novel leaves to the silent spaces of its web the activities that histories are typically made of – economic production, collective public political action. This does not mean that men are left out – not at all – but that they are included specifically and exclusively in their intimate participation in the network of shared confidences that makes up the narrative, shared with each other or with the reader in the overflow of internal thought processes. 'The act of confiding,' observes the narrator, is 'the kingdom, the universe of women.' But this reciprocal exchange of secrets, of intimate self-narration, which the text compares to an exchange of sweets, is scarcely a trivial matter – Far from it: 'In the communication of mints and berries the secret's nuances are personified and achieve their strict and real truth, their deepest, most exquisite and labyrinthine truth through the elementary terms, the reticences and simplicities of common speech' (142). Truth in this novel is an intersubjective construct, achieved in the chains of intimate communication more closely associated with women's everyday discourse than with the lonely meditations of the philosopher.

Such a model of truth and textuality informs Chacel's distinctive style, which flows along chains of discursive links that are broken off by ellipses, then loop back to hook up with other rows of imagery and lines of logic. Her sentences weave back and forth, tracing a weblike truth that emerges in the dialogue between voices, between the utterly concrete and the very abstract, between the irreducibly personal and the expansively interpersonal. In this novel, for example, interior monologue alternates between the first person and the more inclusive impersonal construction permitted by the Spanish use of the reflexive pronoun. Far more deftly than any of the English equivalents – such as the awkward passive voice, the too formal impersonal pronoun 'one,' or the too colloquial impersonal 'you' (the latter being the alternative most frequently used in this translation) – the Spanish construction used by Chacel breaks the isolation of the singular 'I' and hints at the potential plurality of the speaking subject.

Although Chacel's text rigorously, insistently, follows a logic of association, testing identities and differences, her sentences have the elasticity of the knitted fabric, of mental processes, of language itself: they refuse the tautological logic of the same, which has been associated by Derrida and deconstructionist feminism with the phallologocentrism of Western philosophy. In what may be read as an ironic allusion to the deconstructionist critique, one of Manolo's monologues characterizes the paternal instinct as insisting on just such a tautology of identities:

> *The paternal instinct sees itself in everything, feels itself responsible for everything – even the first word uttered on the face of the earth . . . And with the security of an instinct, with the desire to be eternal that characterizes its shots at what it wants to be, it wants to go on overseeing, guiding or directing the words still to be pronounced and will not accept controversies that are never settled . . .* (270)

Chacel refuses to heed the patriarchal claim that language belongs to men, or to accept the controlling tautologies of patriarchal logic. The search for meaning that she unleashes in every sentence – if that term can properly be used for discursive units that do not always have clearly defined predicates – never comes to rest on a fixed proposition, but pushes on in new directions or pauses provisionally to await a new impulse from the multivoiced symphony of social interaction – from language itself.

Chacel's writing is dense and labyrinthine, but at the same time it is open-ended and dynamic, shaping a narrative design that ends with a query instead of a conclusion. This novel can be hard going for a reader, but its seductive power is irresistible to those who allow themselves to feel its enticement. Preserving that power in the translation is no easy task: Chacel explores the Spanish language, that distinctively shaped and shaping medium of thought, culture, and social interaction, as the most intriguing maze of all. The English translation is of necessity a rather different text than the original, an interpretation of Chacel's narrative in another medium. The most one can hope for is that some of the rewards available to the Spanish reader have been made accessible to the reader of English.

The Maravillas District

The bell rang in a very special way. It rang in a special way every afternoon, but on that day it was even more out of the ordinary. The bell's sound gave away the hesitancy, the uncertainty of the person who pressed it fearing that the individual called would not answer, and at that point she did not. It rang as always: first a tentative, scarcely audible sound and then a brief irremediable ring. There it is – it rang now, and one must wait. Elena did not open the door. Before the door did open, steps that were not hers could be heard approaching. But there was no turning back: the door was open.

'Have you come to see Elena?'

Is there any answer to an unnecessary question? Is there any reason to ask a person who does the same thing at the same time every afternoon what she's doing? An affirmative response indicates a certain sense of guilt. Yes, of course, why deny it, just like every day. Why else would one come? All this in a simple:

'Yes, Madam.'

'Well, Elena is not in. She went out with her friends.'

Then a banal, clumsy, evasive good-bye, like someone caught doing something wrong, and a half-turn toward the stairs. Toward the way one goes up, but without doing it, with dragging feet in a torrent of zigzag thoughts, coming and going, spreading out in concentric circles with the impact of each stone, each thought falling as though it were the first time. Well then, who am I? Those, the other girls, what other girls? Her friends. What am I, then? Who am I?

'Isabel!'

This in a vibrant and captious voice from the immense figure which has not yet closed the door.

'Isabel, could you do me a favor?'

'Yes, Madam, whatever you wish.'

'Come in, then.'

To go in alone, alone without Elena, to cross the dark foyer that fills up with light when the door to the parlor opens and then enter the parlor alone; I stay there by myself for several minutes.

'Look at this, it's very fine linen. They don't make it like this nowadays. Do you know how to pull threads?'

'Yes, Madam.'

'My eyes are too bad for me to do it anymore. Look, it's all marked with little crosses. Do you think you can do it?'

'Yes, Madam, I know how to do it very well.'

'I figured as much. You're as handy as your mother.'

My mother doesn't know what I'm about at this point, but I'm sure she would like to. She would say to me, 'See that you do a good job.' I don't know if I like what I'm about either, but I want to do a good job. I want to show them that even though I'm alone . . .

'Sit down here in this chair near the balcony. There'll be enough light for awhile.'

Being alone now has a certain something, a certain distinction . . . they say military distinction is bravery . . . bravery is a distinction. To be here alone and do a good job so that later they say . . . I'd be satisfied if they didn't say anything, as long as they don't say I did a bad job. Alone now with the door closed – I don't know why they closed it, but I'm glad – I'm not afraid. And I have no desire to rummage through things because Elena has already showed them to me one by one. Besides that, pulling threads takes up my time and lets me think about whatever I wish. If the little crosses are not in the right place – and I think they're not – I know how to fix it. Doña Eulalia must have made them. If it had been Elena, there would be absolutely no mistakes. Her grandmother could have asked her to pull the threads, but Elena had to go out with her friends . . . What must they be like? I know their names because Elena has mentioned them from time to time. From the way she says their names, you almost know what they're like. I'm positive she despises them all. For her, they're all little so-and-so and little what's-her-name. She never calls me Isabelita. But she calls them Pilarcita and Encarnita . . . She really doesn't like the latter, because one day she actually called her Encarnacioncita. What a stupid name! And the expression on her face when she said it! The face she makes when she comes out with something like that. And even when she doesn't say anything. It seems like she could kill somebody just by the things she thinks . . . Kill or just the opposite. I don't know what's the opposite of killing, but I think you can say it like that. The problem is that it's hard to tell when she's thinking something good or something bad. That's the way it was with me the first day. And my mother didn't even wait to pay attention to me. I was telling her that this girl had found out about everything and now she was going to tell everyone. 'That's silly, she couldn't have found out about anything.' 'I'm positive, Mama, I'm sure.' She raced up the stairs two-by-two – although it seemed to me four-by-four – like a spider. She was nothing but skin and bone, but with a red dress so pretty that it was hard for me to say she was horrible. Well, she also seemed good-looking, but at the same time . . . well, horrible, no. The only thing I could manage to say was, 'Mama, Mama, there's that girl. Do you see her? She's going to tell everybody!' And we sat together quietly, waiting for something to happen. We didn't wait long. But I was quick to think, making plans and decisions. That girl – there would never be anybody in the world I could hate more. Then she came back up, four-by-four, just like I figured. She didn't even look at me. She asked my mother if she would come down a minute to her apartment. My mother was terrified, and the girl calmed her down as if she thought my mother was just afraid of wasting time. It would only be a minute, to talk to her aunt. She went running down the stairs, knowing that my mother would be following right behind. And of course she went like a docile lamb, taking off her apron and arranging the hair that had come loose from her bun. When she came back up, her heart was still in her throat. 'You see, you're always thinking the worst.' 'What do you mean, always thinking the worst. She wasn't telling everybody?' 'Yes, but not what you were thinking. The lady in question was asking if we wanted the mason to whitewash our walls as well.' I was totally confused. I didn't know what to do with so much hate. I was furious, terribly furious. What people call disillusionment must be something like that. I don't know how long it lasted, but I held on to that feeling like something I didn't want to give up. But then things changed, almost at once . . . Afterwards, she would come up and sometimes we would talk. I don't know about what, anything at all, but it was hard for me to look her in the eye. I felt that she would guess what I was thinking. And she did guess it, although I didn't look at her. I would come back from school and she would be in her little room next to our apartment with her things. She would always say something to me, and I would try to cut the conversation a little short. But one day, everything changed: she invited me to look at her garden. I never went beyond the door, but she pointed to the pane of the dormer and I decided to look at how the sun shone on a little hedge mustard plant which had sprouted between some roof tiles. We stood there fascinated, looking, when suddenly a bird came to peck at it and then went flying off at once. 'It was a greenfinch!' When she said that, I finally looked at her. Her face had changed completely like . . . I don't know, as if it were all alight, as if that green bird . . . No: as though the green color of the bird had filled the room. And I thought that there would never be anyone in the world I could love more . . . But I also tried not to look at her so she wouldn't notice. I don't know if she noticed. At any rate, sometimes I thought it was that she didn't think it was too important, that if things are clear you don't have to mention them. And from then on it was as if we had forgotten that anything had ever happened. Well, nothing had ever happened, in fact. It was all inside my head, me thinking about whether I could hate her or love her. But Elena is a girl that could never happen to. She's never confused between a yes and a no. I ended up leaving it as she wished. Sometimes she would invite me to go downstairs to her apartment, and I would go. Or she would ask me to come into her studio – that's what she called her little room – and I would go in to see what she was doing . . . and suddenly it was decided I would go down to her apartment every afternoon. You come down, even if I don't go up to my studio. Come down around five . . . Footsteps – the door is going to open.

'How is it turning out? Let's see. Very good, very good. You're working fast! It's almost half done. And you weren't misled by the marks. It's correct, a master's hand.'

'It's really very easy, Doña Eulalia.'

'Not really, not really. Have you had a snack?'

'Yes, Madam.'

'What did you have?'

'An orange.'

'That's nothing. What you need is a little cup of coffee with milk.'

'Oh, thank you, but it's too much trouble.'

'No, it's no trouble at all. It's already made. My sister can't get along without it.'

She goes off and comes back at once with a tray.

'Listen, pull the music stand over next to you. We can put it here. They've left the two old ladies alone today. But stop working. First a snack.'

It was a big cup of coffee with milk and a plate with pastries, all on top of the music stand in front of the balcony. I always liked that music stand very much. The mottled tassels of colored wool that hang all around it have such different little faces that you want to talk with them. One day I said to Elena, 'Is this where they keep the music?' She cut me to shreds with a glance. 'Don't ever say such a thing, the music! Say pieces, methods, folios, scores, that's okay, but never say music.' 'Well, then, why do they call it a music stand?' 'Come on, they're not talking seriously. My grandmother is the one who calls it that. I think it's something she learned overseas.' And me like an idiot, 'You mean from those people in the overseas store across the street?' She almost doubles over laughing and starts teasing me mercilessly. 'Those people across the street, imagine! My grandmother babbling about music while they're selling Scottish dried cod . . .' She falls down on the bed and goes into another spasm of laughter. 'You're wonderful!' 'That means I'm an idiot.' 'I always say what I mean: you're wonderful!' 'There's no reason not to be polite.' Of course, I don't mind if she corrects me. Elena corrects me all the time, because she knows wonderful words: alabaster, for example. I had never heard the word, alabaster. I had thought that the little statue on the piano was wax, and she explained it was alabaster. 'It's my grandfather's

Ariadne.' Another blunder on my part: 'Ah, it's his first wife?' 'If she were, she wouldn't be here. There wouldn't be a piece of her left after my grandmother got finished throwing her off the balcony!' Later, she talked many times about the opera inspired by an ancient heroine . . . How beautiful she must have been, and how peacefully she sleeps up there. Could she know, that woman from another time – from centuries ago, I think – that something like this would happen? It's just fantastic to think that so many years later such a serious-looking man as this, whose face looks like that of a pale lion, would remember her and write songs about her. And nobody said anything bad about it; no one said that she was a woman who was a . . . Now that's another pretty word. The first time I heard it was from Doña Eulalia and I didn't understand it, but later Elena explained: a doxy. How could such a pretty word have such a bad meaning? The fact is that they didn't treat this one like she was one of those, because they put her there on the piano beneath his portrait . . . No matter what they say, he must have been more in love with her than with Doña Eulalia. That's why he named his daughter after her. And it's not that Doña Eulalia was ugly: she must have been really good-looking. But Ariadne – wow! – she was in a completely different league. That must be what happens when they perform the opera: they'll never find a soprano who looks the least bit like her. The one who came to study with Elena's mother, that Claudina Toscani . . . And Elena telling me that she was straight from Alcorcón, really Claudia López! 'Don't you see that Claudia's the only name that fits her? Look at those plums!' The fact is that we had never seen a woman with such large nipples. You could make them out no matter what she wore. Of course, she could never be dressed like Ariadne, because it wouldn't be permitted. But even if it were, it would be funny. Ariadne, on the other hand, sleeping there, looks like a saint. To tell the truth, I have no feelings about saints: they're like nice nuns . . . Well, martyrs are another question, and it seems to me that Ariadne might fall into that category. The bell! No, it can't be Elena because she went out with her mother who always uses a key. What do I do? I should go open the door so Doña Eulalia won't have to get up, but she's already coming down the hall.

'You open the door, Isabel. I have no idea who it is.'

Two ladies, two hats and two umbrellas placed in the stand. Shouts of surprise . . . Ernestina! . . . Eulalia! . . . softer exclamations . . . Paulita! . . . Eulalia! . . . Kisses on both cheeks.

'To what do I owe the honor? Because the last time you came to see me was ages ago.'

'You don't owe it to anything,' says Ernestina in her masculine voice, 'it's just that we owed you a visit. All the time saying we've got to go see Eulalia, we've got to see Eulalia, and the days go by. This morning I said to Paula that today's the day, and that's that.'

'Well, praise the Lord! Isabel, don't stand there in the doorway. Sit down in your little chair. There's still light for a while.'

Ernestina asks with a look and shrugs her shoulders. Doña Eulalia answers in a whisper: 'She's from upstairs.' They sit down.

'And what are you up to now, Ernestina? You've spent several years convalescing, but I imagine you don't even remember your illness.'

'No, you're wrong. I recall it perfectly well. It's not so easy to forget.'

'I think you got a bit scared, because angina pectoris seems like something tremendous. But we all thought you would come out of it quickly.'

'Yes, yes, everybody thought so, you're right, Eulalia; especially since the doctor insisted that it was a false angina.'

'But do you think I could have something false . . . even angina?'

'Now it's out! You consider the whole thing a failure. If you had your way they would have told you it was the worst angina in medical history, and they would have singled you out shouting *bravo!* and *encore!*'

'Listen, the *encore* part is what really got me down. I wouldn't have wanted to go through it again for the world, and I knew that was exactly what was coming.'

'Of course, you always want things to be big, you always go for broke – so the whole affair had to do you in.'

'No, Paula, no. What began to do me in was my age, and the angina would have been the perfect way for me to make a graceful exit. But what it did was make me see the . . . conventional (do you like the word?), that's it, the conventional aspect of my vocation.'

'You'll have a hard time discrediting yourself in our eyes.'

'Bah! if I tell you the truth you'll faint. When I realized I was going to have to take it a little easy, do you think it bothered me to put less energy into my acting? No, my little lambs, what made me sad was having to give up the champagne with my admirers.'

'Do you hear that, Eulalia? Have you ever heard such blasphemy?'

'Don't pay any attention. What she's saying is falser than the angina.'

'What do you two simpletons know? The one of you is trying to preserve the decency of our parents' name – our parents, who left us a bit of money so that we wouldn't have to work, by the way. The other preserving the memory of her husband's genius, a genius who . . . Well, we won't talk about it, but you're not going to tell me it was all a bed of roses.'

'Isabel! What are you doing working in the dark? There's no more light at all.'

'There's only one more run left, Doña Eulalia. If I don't finish today . . .'

'It's not important; you can finish it some other time.'
'But, I'll be finished in five minutes.'
'Such a nice girl, Eulalia. Does she study with Ariadne?'
'No, she's the little girl who lives upstairs.'
'Upstairs?'

A question in that mannish voice. A question filled with innuendo: but there's no apartment upstairs. What's upstairs, then? Is there even a garret? And if she doesn't study with Ariadne, what's the little girl doing here? A number of other questions that didn't ask a thing, but only confirmed. A rapid putting-together of things, so conclusive that no response is necessary. Then, the feminine voice once again . . .
'And what is she embroidering? Are you teaching her?'
'No, Paulita, she already knows how. She's helping me pull threads from a piece of linen I've had for a long time.'
'Ah, very handy. She seems quite well brought-up – and as blond as a princess.'
'What do you mean, as a princess?' – this in that solid, mannish voice – 'What she looks like from head to foot is . . .'

Darkness, darkness that explodes like a bomb. But it's a bomb that, instead of setting off a flash, puts out all the lights and means shadows: in one's thought, in one's common sense. A word that's a bomb of emptiness. It is what you cannot understand, what you cannot breathe, what goes against all life. And the word is repeated, and the more it is repeated the darker it seems – more wicked, more taunting, more opprobrious. Because it's repeated with approval, regarded as an arrow that has hit the bull's eye . . . The final thread comes out as though it were shedding impurity, as though it were sticky. It won't come out all the way, it breaks, and you have to look for it in a fabric which is no longer fine white linen but something handled, something dirty. Finally it appears, but it's better to pull it little by little so that it lasts until maybe you can see something. You can't see anything: the only thing clear is punishment, humiliation, to which anyone can be subject, like jail. Because if someone calls you a thief, you know if it's true or not, you know what card you're holding: slander or a just accusation. You can say guilty or not guilty. But you can't say anything to this business about 'from head to foot' . . . The door slams shut, leaving you paralyzed, as though your hands and feet were tied. Elena! My God! Why doesn't Elena get here? It's sounds like someone's coming up. Yes, someone opens the door – it's Elena (the whole piece of linen crumpled into a ball and thrown into the sewing basket, and Elena in the foyer. More shouts, greetings, kisses – an aside, a clumsily hidden aside).

'Elena, I have to tell you something.'

'Wait a little bit. I have to say a few words to those old witches. Wait for me in my room.'

'All right, but don't take long.'

'What happened? You have a terrible look on your face.'

'I'll explain. It was horrible . . .'

Hours, centuries in Elena's room. Hearing those disgusting voices. They can't possibly be telling her. No, for them she has no importance. They're speaking of other matters, which are probably just as disgusting. The tone of their voices . . . I don't understand what they're saying. Even if I heard them clearly, I still wouldn't understand, because they speak only to be understood among themselves. Ernestina dominates the conversation, and they all laugh at her jokes. She seems like a stud, controlling everything. Even Elena laughs! That's impossible! Does Elena understand them as well? Could she possibly think that they are right? If I tell her about this, and she doesn't clear it up, it's the last day of my life . . .

'Elena, I thought you'd never come.'

'But, what happened?'

'I don't know. I don't know how to tell you: something they said about me.'

'Something they said about you? But, you're not going to cry over that.'

'No, I'm not crying. I'm just mad.'

'Okay, was it one of Ernestina's jokes?'

'Yes, yes, but what a joke!'

'Tell me about it.'

'They were talking among themselves – not about very nice things, I imagine – and of course it seemed to your grandmother that I shouldn't be hearing. She said there was no longer any light and that I should leave off my work for another day. That called their attention to me, and of course they started asking questions. The fatty asked if I was one of your mother's students, and your grandmother started in explaining. But that's not the point. The other one, the one with that voice, said, like someone dotting all the i's and crossing all the t's, that I was from head to toe a "Carreño." What's a "Carreño," Elena?'

'Gosh, I don't know! Are you sure? Maybe you didn't understand right. I can't imagine Ernestina saying anything silly. She's no fool.'

'She might not be. But do you think your grandmother even asked her what she meant? Nothing of the sort. And the others all agreed, as if she had hit the nail on the head. What's a Carreño, Elena? Is it something so bad that you don't want to tell me?'

'Don't be an idiot, girl. Why wouldn't I want to tell you? I just don't know what it means. I've never heard the word. But if it's a bad word, it's odd that my grandmother would have said it, because she detests that kind of talk.'

'Well, she repeated it more than once. They they went on talking, but I couldn't understand any more. I think I lost consciousness.'

'Well, I can understand why you were bewildered, but don't worry about it. Are you sure that was the word?'

'As sure as the light of day.'

'All right, I'll look for it in the dictionary and I'll tell you tomorrow.'

'And if it isn't in the dictionary? They don't put in definitions of bad words.'

'Yes, I know, I know. But I don't think it's a bad word. Anyway, if I can't find it, I'll ask my father.'

'Would you really dare ask him something like that?'

'I ask my father anything I want. If he can't explain he tells me it's stupid or garbage. Go on home now. I'll tell you tomorrow.'

A terrible, terrible night. Not a wink of sleep.

'But you're not sleeping. Did you have something to eat downstairs?'

'Yes, Mama, just a pastry.'

'That wouldn't do any harm. Do you have a fever? Let's see. No, you're all right.'

Waiting, bearing the sleeplessness because it's impossible to tell what's happened. If my mother knew about it, she wouldn't see it like me, as something stupid, that you can't understand, a hurtful thing done blindly the way one throws a stone. She would think she understood, and she would think it was because of her, because she was my mother. I've got to bear this anguish the way you do if you fall into the water and have to keep from taking a breath. You have to stop breathing until day comes, hoping that things will be cleared up and fearing that when it is cleared up, it might turn out worse yet. Because it's impossible that things could turn out better. No, it would be impossible for Elena to tell me that it was nothing important. How could there be no importance in the fact that several persons all claim, repeat, and agree that the statement in question is true? That's the only thing I could understand, that the thought expressed with such emphasis was true, like an 'ah, of course!' Hours almost without breathing, without making a sound. It's hard to breathe deeply making believe you're asleep. You can't breathe hard or soft. You just look at the dormer window and wait for day to come. Light does come at last. Who knows how much time has passed. Maybe I slept for a little while. There are moments when you think the whole thing was a dream, and you feel a bit of relief as though your position in the bed were more comfortable, as if this calmness and silence were security and being out of danger. But then at once the anguish again, the threat of what you're going to find out because there is no certainty, because accusation can come along like a dog smelling straight on the track of something hidden . . . But it's not hidden, it's there for all to see. And now, now that there's light, I have to wait until I can go down and talk to Elena. Have breakfast, wash my face, brush my hair without breathing, without loosening this knot in my throat. Footsteps! Elena is coming up to the studio. It's so early. She never comes up so early.

'Elena!'
'I found out everything!'
'What did you find out?'
'Everything, everything you wanted to know.'
'What's it all about? Please, what did you find out?'
'I can't tell you.'
'Why?'

'Because I promised.'

'Who?'

'Myself.'

'Elena, you don't understand!'

'I do understand, and that's why I'm not telling you.'

'Is it so horrible, so shocking?'

'It's shocking, but not at all horrible.'

'Then it's not so bad . . . Elena, you're terrible if you don't tell me! You've found the word and confirmed that it's not so horrible?'

'Not only is it not horrible, but it's something excellent.'

'A Carreño is something excellent?'

'Very much so. One would pay several thousand pesetas for one.'

'For one! Are there a lot?'

'Not a lot, but a few. You'll see.'

'Where?'

'Well, let's see . . . it's now Friday, eight o'clock in the morning. Eight o'clock tomorrow morning, Saturday, would be twenty-four hours. Eight o'clock on Sunday would be forty-eight . . . plus two or three more until ten or eleven would make around fifty . . .'

'Oh, Elena, I can't believe it. How can you do this to me?'

'How can I do what? How do you know what I'm going to do?'

'I don't know what you're going to do, but I know what you're doing. Maybe you too thought Ernestina's little phrase was funny.'

'I don't think it's funny: I think it's astonishing. I told you, she's not a fool.'

'Maybe she's not a fool, but she's malicious; if it's something good or at least likable, why couldn't she say it in a way that I could understand?'

'Well, because if she had said it in a way that you could understand you still wouldn't have grasped how admirably – how . . . etc., etc., etc., – she hit the nail on the head.'

'Do you think I'm so dumb?'

'It doesn't have anything to do with being dumb. If I were to tell you now and even explain it to you, you still wouldn't know. It's not exactly that either. It's that you wouldn't understand what's important. What I want is to bowl you over with surprise, so you can taste the beef in its own gravy.'

'Gravy? Is it something you eat?'

'No, simpleton. It's not something you eat, it's something you see. This Sunday my father will take us to see the Carreños.'

'This Sunday? Where? Ah, I know, the zoo.'

'Cold.'

'Then, why Sunday? Does it have something to do with church?'

'No, you know my father never goes to church. But you're not so cold now. There's a synonym for church which is close to it. Can you think of a synonym for church?'

'No I can't, and it's not important. I imagine it must be any old piece of junk.'

'A piece of junk! Fantastic! A piece of junk as a synonym for the Church. And I won't explain to you what a synonym is, because I don't want you to figure it out. This Sunday you'll go to see them, but not with that air of a victim; because, if you don't brighten up right now, it means you don't have any confidence in me. Then to get revenge I'll tell you what a Carreño is and the charm is broken, it goes up in smoke. If I explain it, from A to Z, then you'll live forever without really knowing what a Carreño is.'

'I think I always understand the things you explain to me.'

'Yes, almost always, but this time it's not a question of understanding: it's a question of seeing and saying, Ah! . . . out of wonder.'

'Do you think I'll be afraid?'

'No, not when you see them. You wouldn't have a black dress?'

'No, I never had one. We have to go in black? What are you going to wear?'

'Me, anything. It doesn't matter what I wear.'

'But it matters what I wear? Then it's because they might think . . .'

'They can't think anything, the Carreños don't think – they used to think.'

'You mean they're dead?'

'They're immortal. But anyway, about the black dress: if you don't have one, you'll have to get it made.'

'Before Sunday?'

'Sunday morning. Ask your mother. She knows how to make something out of nothing. I'm going downstairs. I have to undertake the conquest of the Himalayas right now.'

'Your grandmother, right?'

'You're right.'

'And why do you want to conquer her?'

'It's a secret – something connected to a promise. Imagine, if I didn't keep a promise I made you, what would you think of me?'

'I would think the worst.'

'Well, imagine what I would think if I broke a promise to myself.'

'Oh, go fry eggs with your silly promises!'

'No, I'm not going to do anything in the kitchen today.'

So what does it all come down to? Apparently, it's not a tragedy, but things are still unclear. Not as unclear as yesterday – no, no, not like that, but still something like it. I said to myself: if Elena doesn't clear things up, if Elena agrees with them, if she's playing the same game as Ernestina, then it's all over for me. But she has not cleared things up completely. At the same time, she is not playing their game. She has invented another one on her own which also leaves me lost. And on top of that, she wants me to be happy and she talks to me about having confidence, as though she knew that I did distrust her for a moment. Of course, I can't distrust her, there's no reason for it, and I feel ashamed. It's not that I distrust Elena, it's that I distrust everything so much that my distrust overflows. Well, a lack of confidence is not something that overflows. On the contrary, it's something that sucks up the juice of everything. It's like a sump. It sucks up everything, but I won't let it.

'Mama, do you have something black to make a dress?'

'For whom?'

'For me.'

'For you? Who has died?'

'No one. It's just that on Sunday Elena's father is going to take us someplace.'

'Ah, I imagine. I read in the papers that a very famous children's choir is going to sing in I-can't-remember-what church, and since they're always going on about music in Elena's family, it must be that. But I didn't know you had to go to those things dressed in black.'

'I think it's something very special, but I don't think it has to do with a church.'

'Well, what could it be – in the morning and in formal dress?'

'Yes, I know, but Elena hasn't explained anything.'

'Well, the important thing is that they're inviting you. You have no idea how happy I am that this gentleman should take you with his daughter. He always seemed very nice.'

'I like him too, but I've never heard him say a word.'

'Wait a minute . . . wait, I can make you a nice little dress out of a skirt of mine. It's wool and it's rather worn, it's really old. No, better yet, I just remembered there's something I have in the bottom of the trunk which might be better. Come and give me a hand, we'll put it on the bed.'

'And this shoe box, what's inside?'

'Nothing, leave it alone, it can't be opened.'

'So I see. You've put a wax seal on the string. Did you think I might peek into it?'

'No, silly, it has nothing to do with you. Imagine if I got really sick someday and someone had to come and take care of me. At any rate, you never know what might happen: leave it where it is. Ah, here's what I was looking for – wrapped up two years ago.'

'But Mother, it's an Ursuline uniform!'

'Yes, it is. A lady I know gave it to me when she took her daughter out of the school, and I kept it for when you got bigger. You've grown so much that it fits you now.'

'I can't wear that. Some girl who recognizes it might see me and think I'm trying to pass for . . .'

'I'll fix it up here and there, and no one will recognize it.'

'But it's not even black.'

'It's almost black.'

'That's not what Elena wanted.'

'Call her and ask.'

'I don't think she'll want to come up. She's very busy today.'

'Go down and show it to her.'

'But it smells like moth balls.'

'Moth balls don't smell bad. It's a clean, pure smell. And besides, by Sunday it will have disappeared.'

'No, it doesn't go away so quickly. It'll never go away.'

'Then, you're going to tell her you can't go?'

'Ah, no, I can't tell her that; besides, I don't want to. No, I want to go with her on Sunday.'

'I want you to go, too. Go ahead, go see Elena.'

'But now? They must still be having breakfast.'

If the maid opens, I won't go in. I'll ask her to call Elena, though she told me she was going to be very busy. Who knows what she's up to? And if I call to her . . . No, Elena wouldn't get angry over something like that. I'll call, and she'll understand at once. She'll understand that I'm helping, that I'm collaborating in whatever she's working on. What could it be? What could she have concocted? What kind of 'play' will be put on? I wish I could imagine and guess before she tells me. But, how can I find out? I have to discover a clue, to see if I can find the strand that will untangle the whole ball of yarn. But, what strand? The business of confidence . . . Yes, that's it. Elena wants me to be very happy and she loves torturing me, making my blood run cold. I, above all, have to be very happy. The fact is that I probably am. Maybe deep down I do feel something like some sort of joy.

'Could you ask Elena if she could come out for a moment?'

'What's the matter? Is there another problem? Ah, of course, it's the dress. Let's have a look.'

'Great, Señora Antonia. Don't fix it up. It just needs to be ironed.'

'But, will it really be all right?'

'Perfect. I'll get on with my things. Don't come down today at five. I have to put the finishing touches on the project. Ah, when the dress is ironed, send it down and we'll put it out to air on the balcony.'

Trust. Now she's exploiting my trust. She's domineering. I've heard her mother tell her so, and at the time I thought it was unfair, but now I don't think so: Elena is domineering. But, so what? Even though she's like that, I trust her. My mother is not domineering, and Elena's isn't either. The two of them seem like they're always saying they're sorry, something which I can't stand, and I suppose Elena can't either. We're the same as far as that's concerned. We've never spoken about it, but I can imagine. Elena is domineering and would never tell anyone she's sorry. I don't know. I can't imagine what Elena could do that she'd have to say she's sorry for. Of course, if she makes a mistake, like stepping on someone's foot without meaning to – in that case, you say you're sorry as a matter of course. But for Elena to make a serious mistake, to do something bad – impossible. I don't want to delude myself, but the fact is that she is putting me to something like a test. She wants to see how far my trust in her goes, and, of course, she can only do this if she's certain I won't be disappointed in the outcome. But, what could it be, some fantastic beast? No, because those things are from other climates very different from ours. Besides, she said there are people who would give thousands of pesetas for one of them. No, it can't be a beast. Besides, she said they're immortal. Well, they say that parrots live for a hundred years, but they're not immortal. No, it's not a question of animals or beasts, because she says that at one point they thought. Two days to wait, and my mother will ask me about it, but she'll be satisfied with any sort of answer. It really hurts me to tell her something that's not true. I hate having to lie and, most of all, to my mother. Nonetheless, I can't tell her about the bad word. How could I convince her it's not a bad word? I could never tell her all that went before, the business about 'she's from upstairs' . . . and that voice, no, the look and the silence which said, 'From upstairs, but upstairs there's nothing.' My mother knows about that, of course, and besides she's always thinking about it. She's always remembering how we came to be living there, upstairs. And the fact is that she has trust, not in Elena nor in anyone in particular, but in everybody. In luck, I think, and above all in my luck.

To her it seems natural for people to like me. What I could tell her is what the other one said about the 'little blond princess.' That could have her bursting with pride, but I didn't tell her because to me it seemed disgusting. That's what made me think most about the upstairs business. I almost can't remember. I don't know if this means remembering, because now that I think about it, now I know what it means, but before I didn't know. I was like a baby, I knew how to talk . . . How foolish – as if talking were something one learns. Of course, one doesn't talk from birth, but when do you learn? I could already talk very well, but I didn't understand about things. I understood, of course, what my mother told me – 'We've found a little place, we move tomorrow.' And the next day we moved. 'You carry my little sewing basket.' And I went up the stairs with it, behind my mother who was weighed down with I-don't-know-what. Was I happy with the little place? I don't know, I don't know. I was pleased to be living alone with my mother, because before we were living with some other women. That's the thing: now I can see that my mother didn't like them at all. Here, of course, we had the old man in the other room who was a pain in the neck. My mother had to give him some of the food she made in the little oven. But one day he was too old to climb the stairs anymore, and he began sleeping in the tiny room off the entranceway. Then the business with the plasterer and the appearance of Elena. How much I hated her that first day. So much time, so very long a time – and now waiting until things are cleared up, sleeping, sometimes thinking . . . sleeping that is not sleeping. Lookouts and night watchmen never sleep at night, and when one is in bed it seems like you're not sleeping either, but from time to time you fall into a well and you stop thinking or you stay stuck on a particular thought. You fall asleep with a hope, with a fear, with something which can't go any further because there's no way for it to come back. And it gets light in the dormer and it's the next day. How will I get through the day without going down to Elena's apartment, without indignation, without sadness or disappointment? But all this is forbidden territory; it would be a breach of trust. I have to be calm and quiet here, with no complaints, as though I were in a jar like my dress hung out to air on the balcony. I feel that I'm hung out too, suspended from a cord. I'm hanging and waiting for what might happen, and I don't dare move for fear the cord might break. But it can't break, I have to have confidence in the cord. Maybe Elena will come up. I think I heard the door open below . . . Yes, and now the one in her studio . . . Elena with an egg in her hand.

'This is very important, extremely important. You're going to wash your hair with this. Warm water. If the water is too hot it cooks the egg. Then you rinse well, with a bit of vinegar and water.'

'But you're going, then?'

'Yes, there's no end to what I have to do. Ah, forget about curlers or braids or anything like that. Your hair has to be as clean as silk and combed straight.'

So much the better. A chore, something you have to do, that you can stretch out for almost an hour. Heating the water, putting the basin on a chair, a towel rolled up around your neck. And my mother:

'Yes, you've been really careless with your hair. She did well to tell you so, but I don't like the fact that she noticed it. Afterwards, you have to wash your feet.'

'Yes, Mama.'

'Better wait until nighttime, when you go to bed. Then they'll be clean when you put on your stockings. Can you put on stockings?'

'Yes, I think so.'

'Yes, it seems to me that white stockings always look good.'

My hair takes a long time to dry. First it hangs down over the damp towel, and then it gets a bit lighter. When the towel is taken away, my neck feels damp, but the dampness goes away thanks to the heat of my body. My hair begins to dry little by little and the locks begin to separate. When I run my fingers through them, the dampness goes away completely until they begin to feel like silk. That's what Elena said she wanted. I don't know what it looks like, but it's pleasant to the touch. I can't make a braid, because then it will be a bit curly and Elena said it should be straight. The Carreños must have smooth hair. Well, at least they have hair.

'Mama, the water's too hot. Don't worry about chillblains!'

'All right, I'll throw in some cold, but it's better hot.'

This rose-colored soap doesn't smell like roses, it only reminds you of them. You hold it in your hand and you don't seem to be smelling roses, but seeing them. I don't know . . . it's like cloth roses or roses made of porcelain or roses painted on the walls. I can't remember where I've seen them. Oh, of course, in a confectioner's shop. The smell of artificial roses, which are better because they don't wilt and you can even sleep with them under your pillow. All night long smelling painted roses. Porcelain roses, besides the color and the little sounds they make when they bump up against one another – I saw some once in a cemetery in an arrangement on the grave of a little girl, and I touched them: they were precious – they are also soft, but not like silk, not like my hair: a rough softness, a dull softness. Is dull the right word? The softness of my hair when it's perfectly clean is like a skein when you untangle it to rewind it. Softness – why do soft things make you feel better? I don't like this business of feeling better very much, because just because you feel better it doesn't mean that the illness or the sadness or whatever has gone away. Yes, you feel better, but . . . What I feel in the softness of things is as if it were just the opposite . . . But I'm not sure what the opposite of softness is. I'm not sure if you can say that suffering is the opposite of softness, but it must be something like that. That's why I find no comfort in softness. To me it's like looking into the window of a home that's not mine – a luxurious mansion with mirrors and crystal chandeliers – as if I saw that these things existed and I wasn't inside, but could see them. It's silly, but that's what softness seems like to me: the sensation of stretching out clean feet between just-washed sheets. It's silly, and that's what Elena would say, but if I were to explain it to her she wouldn't say that. I can also explain some things to her. I'm in my bed, and my feet are the ones I'm stretching out, but there's something new, and something not just like always: it's like a house I look into from time to time, like something they let me see, but which I'm not used to. Besides – of course, there is a besides – this feeling of feet and sheets is something I've had before. It was always very pleasant, of course, but nothing more than relief after letting my mother scrub every part of my body, jabbering away constantly about cleanliness. Now it's something else. Now everything is arranged as though something is about to begin, as though I were yet to find out where I might go with my white stockings and my black – or nearly black – dress and my hair smooth and loose the way the Carreños must wear it. No, no, I can't let myself be afraid of the idea of seeing them. No. I have to fall asleep with the idea that I'm going to go into a house which on other occasions I saw through the window and to sleep in a bed that is not my regular bed. Then light will come. And daylight must have come some time ago, because I can hear the bells ringing for Mass.

'No, we're not going to Mass today, because I don't want you to get ready until nine o'clock. Besides, I'm sure they're going to take you to some church. I'll put the rosary in your purse just in case.'

My dress! Nobody on earth would recognize it! In place of its straight, tight collar, it now has a trimming of white lace.

'Do you like it?'

How could I answer?

'Well, that's nothing. Sit down in case you faint. Now I'm going to show you my *capo lavoro* – a real masterpiece, you understand.'

'But this is impossible! How could something like this be made?'

'With patience. It's got twenty-seven little pieces. But I've always had patience with puzzles of this sort. So I would have what I needed, I had to butter up my grandmother and get her to let me rummage among the things in her trunk. There's a universe in that trunk! I spent more time in rummaging than in making the bonnet later. I wish you could have seen it, but I wanted it to be finished first. Look, I got the idea of making it like this from the shape of the pieces of velvet: they're like orange peels. But have you been struck dumb? Don't you have anything to say?'

'What can I say? Only you could make something like this.'

'But, do you like it or not? Let's see. Put everything on. My father must be dressed by now. He wants us to leave before ten because we'll be there – you'll see where *there* is – for at least two hours. Look, Daddy, she's just right, no?'

'Very good, perfect. But the bonnet not off to one side. It should have a more serious air.'

'Yes, you're right. Like this? I think it's all right.'
'Yes, very good.'
'Look, Daddy, look at her hair. Isn't it lovely?'
'Yes, it's really lovely.'
'And this fool doesn't take care of it.'
'Now she'll take care of it.'

The tram as far as the Puerta del Sol. Then another to the Paseo del Prado, and finally . . .
'Ah! Are we going to the Museum?'

Going on to a better life: of whom could this be said? Of heroes, saints, of those who have had a glorious death or those who have lived a miserable life? Of everybody, I think, because *better* implies a comparison, and what we're talking about is the incomparable, the incredible, the astonishing: something as easy as going through a door, a revolving door which seems to move by itself, without having to be opened. You just have to push it and move fast because it keeps turning and other people are coming behind, others who have to go through just like you. And you go through, and you're in a different world. What happens when one goes through? Nothing happens. What do you see? At first, you don't see anything – and what you don't see is a vision that makes you forget everything you've seen before. It's as though, suddenly, you were faced with what could never be. You're seeing, you're smelling an air which you've never smelled before, you're listening to a silence that is like a calm, a light, a gleam on the floor. You have to walk across that floor which reflects you. You have to follow the others, without really stepping on the floor, because everyone walks slightly above it. They advance through a very large room and you have to follow them and walk among those – paintings? No, who would think of paintings? You go past those places, among those people looking at you . . . Incredible people, some of them fearsome, armed, and some just the opposite – no weapons or clothing or anything. They're naked and not afraid of anything, calm as though nothing could touch them, as though nothing could hurt them. The women especially, with little children all around them – cupids, they seem to be. And I have to keep walking because Elena is pushing me, but it's impossible to break this spell, impossible to go farther because nothing better than this is conceivable, what's there before me. It seems infinite, it seems like it could never change but, at the same time, you're afraid it might change, afraid your slightest movement would make the vision disappear . . .

'Let's go. Go on. You've changed your mind about seeing them?'

'Who? Ah, of course. Are they here?'

'Yes, they're here, a little bit ahead. Let's not stop to look at anything until you see them. Then I'll show you everything.'

'You know what they're like already?'

'Yes, always.'

'Then if you knew where they were, why did you tell me you didn't know what they were?'

'Because the way you told me I didn't understand. My father understood at once.'

'Ah, your father understood. Why?'

'You'll see at once.'

Finally, at the end of the main hall, the *Carreños*. I think this is the name of the people represented, but Elena clears everything up. She tells me about the paintings, the name of the painter and the business about 'from top to bottom.' Now it seems to be clear. I look like one of them. Elena adds: 'Up to a point. You'd look more like one of them if you had to spend two months in the hospital, because these people were falling over from anemia.'

'You're right. My mother is always upset because I'm so skinny and pale. And the doctor says I'm not sick, it's just the way I am.'

'Right, that's the way you are. But you can't wear this dress ever again.'

'Why not? I like it very much.'

'Well, I don't. You see, that's why I didn't know what the Carreños were, because I never liked these paintings. The paintings I like are different, and you have to . . . It's not that you have to change, no, you'll always be like this, just like you are. But you see that nowadays people aren't so somber.'

'No, but they're not like these others either.'

'Ah, no, that one over there is a bacchanal, and there aren't any now because they don't allow them.'

'And what do you think would happen if they allowed them?'

Elena shrugs her shoulders. My question seems foolish to her. She takes me by the arm and shows me painting after painting. From time to time, she glances at her father, who's following us patiently. And sometimes he points out something for us so we don't miss it. But Elena, above all, wants me to see the ones she loves.

'You'll begin to learn about the painters, the periods and the works. What you have to do now is see characters that are just to fall in love with. Look at this one.'

He's blond with a light golden beard, a black and white suit – more white than black – and with a sort of large beret more or less on his shoulder.

'Who was this gentleman?'

'He wasn't a gentleman, he was a painter. Though maybe a painter can be a gentleman. He was a German. At any rate, he makes your mouth water. Don't you think so?'

'Just divine.'

'Now, here we have a lady.'

Halls and more halls, people naked and dressed, saints, warriors, angels, white friars, very pale gentlemen in mourning. Finally, a lady dressed in pink.

'This is Doña Tadea. It seems incredible that such a charming person could have such a horrible name. Look at her tiny waist and the way she's putting on her glove. It seems like she's floating on air, like a feather. You can love her very much too, but you can't talk very much with her. She's more like someone you just watch go by. Now you'll see one you already know.'

'One that I know? How?'

Rooms and more rooms, kings and princes on horseback on huge canvases in a large, not very bright room filled with a calm light. Ariadne – immense and immensely asleep. Soft, with the softness you only see in sleeping animals, like the foot of a sleeping cat, as soft as velvet. And the hard marble, sleeping in this softness, in this heaviness. Elena contemplates her.

'Have you ever seen anything so lovely?'

Elena croons, walking around and around Ariadne. The room is empty, except for the sleepy guard. This is a sort of special rite for Elena. You don't need to know if she's done it one hundred times before: it's something she does, that she's always done and will always do. Elena croons. You hardly hear the tune, but the words are not a muttering like in prayers. They're clear, whispered very low, but enunciated syllable by syllable. It's an aria or a romanza, it's the lament of Ariadne.

The waves, calling me, splashed on the hem of my tunic.
The waves called out: Awake, abandoned!

Elena goes on singing and walking around Ariadne. Her father stops looking at the portrait of a king or a horse or whatever and gives Elena a glance hard to define . . . A mocking glance, but tender. A look of connivance, full of secrets, like an affirmation of things repeated. She responds with the same sort of glance, but more evasive. 'Let me go on, we'll talk about it later.'

Exit. The Paseo del Prado as far as Cibeles Circle. Silence, because what can be said after what we've seen? We couldn't talk about anything else, and what's inside our heads can't be talked about either. Elena's father gets that mocking look again. But now it's not just a look, it's a comment intended to justify his mockery, referring to things gone by, to unfamiliar things, as if on hearing Elena sing he had smiled, thinking of a song less perfect than hers.

'How ignorant Claudina is. She's absolutely incapable of giving each syllable its precise value according to the notes. Six months practicing and singing the line with "hem," and she still can't see that's where the phrase reaches its climax and after that it pours out in a cascade.'

The tram again from Cibeles to the Puerta del Sol. Another tram via Fuencarral to San Vicente. A little bit of wind makes me sneeze, and the rosary falls when I take out my handkerchief.

'Ah, remember what I said: a synonym for *church* is *temple*. For me, a museum is a temple.'

Another slightly mocking and conspiratorial look from Elena's father, to which Elena responds:

'You can't imagine, Daddy, what this child said when I asked her if she knew a synonym for church. She said she couldn't imagine and it wasn't very important, but it must be any old piece of junk.'

'Magnificent! It could be a very nice sentence in a story describing a sacristy, for example . . . "There were censers, wine vessels and other synonyms for church . . ." '

The three of us arrive at the entrance-way laughing and giggling. Convulsive laughter that made it impossible to go up without holding onto the banister. One floor, another, and then another. Elena rings the bell with all her might. Doña Eulalia opens. Elena laughs and coughs. She can hardly breathe.

'Oh, we're out of breath!'

'What's the matter? Are a couple of naughty greyhounds chasing you?'

'Oh, no, and it's too bad. I really like greyhounds. I'd let them come in!'

'My God! That's all we need – two greyhounds besides.'

If I had only heard the phrase, I wouldn't have thought anything, because the words weren't anything special. But I saw Doña Eulalia's face and I saw how she said *besides*. There was venom and mystery in the way she said *besides*, and looked at Elena's father. The three of us went in ahead of her. She had kept her hand on the lock and when he went by, Doña Eulalia repeated, 'Two greyhounds *besides*.' How could such a thing have happened on a day like today! It was a marvelous morning. I returned feeling – I don't know – like I was coming back from another country and I wasn't alone. The three of us came in laughing like old friends. It's absurd, or it seemed absurd, but it was the truth. Elena's and my coming in laughing like crazy was normal. And that in itself was strange, hard for her family to understand; it made them uncomfortable to see that Elena preferred to go out with me and not with her friends. But it seemed perfectly normal to the neighbors and the people at the pharmacy, for example, who saw us come down every day to get lithium salts. For all of these people it was quite natural to see us come home with this man who hardly ever goes out and who spends the winter with a blanket over his knees, laughing like a fool! He was like a kid, running up the stairs effortlessly, thinking only of the joke that had set us laughing. The joke itself had been created by all three of us, because Elena told about my mistake – an enormous one, worthy of an anthology, she said. And her father had turned it into a very funny sentence like you might hear in the theater. All this: the contrasts of the world we had just been in, the serious nature of the *Carreños* – the figures really do look half-dead and in fact repulsive, but I don't care if I look like them: they are what might be called elegant today – and just two steps away, the people in the bacchanal, and another woman stretched out on a bed, marvelous! 'What's falling on her is a rain of gold,' Elena says. And then the statues below in the other rooms and, above all, Ariadne, something very much ours. Of course, Elena must feel it more personally because of her mother's name, but anyway it's ours as if it were our saint or our Virgin on the altar of music – of the *pieces of music* that Elena's mother leaves on the piano and Elena and I keep in the *music stand*. Elena's father opened a new world for us, not like a guardian, but like a friend. That is, it seemed as though the escapade was something special for him too, as though the adventure were more delightful for him even than novelty. But that's not exactly it either. For him, even better than something new was being able to experience once again something you know, that you'd like to do every day and can't, almost like it was forbidden. And then suddenly an occasion arises, and you say, 'Let's go there!' All this torn apart and trampled upon in a single word. The most shocking and most important part of it all is that it was such a common word. Because the word that so terrified me two days ago was like a room that seems dark to someone who can't go into it, but for those who have the key there's nothing dreadful about it. This word today, on the other hand, is atrocious even though everyone understands it. Would he understand it the way I understood it? Surely, surely he's fed up with hearing it: for him there could be nothing new in its repugnant repetition. But it crushed me because I saw her face and heard the sarcasm in her voice, and the word opened up like when you take the top off a can of worms. It seems incredible to be horrified by hearing a word as simple as *besides* and to feel as much horror in it as in that obscure word, to hear it as though it were a prison sentence. Why did the morning have to end like this? How can I tell my mother all these things? No, I won't tell her more than the things she can understand. Well, perhaps a little more. That was exactly what I was thinking on the way back, that I would tell her things that would dazzle her and she at once would be even more certain about my good fortune which she assumes and mentions constantly and supposes I deserve, but I don't know why, since I haven't amounted to much yet. And I know she'll be happy with what I tell her. And of course I'll be happy as well, but not because of the same things. Although – who knows? – maybe all the things that make us happy are one and the same. But it's not only that. It's that at one moment – it was exactly going along Prado toward Cibeles – everything was so pretty, so elegant. That was what made me think that the *Carreños* were elegant and I felt a twinge of remorse for not having told my mother what the fatty had said. That was a little mean of me, not to tell her, knowing it would give her enormous satisfaction. And I didn't tell Elena either. If I had told her, she would have understood what the business of the *Carreños* was about; but me with my unrelenting pride – the pride which my mother criticizes and I never change because I understand that my mother has put all her pride in my pride. This is not a play on words – as Elena might say – it's the way I feel. I know that it's as though I had done a very difficult exercise that she couldn't do – I don't know – like walk a tightrope, and she were looking at me from below and shouting to me not to do it, but I would see that she was proud that I was doing it, that she was sure I was born to do it . . . I have to tell her, I have to tell her everything, from beginning to end . . .

'Mama, we didn't go to Mass and we didn't hear music and we didn't do anything you might imagine.'

'Then? . . . But how flushed you are! It's like you've been to the mountains . . .'

'I've been even higher.'

'Higher than what?'

'Higher than everything.'

'Go on! You and your exaggerations! Can you please tell me where you went with that conceited girl who's always showing you things?'

'Ah, if only you knew what she showed me today! Have you ever been inside a museum?'

'No, I've never been in one. But don't think I don't know what they have inside. There are hundreds of paintings.'

'What do you mean, paintings? There are people and countries and everything. They're all alive, looking at us, some naked . . .'

'Naked?'

'Yes, most of them.'

'And Elena's father took you to see that?'

'Of course, he knows all their names. In the first place, his wife's.'

'You mean Doña Ariadne?'

'Yes, but without Doña. Ariadne is there sleeping, enormous. How can I tell you how large she is? Meters, kilometers . . . It would take a century to walk from her head to her feet. She's there sleeping, on the beach.'

'Frankly, I don't understand anything you're saying. Who's there sleeping?'

'Ariadne, of course, but, as you can imagine, in marble. The marble is what the people see, but it's not what we saw. We saw that Ariadne was sleeping on the edge of the sea, and the waves were coming in . . . You don't know, you can't imagine what the floor is like there inside. You know? It's like a mirror that reflects everything, everything that exists and doesn't exist. The color is golden like the frames of the paintings but, since you don't really dare to step on it, it seems like you're walking on air or on water. It seems like a sea which never ends.'

'You think I don't know what a waxed floor is? I know that only too well. And, anyway, why did they take you to see those things?'

'No, Mother, it wasn't exactly to see all those things that they took me there. They took me to see something else that I haven't told you about. They took me to see the *Carreños*. Do you know what that is?'

'No, really, I don't know what it is.'

'Well, the *Carreños* are some paintings by a man whose name was Carreño, and that's why they called them that. I thought it was the name of the people in the paintings, but it was the painter.'

'Ah, paintings of people in the olden days.'

'Yes, but not all that old, do you understand? They're not from those times when everybody went naked. These are dressed, and they're all in black. That's why Elena wanted me to wear a black dress, because you know what happened? They got the idea that I look like those people . . .'

'You?'

'Yes, Mama. Imagine – they're all princes and dukes . . .'

'The ones you look like?'

'Yes, Mother, but don't look so frightened! Elena and her father said it, but not only them. Some ladies who came to visit one day said the same thing.'

'How amazing! But, what did they say? Do they know someone . . . ?'

'Of course, they know the paintings. One of them, especially, one that I think is really smart. But she said it because the other one, the one that came with her, said I was as blond as a little princess.'

'Like a little princess! Oh my God, not really! Heavens! What a headache! Listen, child, put your dress away and go down to the pharmacy. Get me some lithium salts and tell Luis to give you a little packet of antipyrine. I'm going to lie down and see if I feel better in a while. I can't talk, it's like a hammer is pounding in my forehead.' This daughter of mine . . . It makes me afraid when they put such stuff into her head, and at the same time, everything about her is so extraordinary – everything! Because I've certainly brought her up well, just as she deserves. I've never let her do the things other children do. I told her not to draw on the walls, and she never did. Then one day I found a clover drawn and I asked her why she did it, and she told me she didn't, that it was there. I told her not to lie, and what a look she gave me! 'I never lie.' She said it in a voice that wasn't really hers. I just couldn't insist, but she understood that I still thought she was telling a lie, and she became very condescending and explained to me that the clover was already there in the peeling plaster and she had traced it out with her pencil because it was there but you couldn't see it. I would have preferred not to have seen it, because it's just at the level of my head on the pillow, like that blue tile . . . When the nun came in to take my temperature, I was so wrapped up in my thoughts that I didn't even hear her enter. She asked me what I was thinking about, and I didn't know what to say. I told her I wasn't thinking about anything, just about my village. She said yes, that really breaks your heart; maybe not the village, but what you might have left behind. I told the sister no, that I hadn't left anything there. Then she asked if my boyfriend had left me. I answered that I had never had a boyfriend – not there or here. What a face she made! She was about to go on asking questions, and then, how did it go? I had it on the tip of my tongue, but then a doctor came down the hall with an assistant and she didn't ask me anything. She just muttered, 'Sure, this didn't start with a boyfriend!' That nun was really a bad person. Although it was normal for her to think that I was bad. What must I have seemed like to her? A fallen woman. And besides that, she was angry because I didn't lie or pretend and say that I was deceived like all the others do. She stopped just short of calling me a hussy. The doctor checked the chart that was beside my pillow and took my pulse. He gave me a pat and said to his assistant, 'This one will be ready to walk out of here tomorrow.' The pat he gave me was with such a soft hand. The few days I was there I was always hoping for him to come and see me and give me a couple of pats, on the cheek or on the behind when he gave me an injection, the way you pat a little child. It calmed me down quite a bit. It seemed to me that so long as they treated me like that . . . When he said I would be ready to leave the next day was when I began to think about what awaited me. Walking out of there – and limping besides – with my baby girl. Where could I walk to? Should I walk up Atocha or down Atocha? And without knowing . . . My God, the little lord and lady are falling! They're broken to pieces! What was that noise?

'It was nothing, Mama. Did I startle you? I just dropped the scissors.'

'What do you mean, the scissors? It sounded like porcelain falling and smashing on the floor.'

'But, Mama, there's nothing broken. You fell asleep and the noise frightened you. I took so long! There were six people in the pharmacy.'

'Yes, I must have fallen asleep.'

'How is your headache? I brought the antipyrine, but if the headache is gone it's better not to take it.'

'Yes, the headache's gone, but the fright . . . It couldn't have been just the sound of the scissors. I saw how they broke to pieces: they slipped off the round table and shattered.'

'But what broke to pieces?'

'The little lord and lady – some figurines made out of porcelain . . .'

'That's what you were dreaming about. There's nothing made out of porcelain here.'

'Not here, I know. But there were some little figurines, and I was the one who broke them. I pushed the table, by accident of course, although . . .'

'But where did this happen?'

'Oh, a long time ago. In the house of a lady. A long time before you were born.'

'And why did you break them? Of course, you said it was by accident. But what were you doing in that house?'

'I was working there as a maid. I've told you before that when I came to the city I worked in that house as a maid. And I was really upset when they broke. I thought they were going to fire me. But the young man of the house – I thought very poorly of him at the time – defended me. He told the lady not to get angry with me over some old antiques, that they were better off broken. He said we'd be better off sweeping them up with a dustpan and throwing out the pieces. I said no, that I would glue them back together because I wanted one of them for myself. Imagine – a broken thing that's no good anymore for setting out on a table. I was satisfied just to have a piece of it because I had been thinking about it for quite a while . . . And suddenly, bang, in an instant there's a crash and it's smashed to pieces.'

'But Mother, you were dreaming all this. If I hadn't dropped the scissors, you wouldn't have woken with a start and the porcelain figurines wouldn't have broken – and then, what would have happened?'

'I don't know, I don't know if I dreamed it before or after. But what I can tell you is I heard the crash just like then, the same as the other time.'

'But if they hadn't broken, what would you have done? Would you have gone on being a maid? Did you like that?'

'No, I didn't like it. But I would have gone on.'

'And what were the figurines like?'

'Ah, how can I describe them? They called them the little lord and lady. But let it go for now, it's time to eat. I think I'm going to have another headache. It's beginning to get hot. What a summer we're going to have!'

'I don't care, because Elena says she likes it to be hot.'

'Just because she likes something, you have to like it too?'

'It's not that she likes the heat. It's that she wants nice weather for the carnival.'

'Well who knows how it'll be. The weather can change. Come on, eat, and don't sit there daydreaming. Ah, and today you're going to have a siesta. You've been running around all morning!'

'But Mama, I didn't run once . . .'

Or did I really run? I flew, I swam – what else? I rode horses, I went to war, I died and went to Heaven, I saw light . . . That's the thing: you think that light is something you need for seeing, you think that if there's light we can see things, but we don't look at light. There, on the other hand, light went ahead of you. You saw it everywhere, as though it were naked. I don't know if seeing all those naked people, so joyful – no, no, so calm and so sure of themselves – made you want to see something you've never seen before, made you look and see even what doesn't exist. Because light, of course it exists, but it's something you can't say you've seen the way you've seen a bird or a tree or a house. And yet I can say that I remember it. I remember its color and even its smell . . . It's silly, but that smell was like when you pass close to one of those heavily perfumed ladies, and she leaves a wake behind her. . . It made you want to follow, to follow whatever it was that was going by and filling everything – and what it was, was the light. Now I'm going to try to see light everywhere; but of course, it won't be the same. Or, is it always the same? Or is it simply that there's a lot of light or a little light? No, no, it's not that, it's that it's so different, it's that lights are different, just as different as one face is from another. Is it the face that the light has or the face that it makes? Because it's not just that you see it, it's that it looks at you with a friendly or unfriendly face. There, it looked at us with a shower of kisses, as if it were carrying us in its arms. I've always liked to sleep in the dark, but I could have slept in that light. The light coming in now through the dormer, what is its face like? It enters obliquely, now the sun doesn't shine straight in. The light that is coming in looks as if it were reflecting the blue of the sky on the walls, as if it were coloring the walls with a bit of indigo. As if it were more present than the morning and, at the same time, more silent.

The light coming in now through the dormer is siesta-time light, and the silence is like a tribute to its dominion, which spreads throughout the whole neighborhood. The light coming in now through the dormer has a benevolent but imperious look. Who could resist it? This light looks at the neighborhood in a hypnotizing fashion, imposing a truce on the effort, on the labor implied in looking. Its fullness and its force can be managed only by muting it, by filtering it through various screens in various places. Green blinds, sensitive to the wind, trembling like poplar trees. White curtains, as nuptial as mosquito nets; opalescent muslins. Transparent window shades of waxed cloth with brilliant, gloomily brilliant, colors, oval-shaped wreaths of roses framing autumn forests with running deer, oaks or fields or lakes with swans. Intense green in the landscapes, the livid reds of the roses. The light at this time of day is filtered through those screens and looks upon tidy rooms, fluffed-up beds, uncovered bodies. Its look is acquiescent, its countenance harmonious with each window dressing. The dormer has no dressing; it is simply bare, unadorned and open. This light is also acquiescent toward what is unadorned, open to mere necessity. The light doesn't come in to be seen, but to fulfill its mission, and its aspect, its demeanor at siesta time is not all that different from working hours. Its demeanor is neither benign nor aggressive. It is attentive, modest, never dazzling, but solicitously enlightening – Isabel would never have discovered it here, would never have contemplated its nakedness here. The light arrives with the dawn and looks pallidly at covered things: the two sleepers, bundled in their beds, the little household utensils covered with cloths. Their owner doesn't leave uncovered the things that don't want to be seen; it is decorous to cover them, and uncovering them as the growing light permits is like attending their birthing, their coming to light. The light gazes on what appears very clean, brilliant, as it is uncovered. The light corroborates it, puts it in its place. The room has been seen in all its incarnations by the hard, strict, necessary light of poverty – the light that saw them arrive with their bundles, with their elementary, insufficient possessions, which have gradually been transformed, growing and improving thanks to skillful combinations – the skills and crafts of the spider, the thriftiness of the ant, the cleverness of the weasel – all products of sacred maternal zeal; an art, or rather, a handicraft: creation. Nature – woman – abhors a vacuum; she feels, she sees – the supreme abstraction – what is lacking, what is needed, and invests herself with the power to create from nothingness, to make whatever is lacking so that lack will not exist because the nonexistence that is lack is mortal. Necessity dictates the work, works the soil for her after fruitless searches, degrading and debilitating, but not sufficiently so to exhaust her zeal. The saddest, most desolate light has smiled an instant, has winked to signal possibilities in the negotiations with an even greater poverty, with a senility that ceded territory, gave half its space in exchange for a bit of assistance. The light, after that transaction, was also linked here with a smell – odor, a fleeting material that escapes without breaking bonds, without erasing itself on the way, but on the contrary, being the path to the fragrant object – the smell of need, of sustenance . . . Once the room was ceded and the door between the two rooms blocked, the morning light – hard, strict, corroborative and collaborative – joined in essential accommodation with the steam of the little kettle on the oil stove, with the oil itself, with the chemical substances that serve hygiene – bleach, disinfectant, yellow soap saturating the hemp scouring pad . . . Odors as cruel as guardians, as stern as protective watchmen, are sometimes conquered by sensual, seductive cooking smells: garlic and onion, bay leaf, pepper . . . Confused with these aromas, the light abdicates its silence – the silence of a district with little traffic; only hawkers' cries rise from the deep street – and welcomes the busy noise of a Singer sewing machine. This necessary harmony stays inside the room. Outside, in the long attic hallway, the light is more leisurely, its mission is not so pressing because no one there needs lighting. Here the light grows sparer – not from parsimony, a concept antithetical to light – because it localizes or systematizes its beams Rembrandt-style; it falls from little round openings through which soft, heavy, silent cats drop in. The cats fall from them like drops of rain, falling by their own weight and hitting the floor with an imperceptible thud, then running down the hall. There they look for their prey or their adventures and leap with precision through the little window that gives access to the roof. The light there, in the long corridor lined by the garret doors, running the length of the house – the corner between San Vicente Street and San

Andrés Street: five garrets facing toward San Vicente and five toward San Andrés – in the long hall, the light assumes the violent chiaroscuro and the dark, ferocious, sharp smell of the cats. Inside the garrets the light scarcely touches old trunks, broken baskets, tin basins, portraits of people long dead and bronze objects long out of fashion. Then on the staircase there's the scattering of the vertical illumination of the skylight. It's magnanimous at any hour. Resplendent at midday, it is almost overwhelming on the top floor: merciless at the end of the climb. And every floor – each floor has two apartments – has its own kind of light or at least has its own conversation with light, because the light in each quiet corner takes on the demeanor that the dialogue elicits: in each space it takes on the disposition of the whole: the color of the walls, of the furniture and of the faces, because certain specific pieces of furniture harmonize with the style of the food. Certain cuisines give blood a certain color which affects the face. But not just through the blood, no: there is a tone inspired by appetite or the lack of it, by pleasure or accomodation, by resignation or habit, which is the enemy of the senses. All these tones mark human flesh the way curtains color light and both of them – cuisines with their heavy or stimulating spices, and curtains hanging dark and heavy over the sashes or agreeably white with little cupids embroidered on the edges, give the color of their blood to the light: lively, reddish, or somber, or insipid. But going step by step and leaving aside all defining adjectives – which are always extremely ambitious, tireless and stubborn: let's leave them aside – the color of the light, the blood of the light on each floor is – concretely on the floor that now concerns us – the taciturn, dusty light which slides off bookstands heavy with knowledge in a small room where an illustrious mathematician has just carried out vital calculations. A small dwelling, a library, an eating space, a sleeping area with a large, still-shared marriage bed. Still – after more than fifty years – harboring what was a lovingly discordant couple. Concretely... It's so difficult to say something concretely: concreteness limits, and limiting is negative, but delimiting is positive. Ah, how can we delimit without limiting? Above all, if what is being outlined is a very singular and individual uniqueness. At any rate, concretely, in the small room – third on the right – two old folks maintain their discord and care for it like an only daughter, always a little girl as far as the parents are concerned, preserving the conflictive youth of a studious man and a frivolous woman, of an austere, sallow, sober and disciplined body and a rosy restless body that consumes sweets and tangles of yarn in a quick whispering of needles as well as 'ladies'' news concerning other peoples' lives and loves. The laborious discord is attenuated now by new attachments. The light is lit when it begins to get dark. Electric light – is it a hired light or simply light like all light? It's turned on in the late afternoon and creeps into the hallway, accompanied by a nice smell, although a bit somber and melancholy. It's nice because it's new, melancholy because of the wintry and very strong flavor of celery. It spreads through the hallway, little by little, just a bit ahead of the steam from the two cups in which two cubes of Maggi are dissolving in boiling water. The light is more complex and more hard to define in the room to the left. Very different times are arranged, not according to a hierarchy, but according to effect – and thus they create very different effects of light. There is a feminine time – not maternal but matronly. This accounts for the partial subjugation, or frustration, of the hegemony of present time in favor of the nominal rank of former times by the two old sisters. Concretely, to follow the rooms laid out along the third-floor hallway that runs parallel to San Andrés Street, the final redoubt of the building, fortified by respect for a prestigious past, Aunt's room is first. The title Aunt has supplanted a name, Doña Marina, that merely served as a social denomination of the person who remained infertile in her brilliant life as a governor's wife. The light in her room splashes off small and finely woven baskets, made by Indians on far-off islands, and blends lovingly with the smell of aromatic resins, revealing the exquisite tones of a cashmere shawl and the polished yellows of an ivory Christ. In the rest of the dwelling the light wavers, changing its aspect in the different rooms. It enters the kitchen like a servant or a workman. The open window to the right of the cookstove allows the sun to reflect off the opposite wall and the pots hung by the hearth shine in response. The light and smells play rather than blend. It's an interplay of spices from all Spain's territories, perhaps the only form of nostalgia in the ruler of this domain, for she doesn't make a cult of the past. That is, she maintains a cult, but it's for a past that never passed – that never happened, to be more precise. The past of Eulalia the matron was a feverish hope, a confident, more than certain anticipation of success. Seas and lands traveled stayed *there* because she never got *here*, never thought she was living in the present. She lived thinking of a very near future, something which was about to come and never came. Thus, lands overseas lost their category of memories because what was lived in the past never took place. The light, indecisive, creeps through the house of a person who always considered herself a grand dame, a prima donna in the home of a genius, and assumes its own characteristics only in the study with the piano. In the study the light is pleasant and clear. It does its duty shining on worn-out exercises and scores – it carried out its mission for twenty years on scored sheets of paper, shining on the rapid writing and on the even more rapid thought, helping it run with its butterfly net throughout the room. It is only in this room – with its balcony facing San Vicente – that the light has known the present, the real, and has shone upon something that really was. Of course, on that was built the uncertain future; but there were real, although mo-mentary, illuminations. These stayed on and remain still – in the dreams of Ariadne (the light sometimes shines through her waxy, alabaster blood), in the pensive artist whom a modest artisan painted in a friendly oil – his hair not yet gray – before his premature absence. Frustration, escape, one might say. Or a sentence passed by adversity. We said twenty years, but it was thirty or over thirty, perhaps half a century. At that time there was no oil painting, mediocre but faithful, on the wall above the piano, because his hair was not yet gray: it was youthful, Espronceda-like. The hands were elongated and very slim. They toiled every day religiously upon the keyboard. It couldn't be more exact to say that the young maestro worked like a slave. . . Forced by passion, by the force that gave him the energy to try to be perfect. There, then, the light – spring days with the half-closed balcony, maternal carnations arranged on the railing – paid homage to the exceptionally perfect notes. On winter afternoons with the pitter-patter of rain or the silence of the snow the light was modest and left intact the dark corners that harbored the violence of *La Apassionata*. And there were long periods of time when the light shone upon the black cover of the piano with no melodies to accompany it: the maestro was on tour. He triumphed in the salons – the lights of candelabra, of fixtures with a thousand reflecting pieces and a thousand bulbs – of the overseas empire. He was a sensation in Manos during the happy empire of Pedro II and in Mexico during the tragic days of Maximiliano. He had returned from the latter with a portrait Maximiliano of Hapsburg had offered him in honor of his enchanting music – those elongated, extremely slim hands had blessed the royal salon with notes as pure as the reflecting pieces and as warm as the countless candelabra. The small canvas, not larger than eight inches across, faced the balcony, the balcony which opened onto San Vicente. However, the sun never made its surface shine. What stood out with the sharpness of a miniature were the clear eyes and the blond beard, parted into two golden shells beneath his mouth; the handsome image of the ill-fated man dominated the room. The maestro felt for him that special fascination one feels for those marked by adversity, and he had enthroned him in his home that year – exactly in the year eighteen hundred seventy-something – when his parents had died and he brought Eulalia there. She was the wife who would accompany him splendidly in the next trips abroad. She was at his side when he was the talk of the town in Buenos Aires and in Lima and in all the other places where his fame brought him applause. Two cycles had closed, two seasons during which he had harvested more than enough to satisfy the hunger of his *Eros*: beauty created and beauty possessed. But behind that almost excessive satisfaction, the lovely, the somberly lovely Melancholy – elbow on knee and chin in hand, those ample wings nearly closed and the gaze extended in excessive flight; surrounded by the mystic numbers, the hourglass dripping its blood of sand – our blood with it – by the sleeping cupid, the faithful dog curled up in its own constancy – the lovely and irresistible Melancholy spurred him to search for new well-springs of love. Of course, he saw it more simply. It was extremely simple, but there was no solution. New triumphs or adventures could only add more paths to the labyrinth. He had to find the lighted way within himself, and a silenced or repressed or unconfessed passion was crying out like a ship wiring for help amid a tempest, in the sea mist of his mind. It insisted like the siren of a ship, it called like the siren of the flesh: composition, creation – liberation from the monotony of performance. A touch so interior, an embrace so deep bound him to a form – not a voice but a form – that he felt he heard but did not wish to believe in the oneiric darkness. He wished to see it as a form, to compose it as an equation in astronomy, as a statue made of starry movements, as a stairway that *soars through the air till it reaches the highest sphere*. The idea took shape in the water's foam for days and nights along the high seas. Foam is always changing, it can never be understood better a second time. One must flee from its voluble elegance and distract oneself with something – any book, any story. To turn the pages of arid chapters filled with dates . . . Lighter paragraphs, finally, more limpid and luminous brought him to Greece and spelled out a name: Ariadne, 'the very holy.' The cult had a ritual in which a rapid rhythm evoked the anguish of the labyrinth, then a freeing clarity. The sonata was structured not like the foam of the sea, but like marble, the ship sailed *through a sea of sweetness, and slowly* . . . In her cabin or on deck, Eulalia suffered a touch of nausea which had nothing to do with the rolling of the waves. Her hands clasped upon her stomach, she felt her pulse beating even in her throat. Then, Spain, the train, and finally home. The century had less than twenty years to live; the sun was now setting on our domains. Home with its female chorus surrounding Eulalia. Youthful cousins and senile aunts, always praying and watching – contemplating, almost in ambush – the mystery throbbing in the breast of Eulalia as though they were anticipating the preparation of a cake and licking their lips thinking about the pleasure of eating it. The old seamstress abandoning her silent dwelling to attend Eulalia with the whispering sound of her needles and provide her with little booties and white bonnets that grew in a pile in her lap, the product of her pink hands and her arms naked beneath the edging of her dressing gown. The spring days passed and at last at midday in the month of June Ariadne emerged from the conjugal womb. She arrived as though she were breaking away from routine, as though she were cutting all links with the comfortable and healthy warmth of a well-nourished body. She appeared naked, of course, just as her mother bore her. This, which is natural, was exquisite and surprising: she appeared as a virgin project, so to speak. At the same time as the chariot of Apollo – Ah, that's the thing! – Ariadne and Ariadne were twins. Ariadne had also undergone a long gestation in the mind of her father. She had not slept below a heart with a regular rhythm, but had writhed in a fervid spiral like a nebula. Ariadne could not have appeared in this world – like Ariadne – naked, free and well-finished in all aspects. She was forced to suffer transubstantiation, metabolism or hypostasis, which is the musical idea. She had to be condemned first, and then exalted. All the elements making up Ariadne, from her fatal lineage, had to be cast and smelted in the erotic wonder of the mind and emerge bright and pristine with the incomparable proportions before which *the air grows clear*. All this had taken place one midday in the month of June. In the small studio-parlor the summer solstice had leaped from the balcony – the second balcony from the corner of San Vicente. Across the way, over the roof, the cumulus clouds were puffy and there was pure cobalt above, and at the back of the building – the fifth balcony on San Andrés – the midwife, her sleeves rolled up, took from between ample thighs, adorned with the splendor of blood, a little girl carrying along with her her destiny as a woman. (This event would not be worthy of mention if it were not for another similar one – identical, one might say, focusing on the meaning a mere event might have – that was mentioned, indeed, immortalized by a masterly voice and, because of this, was solidly fixed in tradition. In the same way, then, because of its own quality, this event becomes part of the Iberian concert, marked only by its unusual solar affiliation.) The maestro received her just washed – at the foot of the bed in a large washbasin, the midwives drying and wrapping her in cloths and diapers perfumed with lavender. He took her in his hands. He had no idea how to hold her in his arms. He raised her jubilantly up to his eyes in Apollonian consecration, and he named her Ariadne. He invoked for that warm bud of life all the unforseeable powers that beauty harbors. It would be excessive to be sure that the maestro was thinking about all this at that moment, but it is certain as anything that can be that he did not fear the setbacks of destiny, because the muses invoked could only offer gifts which in and of themselves *mingle in the sweetest harmony*. On that midday in June the century had just eighteen years left to live, and the next year Ariadne was crawling about the room and beginning to express her whims and appetites. In the study Ariadne no longer had childlike features, but the lines of pubescence. Yet her face lacked the concreteness of the hand that clutched bread crusts, of the foot that kicked, of the index finger that pointed. Her outlines – lovely, always lovely, infallibly noble – shimmered like those of a statue reflected in the water. At times they burst forth as fleetingly as a meteor shining in the night and at others they faded to the point of disappearing. Ariadne was already gadding about in the hallway, dressed in embroidered garments, and she rolled her hoop in the Buen Retiro Park. Ariadne was elusive – like the reddish light of late afternoon, the shine of polished furniture, the squeak of coarse oil that a poorly closed door lets out. Ariadne's symphonic being was elusive: it kept its distance, without sullenness or hostility. The more she faded away, the more palpable was her lading of love. Ariadne, well behaved, breaks pencil points on the rough reverse side of scored paper. Ariadne always there – gray days, winter days, monotonous drizzle blown against the panes by the wind, silent light, heeding the soft melodic call – always there with her brow pressed forward against the gale, her hair blowing in the air, her garments pressing to her flesh. Ariadne went through her primer, studied catechism and began history. Kneeling up on the piano bench, she does exercises.

The light has other things as well to do in the rest of the house. On the second floor the two rooms are joined. A military wife shelters her widowhood in the smaller and extends her meager pension taking in boarders in the larger one – carefully selected boarders: military men, bachelors, employees preparing for retirement. The light has very little to do there on slippers, cigarette butts left behind by dwellers involved in evening conversation parties. It can do little for the modest bed the *hôtesse* offers her lonely men. On the first floor, by contrast, the light can move in the company of very different actions. The light from the skylight shoots down there in a quiet fashion. It goes down the stairwell as though it were a chimney and early in the morning it welcomes chattering girls to the SCHOOL FOR YOUNG LADIES. Outside, above the San Vicente balconies the light shines on the white sign attached to the small railing. Inside, it spreads over a graduated collection of young feminine souls. At nine on the dot Miss Laura begins her classes – in a gray alpaca that looks like a duster but is an old and indestructible dress – and with sweet severity lays down the conjugation of verbs or square roots. The light passes monotonously through the lower panes coated with white lead so no one can see in. It falls monotonously on the notebooks and the inkwells sunk in the yellow desks. It shines on any number of heads, rhyming with the smell of brilliantine. It weakens at noon – or rather, it lights the weakening brought on by hunger, precisely when the light is most intense and little girls' hearts wilt in luminous depression. At that point the side door to the classroom is often opened and Piedita bursts in. Laughs, shouts and invitations to come and sit at any desk. The teacher is severe: 'I've told you time and time again, Piedita, not to interrupt the class!' 'Well . . . well' . . . Piedita withdraws toward the door – she scarcely reaches the bolt – and disappears.

The light seems downcast in the janitor's tiny corner. It is reduced to a minimum, as though the hammer did not need it to pound away on the sole of a shoe, as if its absence would disguise the desolate smell. But the shoemaker believes the light shines brighter when Ariadne comes down. Her skirt to her ankles, airy, holding back her light step to keep pace with her mother. In the study, Ariadne . . . Ariadne and Ariadne, isochronal heartbeats. Ariadne with hands as agile as her father's moves step by step through a rigorous apprenticeship. As elegant as her mother, she fixes her braid on top of her head. Naked – that is to say as virgin – as on the first day of her life, she is still a mere outline. Ariadne no longer fits in the serene atmosphere of a sonata. Her future, the project she has within her, cannot be written on a blank page. In order to make it her own, she must condense and make a quintessence of the violent past. Ariadne demands all that was so that she can be. The blessing which comes with her father's timorous look as Ariadne turns a page at the music stand graces her brow as though he were blessing her against destiny. When the maestro looks at Ariadne in his mind, he incites her with an almost imprecatory demand to take the highest risk. Concretely, once again concretely. With a boundless devotion the maestro had tried to enclose her in a norm *at whose divine sound, the soul, sunk in apathy*. . . This is what he desired, to clothe her in the signs *of her first high origin*. . . He was not up to the task. He could not enchain her: Ariadne was loved by Dionysus. And why and when and how was she loved? Concretely, it was not just that Ariadne cast the shadow of her story like an unhealthy plant over the mind of the maestro; there was also the technical incitation, the stimulus or fertilization owing to contacts with other works. Perhaps Gluck, his intense *Armida*, his disconsolate *Orpheus*. . . So terribly difficult to distinguish, concretely, the idea which emerges as a form, from its circumstances, but this it was. Dionysus was consumed with love for Ariadne when he heard her lament. How did she lament? With what accent? What notes emerged from her breast? Can pain possibly be of aesthetic value? This has been proved beyond the shadow of a doubt. Can it be an erotic enticement? It can be in a thousand ways, but one must find – one must conceive – the note with the power to enrapture the god of rapture. This is where the difficulty lay: it was not a question of a howl or a roar. The furor of a maenad would be for the god nothing more than a voice in the chorus. The unique, the singular, the personal in the final analysis, had to be a note whose excellence and sublime essence would make its way to the god in ecstasy – *Oh, happy swoon! Oh, death that gives life! Oh, sweet oblivion!*... Without this sweet oblivion there is no perfect love because, certainly, the desire to possess her – to make her his, one says – burned within the violent god. But first – it is impossible to change the order of the phenomena – first there was the judgment. In the god of the abyss, the lord of blind impulses, desire emerged as a result of – that is to say, following – contemplation, which is a testing, a tasting (Can we forget the decisive role of this judgment when the God of Hosts, the Maker, after the *fiat* – afterward, that is what matters – saw that it was good?). A test, a taste, then stuck like a fly in honey, pledged like a pawned belonging, alienated, possessed, lost in sweet oblivion. He must find the exact note, the note that can move boulders, the note that strikes at the heart of all the laws of architecture. All laws, in fact, because in this case – and it must be taken as a case – in this case it is the sublime, exact, unique formula which stops the bolt of lightning, paralyzing it like the hawk which looks, judges and calculates where he is going to land. The note he was looking for – but not in a systematic or speculative search – the note he was looking for filled the head of the maestro like an obscure presentiment. It was not a difficulty, for he had overcome the labyrinth. It was a certitude like that of that gemstone which, *loving stubbornly*, is held in a knot which nothing can break. *And the soul imitates the ecstasy that is its task*... That was it, exactly! It was a question of emulation, of outlining, finishing as with the finest lace trimming the ecstatic trance that enchants without a visible sign. Such a fervent ambition could scarcely be contained in the lines of a sonata – maybe it would fit in a stormy Beethoven. But what was needed was the harmony of human voices. The opera! What light shined on it? It sang in the blue of the Mediterranean and in the gold of the Rhine. It sang in salons lit with a thousand chandeliers beneath soffits decorated with muses and goddesses in flight and covered with laurel and crowns of pearls and rubies . . . In salons with royal boxes, in orchestra pits like baskets with lovely décolletés and in amphitheaters, galleries, . . . truly angelic tiers, the region of cigars, students, and lovers. . . It sang in the street. Via subtle paths through which culture filters, like cuttings, like remnants or perhaps like gleanings of the spirit: like foam overflowing with richness . . . Via subtle paths the opera came to sing in the street. The whole of Italy rang with its song because its voice was the true word . . . even its fiction was the myth so much longed for and confirmed in the realization. It was the inflection that everyone born of a mother understands . . . it was, in fact, like the song of a mother cradling unlearned souls as warmly and artfully as the learned, the pious as well as the cruel, the elevated as well as the commoners. The opera sang for the egalitarian century . . . perhaps its swan song.

It might seem that all this is, concretely, an attenuation, a dilution, but, on the contrary, all this comprises but a moment. If we were to say that it was like a moment at the microscope, that would suggest that we were claiming the investigation is exhaustive, and that is not the case. No, that is not the case because patience often unravels. It mistrusts as well – the special patience which is given the narrator as a little parcel of human, universal and common patience – it mistrusts and feels it will be blocked or rejected by the homogeneous element to which it belongs, it is afraid of being called ambitious or vain or pretentious because it thinks it is bearable when it is not. But really, patience, if it did not doubt its unceasing wellspring, would go into the forest – into the forest, tree by tree; into the tree, leaf by leaf; into the leaf, cell by cell; into the cell, etc. – until arriving at the point where it is no longer a question of one by one because everything is simply one. This is the ambition of patience, love, *the wellspring of constancy* which overflows in an unimaginable cataract and is a single moment.

Ariadne arrived from her afternoon walk to find the lights of the pharmacy and the poultry shop already on. The street in its crepuscular silence – a brief pause as in music – gazed upon her between two lights. From the pharmacy Don Luis and young Luis watched her; from the poultry shop the rather coarse lady who plucked chickens every day kept an eye on her. The latter stayed in the doorway until she went in because, even after Ariadne disappeared up the stairs, something worthy to be seen is left behind – a young passerby who goes off to the corner and comes back and makes a turn and looks up at the balcony on the third floor. The light wears out or gathers up its final veils of evening, it rises above the bespangled roofs and leaves behind in the streets its acolytes or vicars: up and down the sidewalks the gas jets are lighting up. The balconies emit the light of the kerosene lamps, family meals are tucked beneath their skirts; then later, they are only lit for people who are working or who cannot sleep. From the balcony of the study comes a rosy light shielded by a thin silk screen. And there come as well chords or tastes of melodies repeating themselves, never the same, repeating themselves as though – as though between one and the other there was a year of oblivion, a year of care, of nourishment, of trowelfuls of humus. So different and so similar, like one rose and the next every spring. No, no, no . . . because a rose never rectifies another rose. The melodic motifs rectified the profile of Ariadne. They gathered in or faded away in pursuit of the ineffable note. On certain nights there could be heard from the open balcony not the thoughtful notes but the measures of an old master, fleeing from the open balcony – open to let the measures out, so they might stumble along the sidewalks across the street from corner to corner – fugues, fleeting and persistent, took advantage of the freed study because on certain nights the maestro was distracted from his work by other themes having little to do with harmony. He would leave his study and go to a cellar to hear the trumpet blasts of discord: the classical interjections, profuse and crackling. Spain was hit at this time by a sea-swell, not just the peninsula, but also overseas. Ah, the land. When the sea-swell stirs upon the waters the good sailor manages to avoid it all. If he reaches the coast safe and sound, indifferent, he thinks he has won the battle. When the high seas of this earth stir at the root, when you hear its deep convulsions, its moaning, its curses, its threats, can you raise sail with the winds of art which never err, which always carry you to port? The question is not only whether or not this is possible but whether this personal salvation, this escape, is desertion or the contrary. . . Because the malady that afflicts the very roots, that grows slyly like a tumor and spreads its venom through all the sap can also be fought off with . . . with anything at all, with any voice or stroke or stone or number that is pure, true, real. Is this an escape? If it were it would not mean so much effort, so much labor, so much delving into the authentic . . . Whose? The depths plumbed or excavated with the tenacity of a miner, are these nothing more than personal depths delimited by a name and social rank? Is it not the complete truth, is it not the common store of incorruptible health of a people?

The maestro returned home very late with these thoughts jumbled in his head. Turning the corner, he could hear Ariadne at the piano. He was moved as he listened to the impeccable execution. He thought he was listening to himself in his youth – the same sharpness, the same rigor, the same subtlety, shading and intensity. He thought, 'She is working too hard. I have to say something to her about staying up so late, although I'm pleased with her dedication.' He called out for the watchman by his name. His voice was so low that the watchman didn't hear him, but he didn't dare shout or clap his hands; he was absorbed in the music that flowed throughout the whole neighborhood. He never carried the heavy ground-floor key on his person, and he was forced to wait for the little bobbing light of the watchman's pike. Then he called him softly, and the watchman heard him. He came running and opened the door – a task which a nocturnal bystander watched very carefully from the other sidewalk. A long taper maintained its modest cloak of light up to the third floor, illuminating just the zone where he must place his feet. The rest of the staircase was in darkness. Minutes later, the studio light faded. Ariadne at that point welcomed him with the fraternal affection of a comrade in struggle: they fought together. His behavior with her was not a paternal, authoritarian – and so tender! – guidance along the proper path, as it was with Ariadne. With Ariadne in the darkness of his chambers he ran beneath the sun of the divine archipelago and decanted in his mind the luminous notes which could offer the image of that light. We said that Ariadne struggled with him. More than an inspiring muse, she was a sweetheart filled with promise. She displayed herself, she devoted herself, but something always remained hidden. The themes which in the beginning had structured themselves as a sonata took shape now as a prelude. The labyrinth motif developed urgently in the overture with the power of a vortex, and all the others emerged with sacred inflections throughout the work in sudden bursts. A kind of script served as an outline of the bits that achieved a coherent thematic sequence. An impeccable libretto must be written. Difficult, very difficult to outline for a writer – a poet, that would be best – an idea so lovingly conceived. How to do it? Of course, it is possible to ask a painter to paint the portrait of a loved one, but not if that painter must ask where this loved one is and how he can see her, especially if the answer is that she is nowhere at all, only in my mind. Questions like that with their pros and cons came up with the first light of dawn and remained insoluble, blocking the movement of the creative process. They were like a series of family problems, undoubtedly marginal, but unavoidable. And these were not the only family problems. There was something else which stirred far off on the horizon but still threatened with its storm clouds. His concerts canceled, his career as a great performer cut short, the reserves accumulated in the days of triumph could give out. Would they run out before he was crowned by new triumphs? There was an even more marginal conflict that was undisguisedly ignored. The century had four more years left to live. In the month of June the life of Ariadne would gather up fifteen years. The spirit she inherited – more timid and less crushing – was harbored in a magnificent dwelling – the maternal inheritance – and her long skirts now almost hid her feet; a sight traditionally desired by the contemplative. The hegemony of Eulalia managed at times to impose itself. There were even whisperings and chuckling between mother and daughter. Ariadne was reaching the shore; it was time to land on the new coast, to listen to the new harmony so it wouldn't become discordant for lack of attention. It was now no longer a world enclosed in a mind: it was *the world* in all its possible circumstances. One of them had made Ariadne cry, had made her nose turn red. It was time to touch land, time to intervene.

'What is this, my little dove, a hidden tear?'

'No, no, Daddy, it's nothing. I was just rubbing my eyes.'

It was necessary to spy, to see what activities outside the home took mother and daughter out every afternoon, to see what Ariadne had hidden in the drawer of the table of her room. He caught her once putting together pieces of paper with a little jar of glue.

'What do we have here, a jigsaw puzzle?'

'No, Daddy, it's nothing . . . just a sheet of paper that tore.'

'That much I can see. But what was the paper, a love letter? I wouldn't be surprised.'

'Well, no, it's not a love letter. It's a poem.'

'Ah . . . you get poems?'

'Well, look if you want, but it's nothing special.'

'But if it's nothing special, why are you keeping it?'

'I meant there's nothing bad about it. The poem is magnificent. I tore it up because I was silly. I said it was very good and he said it was very bad, that it had lots and lots of bad parts. Then I got mad.'

'And you had a spat?'

'A spat? It was the kind of spat you might have with a friend, because there was nothing between us . . . nothing.'

'And who is this fellow?'

'A boy I met a little while ago. Mama says he's got nice manners.'

'Let's see the poem. You judge a tree by its fruit.'

'It's all torn up. I could only save the end. All the beginning fell into a mud puddle.'

Perhaps the poem described walking alone at night; perhaps it spoke of feelings or illusions. But from what remained – the two final lines – there was only, or mainly, the miraculous surprise of one night.

How brilliant shines this lovely summer night!
No moon, but Ariadne and piano notes in flight.

'Well, it's not bad, not bad at all . . . just the opposite.'

'Now you see! You see I'm right? It's excellent.'

'Excellent? We'd have to see more. What has he published?'
'He hasn't published anything. He tears it all up.'

It is not clear from what branch of learning – scientific or philosophical – we can approach a certain phenomenon. In the first place, the phenomenon itself is not clear. It is a very foggy matter because the event takes place in the human mind. It is produced in the furthest, most closed-off depth and explodes like a sudden illumination. Its power is dazzling and at the same time disturbing because what happens within the mind is nothing more than half the phenomenon. Concretely – for the hundredth time, concretely – something happens in the mind: something like a pretension, a hope, an intention (in an attempt to speak rationally) and whatever it is remains latent, standing there. It remains to a certain extent expectant and somewhat uncomfortable. It does not settle in like something falling by its own weight, like something with which one comes to terms. Up to this point, we have what happens in the mind. But the phenomenon does not end there; the phenomenal – in the most vulgar sense of the word – suddenly happens and this happens at times in another mind, which is nothing at all shocking because at once long-distance communications are suspected. But the same can happen with things, places, objects, elements or worlds which are impenetrable or above all incoercible. This is what is marvelous: the obstinate freedom with which these things answer and act and appear. I don't think this is really clear: it must be worked out very simply, reduced to a simple example. One day someone is thinking about something that has bothered him very much. He thinks about it more intensely than ever. He realizes that he has never really looked into it enough, that he has never got it clear, and immediately – the important thing is this, the immediacy – opens, as if he were opening the door of his house, a book that explains it. Chance, this is already cataloged as chance: there's no reason to complicate matters. But if someone is filled with anguish over a problem of vital importance – not a great deal of importance, just something having to do with his life – and suddenly, immediately, at the moment in which the problem becomes for him as clear as an equation which is so exact that it turns out to be enigmatic, suddenly he succeeds in . . . No, not undoing or revealing or solving the problem. There comes another enigma, another vital enigma from another life, and the confluence brings about a vital solution, making up a wealth of lives, of minds, of loves. We can also say *chance*. We can also say *destiny* or *providence*. We might even say something that now we ought not to say. There are things that can be seen and are not subject to doubt. They are not only seen, one understands the laws of their indescribable appearance, but their incalculable probabilities do not seem subject to any law. For example, smoke . . . the smoke of a pipe which is held in someone's hand. The smoke is imprisoned in the confines from which it is observed: one sees how it thins, divides, dilutes into very thin veils which turn upon one another forming volutes, rings and small clouds which float off toward the window, pass beneath the cone of light from the lamp shade and fade away. As everyone knows, smoke moves according to air currents which tend to move upward, which because of their density or coherence resist being dissolved, and all these necessary forces configure the cloud. As everyone knows . . . Ah, who can know why a desire is formulated clearly, with all its difficulties and all its probabilities, remaining paralyzed before them as though before the impossible, and nonetheless, expectant? Because it is not a problem posed and/or rejected or well on its way to being solved: it is simply an ambition for perfection which insists on reappearing, which emerges during insomnia or any random moment of solitary meditation. It walks arm in arm with the mind stumbling through the night after a friendly chat, after a get-together with all its gossip and plans and decisions and ambitions. Once the voice of the world in all its tortured reality fades away in the final good-bye, in the final handshake or the final hand on your shoulder which slips off and slides down your arm . . . once company is gone like the final drop in a bottle, the desire appears once again, its itching difficulty causing a displeasure which makes minor difficulties worse . . . like searching your pockets for something you can't find while the watchman parsimoniously selects the right key from his extensive bundle. While – at that very moment – there comes walking along the other sidewalk a desire which, far from thinking itself auspicious, dissembles and hides because it thinks it's being indiscreet, while in fact its presence there is as fated and necessary as the rush of streams down their channels. By chance? It might just be by chance.

Because of just such a fortunate happenstance, the maestro, like a Biblical patriarch, blessed the union of the poet and Ariadne. With Ariadne at church, with Ariadne in the study . . . that's the way it was. And regarding the maestro, it was not just a question of the generosity of a patriarch. There was also something of Laban's bargaining with Jacob. Of course, he didn't make him serve seven years for Rachel. Time was running short, and the courtship lasted only several months. But during that time, as soon as the light began to fail in the study, the amorous colloquy came to an end. Candles upon the piano were lit, and the scores began to be mutilated by additions and corrections in red and blue. The libretto was outlined – and more than adapted, it blended perfectly with the score. The romanza or the aria of abandonment, the awakening of Ariadne on a solitary coast came to a climax like a perfect linking of outcry and harmony, like a melody surging forth from the depth of bitterness. The light of that winter – '95–'96 – crystal clear in the snow or severe in the dry wind – put in its reduced time on those short days. Every night it was replaced for hours by candles and kerosene lamps. Brass lamps along the staircase . . . the main door left open late. The comings and goings of the landau that took the maestro to his rehearsals . . . the light of dawn on frozen puddles where the hooves of the horses slipped. The light of triumph during six months of disproportionate upheaval and one single night of cataclysmic light. Desolation. The deeply mourned dead go to rest with a cortege of laments like a funeral march; such music did not accompany this one. The rain wept for everybody, and the house was filled with silence like a perplexity that would have liked to be incredulous, that wouldn't reconcile itself or concede. Something had broken: a heart breaks more silently than a crystal glass. It does not make the noise of the departure from life of a precious object: it goes in silence and leaves silence behind it when it disappears. The result is stupefaction: because now it is not only not what it was, but not what it was going to be. Human life is made evident in human death, in which a pregnancy always succumbs; the dead one carries with him a fetus of the future and those who know of the existence of this embryo try to take it from the abolished womb, to bring the promise to life. Posthumous honors. The foyer of the theater resounded like a veiled kettledrum . . . Comments in hushed voices, greetings which the collaborator and son-in-law – what an absurd thing to call a person – endured, deaf to all compliments and to all offers, squandering courtesies and kisses of the hand, treading upon carpets like dunes or shifting sands, with nothing to cling to but possible notes, the possible voice of Ariadne which never ceased ringing in the ear. The curtain never ever finished rising, and when it had risen it never finished. . . The aria of abandonment swelled throughout the salon, spreading over all the listeners – critics, colleagues, magnates, ladies, ushers, doormen, coachmen waiting expectantly in the door, passersby, the city, the world –

laying over one and all the pall of orphanhood. Ariadne unfurled her notes as if to snatch away the god of rapture. Ariadne sat in silence beneath a black veil in the proscenium next to Eulalia who, also dressed in mourning, received waves of homage. The surge of applause burst forth like a torrent and faded and then rose and crashed once again . . . Ariadne appeared between red curtains that opened to let her through with the poet on her arm. She supported him in his bows and braced herself upon his shoulder to hold back the sobs bursting from her young diva's breast . . . Ariadne, in silence, did not keep silent, but attempted to spread silence; she hoped in anguish that there would be silence in the salon, that there would be silence in the world so that she could leave her box and walk alone in silence. Eulalia deigned to rise from her seat when the applause began to echo toward the proscenium – two thousand hands clapping obliquely in her direction. She stood up and, without raising her veil, responded courteously and in a ladylike fashion. Ariadne took refuge in the box anteroom, alone; but no, Ariadne was no longer alone. The year 'ninety-seven had passed and still the hooves of horses sometimes echoed in the ice-covered puddles along the avenue near San Vicente. A few critics and magnates came from time to time during one month. And then no one came because a more solemn obligation – more mournfully solemn – settled upon all: the year 1898. The maestro was remembered only on a few occasions thereafter in the few columns that the papers set aside for music. In evening get-togethers, on the other hand, friends quite frequently offered him funeral orations inspired by the events of the times. A sentimental gentleman might say, 'He went in time, the poor chap. How he would have suffered!' A more sarcastic observer would remark, 'He was lucky to escape. He took off and that's the end of the story.' And a more envious man: 'He made a big splash, but if he were alive today no one would bother about him.'

In the studio the visits of condolence became gradually more infrequent. Several women friends from his youth came a bit late because they had just come from the other continent with the tide of returnees – artists and travelers of all sorts. Very close relatives of Eulalia came back as well. A long and difficult voyage from the Philippines where they had ruled in marble palaces under bamboo fans. They returned with the remnants of their pomp, refusing to believe that it was over and done with. They lodged like diplomatic travelers, in provisional comfort worthy of their rank while the former Governor assessed the situation. Marina would never come to terms with it. Eulalia, on the other hand, had come to terms with the situation even before the bubble burst. She had understood how things were going to be in her house since. . . She had argued discreetly but energetically with the maestro. 'I'm not denying that this young fellow has talent, but aside from his poems . . .' And now she tried to unburden her silenced anxieties to her sister, hoping that what remained of the bygone power might offer a minimum of support, a helping hand, a solution. . . The midafternoon light in the dining room – the corner room, San Andrés and San Vicente – was unable to surround the dialogue in a properly serious atmosphere. The two balconies could no longer be closed, there was no longer a brazier lit under the table, and the aroma of coffee no longer filled the room because April airs passed from one balcony to the other carrying away the voice of Eulalia. Eulalia raised her voice appropriately, she deepened her tone to give the proper weight to her words and, as a final resort – something final which was really primordial – she concluded: 'Don't forget that Ariadne is expecting in two months . . .' This was a pleasant idea for Marina. She had never managed to reach this state of expectancy, and she was pleased about the approach of the happy event: she wanted to be there, to be the godmother. 'Yes, Marina, yes, but the child needs something besides nice swaddling clothes . . . it needs to have parents, a father who . . .' The light grew, the days were longer now, and they brought dazzling cirrus clouds over the rooftops at midday. In the early hours the May light was cheerful from the moment it dawned, and it filled the kitchen well enough for the coffee and toast that awaited the daily departure of the poet. But it was not as a poet that the morning light warmed him; rather, the man the light followed quickly down the stairs was a new employee – an official scribe – of the Ministry of Public Education. His name: Juan Morano. The light comforted and kept him company all along the right-hand sidewalk until he reached Fuencarral. Everything was easy – with the easiness of the possible, of the feasible – until the overflowing light of June, a naked, violent midday light – shown on Ariadne as she gave birth – brought to light, so to speak. The large washbasin at the foot of the bed, and the midwives in that same back room of the house – fifth balcony, San Andrés. There where she herself had been born Ariadne brought into the world a tiny woman who some day would be able to say, 'where my mother was ravished . . .' The two – mother and daughter – had been possessed in their nakedness, in their forthcoming virginity, by the light of June. Eight days later she was taken to the font in the parish church of Maravillas by her aunt and uncle, the ex-Governor and his wife. Marina held her as she received the salt, the oil and the water, and the priest pronounced her name . . . a name which had been discussed and defended by her parents to the point of no return. Above all, they would never consider a name vulgar enough to lend itself to diminutives or family deformations. And they would never have accepted a name without feeling secure that the late maestro would have approved it as sufficiently noble or exalted. They decided on an irreproachable name: Elena. The parish priest pronounced the sublime name in the name of the Father and the Son and the Holy Ghost. The candles and the night taper behind the red glass trembled when they opened the door of the church. The door closed and the small group was bathed in sun on Dos de Mayo Street.

If Elena comes with us, she'll want to bring Isabel along too. It's not that I care, no, but if the other girls find out they'll say . . . They're already saying it, it can't be helped. The ones doing all the talking are jealous, because if she weren't the first in the class nobody would pay any attention to her. But since she is, they say that I single her out. They say *even though*, *well*, *in spite of*, etc. How can I tell the girls that I don't care a thing about this *in spite of*? I couldn't say this to the girls, I couldn't explain it to them reasonably – I can't even explain it to myself – and even less to their mothers, and it's the mothers who spread it around. The girls have learned it from them, they've picked it up from their gossip; and that's what can hurt me, hurt the reputation of the school. And the gossipers are also worried that the fact might have an effect in some way on their daughters. Their reputations? I don't know if it's a question of that, because can you see any effect on the reputations of a handful of daughters of shopkeepers – to be more specific, of butchers, bakers, greengrocers and even a well-to-do electrician? Could their reputations be hurt by having been educated – we can suppose they're being educated – in a school where we admit a girl whose father is unknown? Or maybe the gossipers are afraid the contact with this little girl might have some effect on the morals of their daughters. For sure they're afraid of something imprecise, a vague damage . . . just the way I fear their fears might damage my reputation – not mine, I'm too old for that – but the reputation of the school. I'm worried just like they are, but not for myself. It's strange. This fear mothers have for offspring is natural, and I have that same fear for Piedita. Of course, Piedita is the offspring of my parents, just like me: maybe it's egotism. But no, no, it can't be because the fact is that Piedita is what I'm not . . . it's as though she's being it for me. She was such a beautiful creature, right from the day she was born. And I've spent twenty years caring for her, twenty years trembling for her . . . well, almost twenty, because she hasn't had her birthday yet. My God, twenty years! She's spent them shut in here because I'm afraid, afraid of anything that could affect her. Am I too afraid about this business of reputation? Of course I am. It's just that when you move among educated people, you put your reputation on another level. And I'm also pretty much afraid of educated people. My God! Why are we always afraid of each other? It's an endemic sickness in the human race. And we find all these optimists claiming it is necessary to rid ourselves of this fear, that there is no reason for it, that people are in the final analysis good and that fear only confuses things. What is fear? My God! But why am I saying my God? I've said it around sixteen times, now . . . why? I don't even believe in God. It's out of fear. I don't believe in God. I'm not afraid to say so, but ten minutes later I'm shouting my God! And the more often I say it, the more times I repeat that I don't believe in God. Because when I shout my God! it's a curse, it's almost blasphemy. I'm afraid to utter a blasphemy. But I'm less afraid to say *I don't believe in God* than to say *my God!*, because if I say I don't believe in God it's something merely mental which has nothing to do with any other zone of my being. But when I'm angry, sick to my stomach, filled with hatred for the whole human race, I shout my God!! What dregs, what venom I vomit in that curse! The gossipers get upset because their daughters go to school with a girl whose mother has had . . . well, you know. And they entrust them to me, who laughs at all that, and at everything else, everything else. Of course, I don't laugh in their faces, of course not. I offer them the most well-mannered teaching imaginable – they wouldn't be able to take any stronger medicine. Is that the reason I don't give them a stronger dose? Or is it because if I gave it to them their mothers wouldn't entrust them to me? Who knows? If I didn't have that fear – the fear of ending up without them – would I dare to use a heavier hand? Maybe I have the same fear the mothers have. Maybe I have a disinterested fear on behalf of the offspring of others. Am I capable – still – of feeling such a fear? I doubt it. Or maybe I'm just afraid of myself, afraid of spreading what I have inside. This could grow all by itself and turn against me and make me afraid. What I'd be afraid of in this case wouldn't be that it might turn on me in a real way – with concrete results – but that it might stand before me, that I might have to look at it. Everything about me is rational, incredibly rational. I'm not afraid of discovering something muddy at the bottom of what I think is crystal clear. What I'm afraid of is seeing it, of simply seeing its . . . well, its face, I'd have to say in this case – its physiognomy or features or expression of desolation. This is stupid because if I know that what its features express is desolation, why should I be frightened of seeing something I spend my whole life thinking about? It's a rather indecent fear: I'm afraid others will see it, that they'll see that it belongs to me. When I think about it by myself, only God and myself see it – That's just a manner of speaking. Right now I can't imagine saying my God! No, it just doesn't come to me. Goodness, Elena is here! And she's got somebody with her.

'Piedita told us to be here at three on the dot.'

'Ah, Piedita was keeping track of the time? Let's see how long it takes her to get ready.'

'No time at all! I'm ready.'

'That's a miracle!'

'Oh, Piedita, you look terrific. And that hat! It's darling.'

'Darling? It's a dimestore sun hat.'

'What does that matter? She looks great in green, don't you think, Isabel?'

'It goes well with her hair.'

'Only with my hair?'

'With your hair – and everything else. You look like . . . let's see what you look like . . . ah, yes, a Divine Shepherdess.'

'Elena! You've got an incredible imagination. Let's go downstairs. The mailman's here.'

'The lady of the house . . . Miss Laura.'

'Yes, thank you. It's from my brother. I'll read it when we're sitting on the grass. I can't read on the tram.'

'How long will the tram take?'

'I don't know. I imagine around a half-hour. But that's better because your stomach will have settled so you can drink some iron-water.'

'I never drink that. It tastes like toads.'

'You'll have some, Piedita. It doesn't taste so bad.'

'To me it tastes great.'

'Elena!'

'It's not exactly that I like it. If they gave me a glass at home, I wouldn't drink it. But the notion of drinking from the pipe, that's what I really like. You know the taste is from the iron, you think you're drinking iron.'

'Yeah, you're right. When I was little I liked to drink from the taps.'

'Ah, you remember? You got some good scoldings.'

'I also got the devil from my mother for drinking water right from the faucet.'

'Do you do the same thing, Isabel?'

'I do, and so does everybody else. Don't you ever do it, Doña Laura?'

'Elena! Come off it!'

'But that's crazy, like it was something bad to drink right from the faucet. You think a person shouldn't ask?'

'Why not, Elena? You're right. There's nothing bad about it.'

'Then, do you do it or don't you?'

'You're impossible! But just so you're satisfied, I imagine that at one time or another I must have done it.'

'That's what I wanted to know, because if you've never done it you can't even imagine what the taste is like. How would you describe the taste?'

'Describe a taste . . . that's not easy.'

'Of course it's not easy. That's why I asked you, or you, or you: because we all know what it tastes like. Let's see if I can describe it. It's a taste that almost hurts. Yes, that's it. You come to the point when you've drunk awhile and you can't stand it any longer . . . it's like a sharp taste. Not stinging; it's just that it gets sharper and sharper. It's something like the taste of mint, but mint is always cool and water isn't. It also tastes a bit like blood, but the taste of blood is heavier. When water comes out in a squirt it's very fine and clean.'

'You're getting warm. Maybe the taste of blood has something to do with the taste of iron.'

'Yes, maybe blood tastes like iron, but not like the spout.'

'You'd think that the spout was, for you, the best candy on earth!'

'Candy? No, the taste from the spout is like a sound you hear vibrating while you're thinking about something else. You're thinking with your mouth at the spout, and you think about the color of the taste. Ah, this is important . . . the color. It might taste like blood, but the color is not just red by itself. It's a red that you see sometimes in church, in draperies, in heavy curtains . . . a red filled with blue. Yes, that's it. One drinks from the spout and the color – or the taste – is mysterious . . .'

'All right, here comes the tram. Let's go, jump on. Don't stand on the platform. You can talk about your mysterious spout later.'

The faucet, in the sun for the whole morning, is warm; but the water is cool, though not very cool. And it doesn't taste exactly like a toad but like something alive, something intimate, iron buried deep in the earth. It tastes like something substantial. You can split a hair into four hundred parts – four hundred is a perfectly conceivable number, and a hair could be split infinitely, impossibly, incalculably because the seams of the earth are absolutely inconceivable. They are inconceivable because they are not veins – with the arrival and distribution later via veins – real veins – of the children brought by mothers full of faith to this wet nurse. They bring them and they make them drink. They hold the little ones close to the spout as if it were the tit of a country nanny; and this open vein is not closed off. Its prodigious richness is within the reach of all. Where it is marked off as royal property, you must have a card to get in. You have to go in with it via a gate and pass by some guards – you walk by them, you pass with their permission. A zone of opposition, of fear, of mistrust. Will you be allowed to get in? Will the card be accepted? Will it be in order? Has it been canceled?

On the avenue where you go in – enormous – the gravel crunches underfoot like something hard to munch, something artificial placed there to delimit the ground with a hardness that does not sound like the country. Then, there is no sound at all. You begin to walk upon real earth. It is not soft, but it seems smooth and silent enough to make you forget it. You can run down side paths, or even where there are no paths at all, or even through underbrush where sometimes you see insects that were hiding there, but it seems like they just squirt out of the earth like water. Some go flying off, some run, some slip away in the grass, swiftly, leaving a furrow, a furrow already made, before, by their very same kind, by them. They shoot like a stream of water through the sand and then they sink into it through another opening. And then the flowers – unnameable for the ignorant – spell out the season of the year. They are not the most prestigious wild flowers (daisies, cornflowers, poppies); nor are they the vulgar kind (dyeweed, rockrose, French lavender) that never grace the gardens of gentlemen. They are the *fioretti* that Francesco and Sandro liked – tiny, exquisite, unnoticed if one does not seek them out to contemplate them. They are hidden away and never mentioned. Suddenly, in a shady place around a corner – a corner which is nothing more than the end of a thicket – in a place where the rising sun shines brightly, where midday is hot and where a fleeting light stays in the afternoon . . . right there, resplendent, covered with whiteness from top to bottom we see a bush in full bloom showing off for itself.

'Ah, Doña Laura. It's so lovely. What is it?'

'A thorn bush, a hawthorn. I don't like the name. It's too stupid. I always say *une aubépine*.'

'Yes, it's prettier, it sounds better.'

'It's not that it sounds better; it means more. Listen, if I say *hawthorn* it seems trite. I could say 'white-thorn,' but that sounds very old-fashioned.'

'You're right. You'd have to say it speaking in verse. But the sad thing is . . . no, no, I know that you can't do it . . . the sad thing is that we can't take a branch, because it's so lovely you need to sit and look at it for at least two hours.'

'Oh, no, Elena. Cut flowers . . .'

'Now it's out! These are things that Mrs. Smith teaches my little sister.'

'She doesn't teach me. She just says them, and I think she's right. Something dead . . .'

'But Piedita, it's not a thing, it's a flower. Dead or alive, imagine what you'd look like with a crown of those flowers.'

'Ah, Elena, you really know her weak spot. She's not going to answer you that.'

'You know, Piedita seems more like Elena's sister than yours. And she even seems like Elena's little sister. Isn't that funny?'

'It certainly is! And now you're the one who's setting Elena straight.'

'And tomorrow you'll give her an A.'

'I always give her As. She's first in the class and that's that.'

'It's because you're very patient with me, Doña Laura. Besides, you understand me; you understand everything.'

'I'm very pleased you think so, but I can't let you be mistaken, Isabel. There are a lot of things I don't understand.'

'No, that's not true, you understand everything. You understood what I said about Elena and Piedita, and not everybody would understand that.'

'She's right, Doña Laura. You can believe her. You can believe everything she says. I'm almost fed up with telling her she's fantastic.'

'You're fed up! I can tell you a thing or two about being fed up!'

'All right, now don't get into a fight about it.'

'No, no, don't worry. We never, ever fight. Sometimes she's so sharp you want to kick her in the pants. Remember what she said . . . Piedita seems like my little sister.'

'I said Piedita because we were talking about Piedita; but everybody, no matter who, always seems like your little sister.'

'Isabel! You've got such a sharp eye, it's almost dangerous. What do you have to say about that, Elena?'

'I already told you. She's fantastic . . .'

'Come on, girls! You're too old to be rolling around on the grass.'

'What am I old enough *for*, Doña Laura? I don't know – I just don't know – and that girl is so smart she can sniff out anything. She asked me once why I use the familiar form of address with Piedita when she's grown-up and all, and I tried to explain. But it could take forever. How Piedita used to go running down the stairs with me in her arms! My grandmother would shout out that she was going to drop me, but I wasn't afraid. I really liked the strength she had. She carried me with just one arm, and I must have already weighed a lot. I must have been around two and she must have been around twelve, no? There's a bigger age difference between the two of us than between Piedita and my mother. When you came here to live Piedita must have been a little over three and my mother maybe nine. At that point it was my mother who would go down for her and bring her upstairs. She would bring her up running, too – harder but less dangerous. It's strange, but can you believe that I remember so clearly when my mother would come up with Piedita just like when Piedita would go running down with me in her arms? The same, exactly the same! The light on the staircase going up or going down, repeated over and over for so long, with some little changes. No, not little ones . . . big ones, very big ones, but slow as the minute hand, a minute hand that measures years instead of minutes. And the changes from the familiar to the polite form in front of the students. Piedita calling my mother Doña Ariadne. That's horrible! And all the things that happened in the house, that seemed like they kept on happening because people talked about them all the time. The catastrophe with my grandfather, the arrival of my aunt and uncle. Then, you came. I recall something really well. Can you imagine? When they put up the sign on the balcony railing . . .'

'But Elena, when we came here to live you weren't even born yet.'

'You're right, of course you're right; but I still remember. Not the way I remember how my mother ran up the stairs with Piedita. I can remember it with certainty, with the certainty of having seen it. But how could that be?'

'Ah, yes! Elena's right. Now I remember the sign we had at the beginning. It was some sort of canvas or oilcloth with painted letters, and then you put up the white sign we have now.

'That's right, Piedita, you had to remember it; because what I remember is that you were holding me in your arms and we were looking at the men who were hanging off of the balcony to put up the sign, and we thought maybe they might fall. Then we looked up at it from the street, and it seemed really pretty.'

The garden, the hawthorn and the spring did not fade away . . . they were not forgotten. They became part of the house, of the history of the house. Here at the present moment, there was all that past as if all this now could only be seen in its reflection. As if the only ones who could see it were those making up that fabric of memories, those who in picking those little flowers and herbs and collecting little stones that spring could remember the whole road taken. That road had not been all happy, but always worthy of fidelity, always pleasurable, sadly pleasurable, painfully, tragically, monotonously, brightly, darkly pleasurable. The road had been a chain of contacts stretching on to eternity and tightly linked . . . And yet, in this present moment there was something not connected to the chain, someone so real in the present, so faithful to it, so involved in what is going on, someone who has lived her road with such devotion . . . But not linked to the past with such regularity. This other history cannot display its chain of connected links because there was no dialogue in them, no connector, no continuing response. There was fear, shame – it is hard to grasp the concept of shame clearly – solitude. It was a past not shared, a past about which one cannot ask, 'Do you remember?' It couldn't be said; but even if the question were never heard, it had a firm answer. There was a watchful gaze – dominating without a doubt – ready to level every obstacle, demolish every barrier. A gaze that dared to say:

'I remember! I remember your memories and I take them as mine so long as you trust me.'

Thanks to this gaze and this trust, one could go on, one could tolerate the ironic remarks without meekness and without humiliation. You could put the conflict on a masculine level, go rolling around the floor like boys in a street fight . . . This dominating gaze imposed another outlook; it carried the other's gaze to a very new place with no memories.

'Look, look at the little boat,' addressing one, not all the group. 'Look at it over there on the other bank of the lake! My father said we shouldn't miss seeing it. That must be the one . . . right, Doña Laura?'

'Yes, that must be it. They control it from that little brick pavilion.'

'And it goes by itself?'

'Absolutely. All by itself.'

'Oh, I want to go on it!'

'Piedita! You who wouldn't pick a flower, want to take away the little boat's mystery.'

'I wouldn't take anything from it. I would just get on board and it would take me away.'

'Well, I wouldn't go. What I like is seeing it from here. Look, Isabel, look how it goes by itself.'

'Come on, girls, it's time for lunch. I told you, Elena, not to bring anything. We've got veal sandwiches and tangerines.'

'But I wanted you to taste these little black-and-whites. They're really different.'

'What are they like?'

'They're really simple. You put a good-sized piece of chocolate between two pieces of bread and stick it in the oven.'

'Hey, that's a neat idea!'

The little boat went its way then along the lake. It came closer then it turned a bit and finally came to rest at the little brick pavilion the way the swans come to eat out of your hand. And the veal sandwiches were exquisite. They were made with slices of veal from the pot, and some of the juice had colored the bread. They tasted like real home cooking. There outdoors they reminded you of dinner and sopping up your plate. You had to drink water – from the fountain right there – to fully experience the black-and-whites, toasted and filled with chocolate. And the little boat began its second turn around the pond. The silence was so great that you could hear the absolute silence that powered it. The tangerines relinquished their skins easily. As their skins came off you could hear the breaking of the veins connecting them to the segments. And the vegetable aroma, the almost floral smell, made a perfume that erased the greasy and dense tastes of eating, a bath of cleanness – there's nothing out of the ordinary here – speading out in the wake of purified sensation.

'Ah, I forgot to read Manolo's letter! It weighs as much as a briefcase.'

'Then while you're reading it, may we take a walk around the pond?'

'All right, but don't go far.'

'Well, out with it. What's the situation?'

'I think things are decided.'

'And will your sister let you?'

'Yes, Mrs. Smith has convinced her. She's told her she needs me, that she can't find another partner for her Leandro. Leandro isn't her son, no. Her stupid son is going as Samson. He's got it into his head that he should go as Samson because of his build.'

'And Mrs. Smith's daughter, your student?'

'She's going as Ophelia, and the role fits her like a glove. But Mrs. Smith, who is very good-looking, is going to dress up like an old lady. Imagine: just so we girls don't go alone, she and her mother-in-law and a friend have decided to go as the Weird Sisters. The front part of the float will be a grotto with them as the Weird Sisters weaving, wearing grey gowns as thin as spiders' webs and gray locks down to their ankles. Above, as though the grotto were in the mountains, high above there'll be a cupid with a bow and arrow.'

'And who's going to be Cupid?'

'No one. Cupid will be made out of papier-mâché. Somebody from the factory in Valencia made it, a fellow who does *fallas* there. And he'll make paper roses too, hundreds of papers roses flowing down from Cupid in garlands upon the famous lovers. Each couple will be tied by a garland of roses. Even the horses – four white Percherons – have reins made of garlands.'

'And who's leading them?'

'Ah, that was a really tough one to solve. Mrs. Smith didn't think there should be a couple of coachmen in front blocking the view of the Weird Sisters so she got the idea of putting in front of the grotto two little boys dressed as little cupids with rose-colored shirts – imagine – holding the reins. But little boys couldn't handle the horses; so then she thought up four big fellows – I don't know where she'll find them – who would walk ahead leading the horses by the halters.'

'But that's fantastic, Piedita, just fantastic! Nothing like that has ever been seen here. Naturally, Mrs. Smith must have learned such things in Nice and in the other places she's traveled to. I think she's been to Japan too, no?'

'Yes, she came back beside herself. She wanted to make a dragon like they do there, but no one backed her because it's carried by people inside and they wouldn't have a chance to show off.'

'Of course. But with this one you'll be real stars. And you know that you have better looks than anybody, but you also have to be full of life, you have to talk. How's your Leandro?'

'Well, he's all right: blond, slim and very tall. Mrs. Smith curled his hair with tongs. He didn't want to let her, but she held him down. My sister says she's a frivolous woman, but she's wrong. She's interested in the occult sciences.'

'Ah! No, no, let's not go straight ahead. If we go back a little and end up on the other side of the grove where the hawthorn is I have an idea.'

'No, Elena, we could be in trouble if you get caught.'

'I won't get caught because I won't be hiding anything.'

'And now, what?'

'Now you take off your hat and give me two or three hairpins.'

'My bun will come apart . . . Oh! You can't dare to cut such a large branch!'

'It's not so large, and I like cutting it. It's just right to go around the crown. Look. Could you possibly imagine the hat wasn't always like that? Let's see. Put it on. What do you think, Isabel?'

'Phenomenal!'

'But I don't know if I dare go by the guards like this. Besides, my sister won't allow it.'

'Your sister won't even notice.'

'Do you want to bet?'

'Anything you want.'

'We're a little bit late. Were you thinking we got lost? Bad news?'

'Very bad.'

'Manolo?'

'No, Magdalena . . . by this time they must have operated on her and it's serious, very serious.'

I don't know if I dare to tell even Isabel, although I don't know either if I ought to tell her . . . I just don't know. Is it better to talk about it or not to? If I tell Isabel, I involve her; if I don't tell her I won't know if the very same involvement is already going on inside her head. I suspect . . . my intuition tells me yes, and maybe it's even more complicated. What seems serious to me will seem exaggerated to her, and she'll think it's serious that I think . . . I won't tell her. I don't want her saying to me that it's something stupid knowing, as she knows, that it's not stupid. Who could understand it better than she, after having seen what happened? Doña Laura upset – she must have cried and cried while we were walking around the lake – over the illness, over the death, most likely, of her sister-in-law. What must Magdalena be like? Facts: the boy, Ramón, is very handsome they say, 'as good-looking as his mother.' And Don Manuel, 'Manolo's head over heels in love with Magdalena.' 'It would be terrible for Manolo – He couldn't survive it.' If she does die – because maybe she won't come out of the operation – what would all of them do? They would sink into darkness! I can't imagine the father and the son, but Doña Laura, who loves her brother so much, I can imagine sobbing and in mourning. That's the first thing I imagined: Piedita dressed in mourning. Even the most ignorant or evil or selfish person would have to realize that the death of this lady is more important . . . more impressive. I don't know, I don't know how to say what it is, but I feel it as much as anybody. I can see that it's tragic, that it's enough to leave you crushed, and yet I think about Piedita dressed in mourning. Well, what I'm thinking is not how she's going to be, but how she's not going to be . . . how everything she's thinking about doing is going to turn out to be impossible. What really distresses me is that it hasn't happened like it does when there's a catastrophe. If that lady had died, we would all be very sad, in awe as though we had seen half the world crumble to dust. We would all feel as though something of our own had crumbled – a different thing, but the same in the fact of crumbling. One has a sense of proportion, even regarding things you can't measure: a horse is larger than a dog, for example, but you can feel more deeply about the death of the dog than of a horse. It's in these things that one has an idea of measure; but not because we learn them as kids, no. If it were only a question of that . . . but it's not. It's that we've all measured things inside our heads, we've imagined everything that might happen to us, so when they happen to others – these things we've imagined – we have an idea. That's why if a catastrophe had taken place, we would all be thinking about those who had lost the most . . . but it didn't happen. That's what's really hard to calculate. To this, they'd reply . . . What would they say? Who could I go and tell this story to? Only to Isabel, of course, but I don't want to because . . . At the same time, I think it's the only solution. I can't bear this problem alone . . . Problem, calculate: people get nervous when they hear these words, as if you had brought home a snake. They say, 'But that little girl! What a way to talk!' They can go to the devil. Isabel understands these things, which means that I'll end up telling her. If I haven't told her already it's because I know there's something in this that doesn't please her in the slightest. Anyway, the fact is that the catastrophe hasn't occurred yet. It's looming. We'll know any moment if it's happened or not. No, no, if it happens immediately, we'll know, but it'll likely be several days before the situation is cleared up. Well, here we have a couple of things. I must lay out the problem very clearly, calculate everything, even the most minute detail. But the one stumbling block is that I'll have to find out several details for myself, because I don't want to intervene in them, make them up myself. Tomorrow just by seeing Piedita's face I might understand, or maybe not, because who knows if she herself has thought about the problem. If for her there's no problem, I'd see it immediately. If she's crushed by the news, if she's unable to think about anything else, if she's convinced there's just no hope, then there's no more to be said . . . But, if that's not the case? And if she's trying to keep up her hopes? It's probable that she's clutching at the idea of keeping up her hopes. That's natural. That must be what's happening with her sister. She must have spent a sleepless night. She must have been praying . . . I don't think so; she seems like one of those people who doesn't pray. Although maybe on this occasion, if she's not praying, she's doing something like it. And maybe she even was praying, like any ordinary person. But Piedita – that's the other side of the problem, the one that would bother Isabel: are Piedita's affairs so interesting to me that I lose sleep over them? Not because they're Piedita's – that's what I'll never get her to understand – but because this business, which in this case is Piedita's business, is something anybody would lose sleep over – anyone capable of losing sleep over a problem. Not very many people stay awake nights because of a problem with no solution. In this case, if there is a problem, there's no solution. There is a problem if Piedita is still holding onto the hope of her plan, something she wouldn't confess to herself. I don't want to make her confess it to me. I don't want her to think that I'm suggesting it to her. If she has posed the question to herself, of course I'll try to help. Naturally, the only thing I could do is help her bear it. That will be the hardest thing to bear, not knowing how long the uncertainty will last. There's something so tangled up here that I can't think about it clearly. Uncertainty is unbearable. Let's say that it lasts ten or fifteen days. Depending on how the thing turns out, the uncertainty can be resolved or mitigated very differently. Let's say that after ten days of horrible anguish, this lady dies. Then our own suffering will seem brief. It will seem that she was worthy of more, much more than our pain, which was like an offering to her. We will try to console ourselves thinking that we have accompanied her in her suffering and that somehow she was aware of this, that she felt our leave-taking. I can't stand people who say, 'I don't like good-byes.' – as if it were something to be liked. Nobody likes to say good-bye, but if it comes to that, why not wait until the train is no more than a speck in the distance, and then not even a speck? But that's not the case now. She will have felt and received our pain like those things they used to put in the sepulchers of people in ancient times to keep the peace with the dead. That is, if she dies. The pain is left in peace; but if she doesn't die? If after ten or fifteen days she gets well? Naturally, everyone will be very happy. Of course, of course, everyone – and myself – very happy. But those days of pain? No, no, no . . . if I look at it superficially it seems like I think it would have been a waste. But that's not it, that's not it at all: it's that during those days so many things died. If she doesn't die after fifteen days the joy in the fact cannot be used to go back and find the joy one should have had, the joy one might have had. Now I'm in the same predicament. Of course she was worthy of this interruption . . . I have to grapple with this business as though it were my own in order to get to the bottom of it . . . She deserved for us to wait breathlessly. But she deserved – or deserves – our real and complete joy if she comes out of the crisis. She deserves that change of light: 'Oh, the storm is over! We can live in the sun again. Everyone is happy!' But no, it won't be like that . . . on Piedita's part. It will be like that for Doña Laura, although it can't be really, because if Doña Laura notices any uneasiness in Piedita, any kind of disappointment . . . No, no, not exactly disappointment but the kind of uneasiness which stays with you when something turns out wrong, when you want to correct or add something. Because Piedita will want to return to these days, to this anticipation. How is Piedita going to be able to recover the joy of this morning? Today, no, yesterday: it must be near dawn. Her joy: that's what I want to imagine, because if I think about mine it's very different. It's the difference between a portrait and a mirror. I will always be able to see the portrait, the description of the float. It seemed like I was seeing it and I will see it, in a week, with or without Piedita, I will see it. But she, from today on, as soon as she gets up, will be different. I don't know what the change will be, and that's what I want to know. Think what you like, that slightly foolish expression (quite idiotic according to Isabel, a bit expectant as if she's always saying 'Let's see what's going to happen') that expression will never be quite the same. It won't be like it was when we went running down the little hill to where Doña Laura was sitting . . . Piedita, with the hawthorn on her hat. It seemed like she was running to the lake. The lake was in the distance, but it suited her as a blue background with its little, solitary white boat. We couldn't have imagined we would come upon that unsettled face covered with tears. No, not even Doña Laura could recover that joy; that is, if there is reason to recover it. She'll always feel she's a bit to blame for the disappointment – joy and disappointment together; it's exasperating! – for her sister's lack of resignation, and she certainly would feel this lack of resignation if . . . if the moment goes by. Yes, you could say if the moment is missed because it's like someone who could miss a train. The float is going to pass by in a week, but it's not like what you see sometimes in the station: someone arriving out of breath with his hat falling off. He jumps and they grab his arms to lift him up into the coach of the moving train. No, here Piedita has to be taking the train beginning today. She has to get her ticket and tell Mrs. Smith that she can count on her, that she'll do it no matter what. Because Mrs. Smith will not let her say that she may or may not do it according to developments. And here the role of Doña Laura will be major because the decision to carry on or not must be made today and . . . Suppose that Piedita at bottom has already made it. She has to tell her sister before explaining to Mrs. Smith. What will happen if there emerges between the two a difference of . . . feelings? I don't know, I don't know if it's a matter of feelings. Feelings for Doña Laura are feelings and nothing more. The news has come as a shock and in the middle of her rather boring life, feelings are something: you plunge into them, and you forget everything else. But Piedita on the other hand . . . It wouldn't occur to me to think that she doesn't have deep feelings; but to tell the truth I don't think she's capable of truly plunging into them. I think what she would do is to try to pull them out the way you do an aching tooth. But maybe I'm wrong. I really can't figure it out. I ask myself if Doña Laura would be able to see . . . and if she sees, what would she do? Because if Piedita gives in to feelings, if she figures everything is lost – everything present, or rather, from yesterday – there will be harmony between them. Not because they'll be in agreement, but because they'll coincide. But, what if Piedita wants to hold onto hope above all? Of course that very position, clutching at hope, will be the same as her sister's. And then there will really be discord. Could this matter bring about discord between them? Could Doña Laura utter any of those shameful words – shameful for the speaker and for the listener – those words that put things, not clearly and nakedly, but crudely? 'How can you go on thinking about that when you know about your brother?' No, nothing like that could possibly happen. It's useless. I don't know what to think. The sun's been up for a while . . .

'Isabel!'

'It's really early to be calling, but I couldn't help it. When I went down for the bread I met the telegram boy in the doorway. I went up with him and Doña Laura read it. It said: "Operation completed. Will write." It didn't say anything else.'

'When they don't say anything more, there's no disaster.'

'That's what it looks like.'

'Let's go down and see what they think. Was Doña Laura pessimistic?'

'I think so, but she covered it up. I think it was so as not to worry Piedita. O.K., I know what you're thinking.'

'And what do you know?'

'What you're thinking is what I just told you. And I'm sure you've been thinking it for a while.'

'Ah, and you, no?'

'Yes, me too . . . It could occur to anyone.'

'Well, then, how do we act? It's not a case of putting on remorseful faces. What I want to say is, how are we going to hide the fact that we're thinking what we're thinking?'

'Do you think it's so bad to think that? For Doña Laura, yes, of course. But is it really so bad? Is it possible not to think about it? I'm not talking about you, with your weakness for . . .'

'I don't have weaknesses. You wouldn't call thinking about things – good or bad – a weakness. Not that you'd have what you call a weakness. I was feeling so happy that you think the same as me, but if you come up with this business about weaknesses, then you don't think the same as I do. You don't understand that it obsesses me like a puzzle that has to be put together.'

'All right, let's put it together – but how?'

'I don't know. We'll see when we're downstairs what they seem like.'

A change, a transposition in daily life made this thing unfathomable. Differences in schedule played the role of obstacles to investigation. The girls in the classroom wrote in an orderly fashion, in respectful silence. Piedita was giving the Spanish history class. She didn't want to send them home, since they were already there. But there would not be a normal school day because the Director, after such a night, according to Piedita, was unable to appear. In Doña Laura's room the shutters were closed. The slightly opened door permitted an inquiry as to how she was feeling, if she needed something, whether they could bring her anything. The maid wouldn't be in until late, and she had to take something: they could go down to the pharmacy for some kind of relaxant, they'd ask Don Luis. 'All right, all right, ask him . . .' 'You go down, Isabel. I've got something to do meanwhile.' On the stove the aluminum coffee pot still had some hot water. She just had to move it a little so the water would boil to make some linden tea, then go carefully to the room and pour several drops from the small flask. What a sad smell! So sad that it seemed impossible to serve it as a remedy for sadness. It seemed more like a consoling corroboration that would make sadness acceptable. 'This exquisite aroma is sad: dissolve your sadness in its painful aroma, and sleep, wrapped in its sad vapors.' A tiptoeing out of the room, and from the door of the classroom a discreet good-bye to Piedita. Then running up to the studio with a large package.

'No, I won't open it here. You know I don't want to bring sewing stuff into the studio and get threads all over the floor. Let's go to my room . . . Now, see? She's made very little headway with it. We have to finish by the day after tomorrow. Do you want to put on the blue ribbon or do the black needlework?'

'I don't care, but maybe it would be better for you to do the ribbon and me the needlework because we have to sew the ribbon first, no?'

'Right, you do the needlework with the black silk thread. Make it double so that it's good and thick. The first piece is marked, but I think you can go ahead by yourself after that. Don't make any mistakes.'

'How could I make a mistake? The pieces that go vertically, to the right; the horizontal ones, below.'

'Exactly. That way it looks like a Grecian relief, don't you think? My father drew it, and I traced it on the cloth. It's a wonderful effect.'

'And what are they going to say here in your house?'

'Well, everyone will say what they're supposed to say. Everybody knows the script by heart.'

'Do you know it?'

'No, and neither do you. We'll improvise. My father would also improvise if he wanted to; but he doesn't, because he's indifferent to everything (or almost everything). My mother repeats her part out of boredom. She gives so many lessons in one day! What does one more matter? The one who never gets tired of repeating it is my grandmother: she lets loose and puts everyone in his place.'

'Yes, she normally puts people in their place.'

'But I don't think she's ever gotten after you.'

'No, after me, no. Look, is this all right?'

'It's turning out perfectly. Listen, downstairs in the class, do you girls draw much?'

'Yes, we draw some. I've got a folder filled with doodles.'

'Why didn't you ever show them to me?'

'Because they're really bad.'

'I doubt it. You draw. Look, it's something I thought of just this moment . . . No, no, it's not something I thought of, but something I can see. I can't understand why I didn't see it before: you draw.'

'Not really, they were just silly things I did for class.'

'I didn't say you *did* anything. I said you draw. Listen, your putting the shadows just where they should go without their being marked shows that you draw. And you're going to begin to draw immediately, tomorrow morning.'

'Tomorrow! Where?'

'Upstairs in my studio. There's a very large portfolio there which you can use as a table. There's enough charcoal, and we'll buy paper tomorrow. You don't want to? What's that face for?'

'But Elena!'

'What's the matter? What's the big catastrophe?'

'There's no catastrophe – I mean – I don't know. Ah! Look, I made a mistake. I just put one on the left. See? So much for your bright ideas.'

'I'm not getting bright ideas. Undo it and put it on the right. It's about time you stopped getting upset over nothing. Let me tell you what Doña Laura said: "You're too old for that." Well, you're too old to act like a scared rat. Look at the size of you! You're a couple of centimeters taller than I . . .'

'Fiddlesticks! I'm not a bit taller. We're the same height.'

'No, sir, we're not the same height. You'll see. Let's measure ourselves on the door frame. See? A centimeter and a half. Only eleven years old and taller than me. You've got to convince yourself that you're not a little girl. Why are you laughing?'

'It's something really dumb. It's that Don Luis wasn't in the pharmacy, and Luisito, who has as many whiskers as his father, waited on me. And he says to me all of a sudden, "I'm glad you're teacher is sick! Because you've had to come down and talk to me!" Imagine – what a ninny!'

'What's the date today? Ah, it's the 7th of April.'

'But why did you write it on the door?'

'Because it's the first day we've measured ourselves . . . and because it's the first day . . . unless you've hidden other things from me.'

'What other things? Don't think for a minute that I'm interested in that kind of stuff.'

'Be quiet and sew.'

Luis – Luisito – was already old enough to shave, but he left his mustache. One day he shaved it off, and his father told him, 'You look like a priest.' The conflict between his parents on this issue was dramatic, and weighed upon him, not like a sentence, but like a ball and chain dragging on his leg since . . . since before he was born. It was a chain that his father helped him break. Now he had broken it. He was free, completely free: the chains would never limit his future . . . no, never. It was settled. All that was left was the pressure of the irons on his ankle; he wasn't immobilized, no, but the pressure of the irons didn't disappear and the feeling inspired by that pressure was unusual. It wasn't the desire to escape – he had been set free so easily! – it was the desire, the duty . . . Can there be a desire for duty? Can duty be seductive, bewitching and as tyrannical as a temptation? It wasn't the desire to escape, it wasn't the otherness of any shackle or chain that was to be feared. What couldn't be overcome was the mark the irons had left, something like a longing to remain true. But there is no fidelity without a promise, and he had promised nothing. It was he who had been promised. Can a woman communicate with a fetus that can scarcely move in her womb? This being that begins to take shape with its little fists clenched against its eyes – can she fasten it with an indestructible chain? We are talking now not about the dawn of life, but the jaws of death. The mother, on the verge of death – or so she believed – had promised God that if she regained her health her son would be consecrated to Him. Her health was returned, and the child appeared in the world with no signs of the danger undergone. This terrible promise spread the power of its dramatic essence through buried roots. On the surface it was manifested in the infantile forms – the games, the comfort – through which women nourish their children. It was all glossed in talk with the other mothers. 'You see? My little priest has everything . . . tiny candles, the candlesticks, the missal. I made the cloth for the little altar myself. Look. It's all brocaded.' The game was charming in its seriousness and in the innate ability that could be glimpsed in the tiny hands endowed with an intelligent touch. Gradually, however, the ecclesiastical toys became chipped and broken, exactly like the other toys, and at the age of seven the game moved up to the level of the parish church. Then it became the surplice, the censer and 'Look, look how well he manages the candle snuffer!' When he was ten, the arguments between his parents were becoming more frequent. They were about him, but he went off by himself to think about them. He studies the pros and the cons. Which one of them was right? He did not dare judge them. Which of the two do I want to be right? He had no doubts. Terrible, brutal exclamations exploded in those disputes. He fled from the murmuring voices and they dissolved into confusion, into sprinklings of intermittent phrases which were mostly cut short. Some, though, went off like shotgun blasts, and the full force of the reports reached you no matter where you were. Brutal, definitive despite the question: 'How could I let you make a queer out of my son?' Or heartbroken, howling like a dog, 'You want him to be damned, to lose his soul!' And the cutting response, hatchet and broom all at once, sweeping all before it: 'If there is Justice – listen to me now! – if there is Justice, the only one damned will be me!' So, if there is Justice, it is certain that one can accept the sentence voluntarily, stand before the judge and plead guilty. His father was willing to do it. The only thing left to know is whether or not Justice does exist – and this means asking at the place where nothing in the code can be overlooked. If he had asked in a simple way, perhaps he would have found an answer appropriate to his innocence. But he started with a preamble, he wanted to stress the seriousness of his inquiry, and he revealed a tormented conscience, obsessed by the concept rather than the feeling of guilt. The pettifogging confessor – a bureaucrat used to the routine of a humble neighborhood's confessional – avoided the answer and used his authority to conduct the questioning along lines that led to the sins common to boys. He answered nothing: he kept asking relentlessly. He asked about solitary pleasures, fondling, little glimpses under girls' skirts. No, no, no! Luis denied everything. He denied what he thought he had confessed other times. Even if it was true, he denied it cynically, ferociously; and not in a weak no-no-no way, but with a loud, clear NO. To every question he gave a NO heavy with contempt for the word he had heard for the first time, for the obscenity he had just learned: fondlings . . . No to the stupid questions, NO to the banal penance. Settled in his NO as if it were a newly acquired dwelling, he received communion. Then he began his studies: the rigors of chemistry, the aromas of botany. Going out with his friends, never without a few pesetas in his pocket. And with the impiety common to all forgetting, even when what is forgotten is detested, silence fell on the family disputes, as if now . . . In a way, everything having to do with the family was subordinated to the external. Before, the city had always been a place of transit, the space between one house or family and another: streets were a space for going visiting. Now it began to be a presence – not a visitor but a host, something to which everyone was obliged, both by the strength of its reality and by gratitude. The city's tremendous, imperious reality was gratifying, worthy of gratitude because full of favors. Reality with all its impurities – always heavy with the grace of its being, always lit by the danger of its no longer being, by its mortality. Everything: children's games, which were no longer child's play but could seduce adults – the merry-go-round and the slide most of all! in the open area of Cibeles Circle, across from the Bank. The slide, a pocket edition of orgasm, anticipation more than initiation! Something like the tasting of a dish as you're preparing it. And the cinema, a pleasure that is immeasurable because it surpasses all sensuality, because it encompasses – or rather, envelops and makes real just by indicating it – vision, the supreme form of sensuality that spreads out, infiltrates and appropriates by making things palpable to the mind and to the emotions with equal power. The discovery of an inexhaustible New World, a place to emigrate to, an Eldorado for all the poor and the ambitious, a seedbed for ambitions, a showcase for beauty; lacking a canon, but in its place initiating, creating with the simple power of its luminous finger, projecting its FIAT. The cinema, reality in disembodied images, shadow and light – and silence, that is, attention. Unblinking attention, opening your eyes and seeing, seeing swiftly because it passes . . . the image escapes and does not return, but it etches itself so that it cannot be forgotten, because if it, the image, is not etched, the one that follows loses reality and meaning. The chain is unbreakable. It fills the entire night with vision, with the most extreme scenes of love or of death, crying out in the silence.

Outside, an uproar can be heard, first far off and faint, then getting closer and closer with the sound of a metallic clanging. The clapper of the firemen's bell beats incessantly. The sky is reddish above the glass of the skylight, and the two – the two sisters – go up to the balconies of the third floor to watch. The Noviciado Cinema is on fire. An enormous blaze rises above Ancha Street; everyone is out on the balconies. The fire has taken them from their private affairs. The Cinema has called them to the spectacle of its own destruction, of its own death – which would strike who knows how many people. Its apotheosis, by its magnitude, is able to bring these people together and rob a bit of the attention they fasten on their private lives. Their gazes send a rain of pity upon the flames. The two sisters dwell on the terrible scene, not because they rejoice in the misfortune of others, but because the lamentable occasion offers them a bit of freedom. It is restful to commune with the suffering of many, putting aside, as if by hand, the dim pain of the uncertain, of not knowing if it has happened. The threat of pain is possibly worse than pain itself: 'If it has to be done, let it be done quickly.' As long as one doesn't know, it's necessary, freeing, even comforting to lament something concrete, a real pain, as if one feared the failure of fear, as if the intensity – the truth, above all – of the pain suffered yearned to be justified by the very fact it abhors. A chorus of neighbors crammed onto balconies makes banal comments . . .

The liberation and rest which comes from communication can also cause nausea. Degraded by the shouts, remarks, reflections and even commonplaces uttered by the neighborhood women, suffering can prompt rejection and sever the current of communication. Laura makes believe she doesn't hear and stares at the flames in shocked silence, concentrating her faculties as though she were in the cinema watching a magnificent film. She listens – with the delight inspired on other occasions by the intriguing hum of the projection booth, a kind of crackling of light – to the sputtering of the fire, the crack of falling beams . . . Piedita squeezes onto the balcony next to Elena. 'You took something from my room, didn't you?'

'Of course, it's got to be finished.'

'Do you think so?'

'I don't think anything, but don't you worry about it. It'll get finished on time.'

'But, if . . . ?'

'Oh, if . . . Your sister's sneezing.'

'Of course. She got up out of bed.'

'That's all we need . . . They seem to be getting it under control, the flames aren't any higher than the houses now, just the ashes are glowing.'

The gathering is beginning to break up. Those closest to the sisters are the last to leave. Ariadne embraces Piedita without a word. Eulalia calms Laura. 'There's no reason to be negative. Who knows? Today, with so many new advances . . .' The night has passed its climax. The firemen leave, their bells softer now in opening a path . . . 'Isabel?' – 'The sight was more perfect from the dormer window.' The sky was no longer reddish above the skylight. The staircase awaited the day just like always, and morning came, putting things in order. Isabel went down like always in case there was class, but there wasn't.

'Elena, you should come down at once. Another telegram arrived, just as we feared: "Still serious. There's hope."'

'I was just going to come down.'

'Wait a minute. Doña Laura is in bed with a cold, wrapped in blankets. She needs some syrup. Piedita asked me to get it for her, but I don't want to. You go and I'll wait for you down in the entrance.'

'But, child, are you an idiot? Do you think the bogeyman will get you?'

'I might be an idiot, but I'm not going.'

'All right, let's not argue about it now. I'll go, and we'll talk later.'

A woman is waiting down in the pharmacy. There's not the slightest sound on either side of the counter, but somebody must be preparing what the woman is waiting for. Luis comes out, corking the flask. 'Syrup of Tolú.' Luis finds the syrup in the display case. 'Put it on Doña Laura's account.' Luis raises his eyes and looks at Elena, nothing more.

Joshua stopped the sun . . . Some legends, phantoms and poetic shadows from other times have vanished in the light of our rational era. Others, by contrast, are only just now beginning to bloom, to reach their suggestive effectiveness. The notion of the sun obeying – humoring, rather – Joshua: we cannot imagine the sun detained by an order. We do not wish to see the event as a game of strategy, but rather as a vital conjunction or association. This one, for example, is understood or experienced today – who has not lived it! – as an instant in which Joshua held his breath. His life, the flow of his blood, is suspended while the torrent of his will – 'The will is only that which says YES or NO' – rushes in a grand cataract of affirmations and everything, the world, the atmosphere, the stars, stops – no light glimmering on the waters, no change in the dunes' shadows – and gathers energy . . .

Elena thinks first of all that she's thirteen and then, simultaneously, she thinks that she's known Luis for thirteen years. She thinks this during the time that Luis's gaze focuses on her eyes. And the important thing is that it was not a meaningful look: it was simply a look. It was not a melancholy or anguished or reticent look: it was a slow look. Luis raised his eyes and looked at Elena, nothing more. It can be said in no other way. She thinks about, or rather sees those thirteen years of being neighbors, of being friends, for Luis is sixteen but their friendship is thirteen. In that instant she sees the friendship which exists between them. She sees, above all, the enormous familiarity she has with Luis – toward Luis; she sees him – Isabel would mock her for this – as her little brother. A little brother who might suddenly find himself lost, upset because he didn't have something he wanted madly, and she could put her arm around him and tell him not to cry, that she would get it for him. Elena sees the form or presence of this familiarity in the way the syrup is wrapped, the way Luis moves his hands. He places the flask on the paper spread out on the counter. The paper is blue-gray and has letters on the shiny side that don't show through on the dull side. The flask in its box lies on the grayish surface which is like the gray of a cloud. As the flask lies on this surface of uncertain tone, Luis raises the right-hand side of the paper, and then the left. He adjusts the box and folds the paper, closing it at the corners, putting one edge on top of the other, just as he would have done with his hands if he crossed them rapidly. At the narrow ends, head and foot of the box, he turns up the ends on an angle so that they come together, forming a triangle that, when it is raised, closes the package. Meticulously – not slowly because the time consumed in the work is purely mystic time – with a perfection that speaks in each fold, narrating confidingly the essential meaning of what is being experienced. He passes his index finger and thumb along the corners, adjusting them, pressing them firmly. Then he slides the edge of his hand over everything to make sure there are no wrinkles. This movement is decisive rather than rapid. Nothing is left undone; that is, there is nothing left to do: the perfection of the perfectly complete. The hands that played with religious objects move, work, execute each movement as if elevating their own act. Elena is discovering in each of them the reason – the reason for being – for her sense of familiarity. In each one of them she reads the solidity and the quality of matter – the soul or personality or humanity that is the substance or the theme of her meditation. Of course, Elena is not meditating, she is living the infinitesimal text in myriads of stellar phases. She is confirming the authenticity, the accuracy of her first certainty, the one acquired in the exchange of glances that now is not repeated. They do not look at each other again. Luis looks, not at the package he is wrapping, but at the space around him. Elena looks at the hands of Luis which have been granted – by no one, by simply being the hands of that soul, personality, humanity – the capacity to relate minutely, to affirm with the firmness of what they affirm, pledging . . . And then, without their glances crossing again, without even a good-bye, a thank-you – an excessive lack of any sort of etiquette, of politeness, we might say, the behavior of old neighbors who scarcely say 'good morning' – Elena goes running upstairs, because Isabel wasn't waiting for her in the entrance, but on the landing. She had felt too exposed in the entrance.

'What did he say to you?'

'That you're a complete imbecile.'

'He said that!'

'No, he didn't say it, but he thought it. He didn't say anything, he didn't mention you. What did you want him to say, that he couldn't sleep last night?'

'No, why should I want him to say anything? What's it to me?'

'Then, why did you ask? Why did you come up here to wait and see if I had some news?'

'Oh, don't make up . . .'

'What's the matter? They didn't have any syrup?'

'Yes, they did, Piedita; but we're talking about *something new that* . . .'

'Oh, good. You can tell me later. We've got to give her some now. She's been coughing for ten hours.'

Coughing is also something new for someone cornered by uncertainty. Sunday, the letter; Monday, the telegram; and that night, all the commotion of the fire, bringing a release of tension that restored equilibrium if not peace of mind. Anguish, suffering, tension – manifested, expressed like someone rehearsing a text or copying a model. The horror is there, rising above the rooftops, and our laments attempt to equal it in dimension. But the fire is over, and the cries fade, because the horror is mixed with a certain dose of perplexity. What is going to happen? What is happening? What has already happened? There, in that other place two hundred kilometers away, what is already obvious at this moment, verifiable, making the pain's true dimensions evident? What must that distant reality be? And how is one to bear this uncertain, mute, impotent waiting until one knows for sure? Something must be found, a discomfort that is not a selfish distraction, but which offers a diversion – an incursion into the painful fixation on something different – that carries its expiation within itself. Coughing, coughing until your throat is torn apart. Coughing hoarsely from the depths of your lungs, exchanging the habitual sigh for ferocious hawking, bringing up phlegm, soaking handkerchiefs with nasal fluids, with sweat that turns the pillow into a soggy object smelling of wet wool – like a lamb in the rain, the imposed passivity of material things: the pillow or the bronchi, the blanket or the nasal congestion that blocks the passage of air, the nightgown and sheets plastered to your legs, wrinkling more with every movement, knotting around your legs in cords that your hands can't loosen, holding your body imprisoned in a wet spot because stretching out your feet to the cooler regions of the bed takes too much effort. Another sneeze, more mucus, hawking, and now it's too much even to move your hand to your face and push away the hair plastered to your forehead with sweat, or the drop on the tip of your nose, which is as cold as if you were outdoors. All of this interrupting, or rather, rejecting the spring that was beginning, but can't come into the bedroom. The cubic space of the room is swollen by turpentine, by the vapors of eucalyptus boiled in the earthenware pot, leaving no cracks through which spring's mild gusts might filter as they shake old seeds from the banana plant and shred them into fuzz. No, spring can't get into the room; it can't make itself felt. But amid the sweat and hawking, it is present in the idea of time passing. The vague time of uncertainty is certain and fixed for what is outside in the street, mathematically fixed for those walking around outside. It's fixed not only for trees and seeds, but for people. For Piedita. Her plans for fun, luxury, novelty, defended so obstinately. Had there been a kind of presentiment in her opposition to the plan, a fear? 'Don't risk your happiness on a desire that will be difficult to sustain, in a climate of luxury and ostentation that is too costly, too unusual, too discordant in your life.' And it was that consideration, that her life had neither brilliance nor discord (not that discord was a desirable thing, except in the context of what was not harmony, but monotony), the very consideration on which the opposition was based, that in the end won her consent. The fact is, it wasn't purely tenderness or compassion toward the whim – let's call it illusion – but ambition of another sort . . . practical, practicable: a vague, probable – at least not impossible – germ of practicality. It was a dangerous play, but it was a play. Giving consent was accepting the game. There's no reason to deny it: she had become part of the game. She hoped for more, so much more than Piedita, from it. Because . . . what was Piedita hoping for? To play, to shine for an evening on Recoletos, to go in costume, to embody the legendary lover – her classical beauty made it possible. She would be splendid in the tunic designed by Mr. Morano. But apart from that, what did she know about Hero? What does she know about a love that leads to perjury before the gods? Of course, I have put plenty of books in her hands – many more, naturally, than have ever passed through the hands of those young people, those children of the . . . rich, shall we say? With the exception, certainly, of Mrs. Smith who is the daughter and mother of wealth, who is a snob by nature. What can any of them know about the types they're going to parade on a float, the lovers – THE CHARIOT OF

LOVE – and the Weird Sisters weaving. It's not that Mrs. Smith doesn't catch on, no, she has her little ideas. They are probably very well-received in her own circles. They all must be eager for the arrival of that day, that radiant Sunday – radiant only for a few hours, the time it takes for the float to go along Castellana and Recoletos. Sufficient time for what they want, a few hours of pleasure. What prestige, what majesty there is in that word if I compare it with what my hopes were regarding this game! Because I've thought about it a lot, as much as Piedita, and maybe even more. But I haven't been thinking about the float full of lovers in their elegant costumes; I haven't been thinking about their afternoon – because the parade, as always, will take the whole afternoon. Right after lunch preparations begin. Some will not have eaten out of impatience. Then it gets darker and the first street lamps are lit. Everything breaks up, each one goes home with the memory that is left. Of pleasure, that's it: of any pleasure, no matter how small, as long as it's truly a pleasure. 'It's going by!' they shout. Of course it's going by. It goes by like a meteor. What I wanted – longed for, hoped for – was nothing so brilliant and so fleeting. I agreed to it, thinking that perhaps in these brilliant gatherings, in these meetings, perhaps there might emerge . . . well, something lasting. Yes, that is what I thought. I decided to risk whatever it was because there was no real danger. There was the risk of this fleeting splendor. It is so difficult to know what lies within that too-feminine soul! The fact is that I spend my life trembling for her, afraid that at any moment she might let herself be deceived by something . . . and other times fearing that she'll go through life without feeling anything. Too feminine, too good, too healthy. I keep wanting for her a punishment for all those virtues, yearning for the appearance of a master for all those excesses. Because a man, perhaps, would not see them as excesses. And suddenly it has all fallen apart, everything has been interrupted. She must certainly have lost her enthusiasm, her humor, her gaiety. Her loss of gaiety is obvious; but I don't know if it's because, for the most part, her gaiety has been lost. It's more like, well, I don't know, like something being crushed. I, on the other hand, since it was not gaiety or any form of pleasure that I was seeking, but a greedy hope for . . . rest. I am always wanting a rest from this burden which does not weigh on me . . . no, or if it does weigh me down, it is a burden which I adore. If I want to rest, it's my way of drawing back a bit so I can see it, see how it adapts itself, see if it reaches a stability of its own, rather than one maintained by me. A person can rest a bit by pulling back, without loosening ties. The ties that neither weaken nor break are those which one had not noticed, never imagining their existence, until at a particular moment the knot tightens to the point of asphyxiation . . . Like now with this catastrophe that is taking place in Zamora. Three days ago, we thought about Zamora without the horizon clouding over . . . Even if we had heard about some cataclysm in Zamora, I don't know what, the derailment of a train . . . Names, names would have been the first thing we asked about and, if our own names weren't included, we would have been very sad about the tragedy, but our horizon wouldn't have clouded over. And so they condemn the family, the clan – as if clan and family were abstractions, things instituted in law codes that could be abolished. And what haven't we abolished, we freethinkers in our family – freehanded destroyers and levelers! What worthless rules wouldn't we obliterate? What bonds could they impose on us? Bonds, let me see, if I were to claim that bonds exist, they'd say that a bond is an effect of the irrational, a sentiment left over from an earlier stage, when what it is . . . , when in it culminates . . . Let me see, what is it that culminates? What is it? Knowledge, that's it, knowledge. I don't know what might be happening in Zamora at this moment, and not knowing is dreadful precisely because I know what it is – not only how it is, but what it is – no matter what might be happening. I know what is taking place within a mind, in certain eyes, on lips that are smoking or not smoking, drinking or not drinking, according to the circumstances. I know how all this is; I'm responding from here to each of my brother's movements, and – this is the thing! – if I say I respond without realizing it, they'll say that's the irrational part, when it's a case of a more rigorous knowledge than any other kind: a response, a correspondence – the vibration of the tuning fork . . . My God, my temperature must be going up! Who's shouting like that from the balcony? Ah, of course. It's that crazy Araceli, talking to Piedita.

'Yes, Elena was here with me, but she went to open the door because we saw the postman at the entrance. I'll talk to you later, Araceli.'

The promised letter doesn't arrive, but no more telegrams come either. The situation has come to a standstill. A telegram can still come, even at midnight. That would mean that something serious had happened. May it not happen, please God!, may it not happen.

'We're going to finish the tunic. Ah, don't you remember that we were going to begin something else?'

'What?'

'Do you dare tell me you can't remember?'

'No.'

'No, what? You can't remember or you don't dare tell me?'

'All right, well, yes.'

'Yes, what?'

'Whatever you wish. Whatever bothers you most. So long as you remember, I certainly won't get out of it.'

'Ah, but did you want to get out of it?'

'No, no, no, I didn't.'

'Well, what did you want, if you don't mind telling me?'

'You already know perfectly well what I wanted. What I didn't want was to begin now. Can't you see the storm clouds overhead?'

'And what does the storm have to do with it? Besides, it's still a long way off.'

'The storm does have a lot to do with it because there will be a horrible light in the study, everything will turn out badly and I'll be convinced that I'm completely worthless.'

'Just as I, from the start, am convinced of just the opposite.'

'But since I'm not . . . Let's finish this even though we have to light the lamp. The sash is almost finished. Did you hear that?'

'Yes, it's approaching quickly.'

'No, I didn't mean the thunder. Didn't you hear somebody shout "Elena"?'

'Ah, I can imagine who it is. Exactly! It's her in person. And now she's shouting louder. She's afraid the louder thunderclaps might drown her out. I'm going to lean out the window before the showers begin.

'Araceli . . .'

'I've been calling you all day, Elena. Where have you been hiding?'

'What did you want?'

'I ran into Piedita downstairs and she told me . . .'

'Wait a minute until the noise stops. You can't hear a thing.'

'Are you finishing her tunic? Is there a lot left? It must be gorgeous.'

'Wait, wait a bit. I can't hear a thing.'

'What do you mean? I can hear you perfectly.'

'But don't shout: I'll come over in a minute.'

Doña Laura must have heard her. She must have realized that we're getting everything ready here upstairs as though nothing else were going on. These thunderclaps must be a horror for her, covered up in her bed and realizing that everyone else is untroubled, thinking about clothes and going along with Piedita's whim. Because she'll be thinking that Piedita is persisting because we're behind her. Well, that might console her a little. It is probably easier for her to think that we're to blame and not Piedita.

'My heavens! That was really a blast!'

'It must have hit the house.'

'No, it couldn't have hit the house.'

'How do you know?'

'Well . . . I'm not sure. It's not that I know it didn't hit, it's not that I know how to tell when it doesn't hit, but I'm certain that if it had hit there would be no room for doubt. Come on, let's see what that crazy girl wants.'

'But what do I need to go for?'

'No reason, just to see what she wants.'

'But I'm not the one she wants to talk to . . . and now the downpour is starting.'

'Who cares? It's just across the street.'

Oh, what a marvelous smell, and what a clamor! Of course, since it's not water, but hail. You want to gather it up by the handful . . . look how it piles up in the gutters. It falls, smashes against the paving stones or bounces as if it were all little rubber balls. They make curves, short white parabolas that stand out on the ground like necklaces. They leap with the impetus of their abundance, as though a never-empty cornucopia had been turned upside down. It rains pearls and Felipa stands in the doorway of the poultry shop shaking her head sadly. 'This is a disaster for many!' But it's not because she's an old soothsayer; it's because she's thinking of the country, of her village. The smell of wet earth – she has gone out to smell it as though it had called her – is like a familiar face, like all the faces of brothers and sisters who might be miscarried because of a storm like this.

Faces that pass through her mind, that surge up in her memory with that same cornucopian abundance because they are countless. They are the unforgettable, the known, what was seen a thousand times and what was never seen, though one knows how they must be: one knows how a face that one has never seen crying must look when it cries. One knows how the white curtain might be falling over sown ground, knocking down the flowers from the trees and sending up everywhere that marvelous scent, as though the color green were giving up its soul to that smell. And it gives its soul, of course, and receives it. A few buds fall, a few spikes lie down, and those that do not fall or lie down drink in without expression the grace raining down upon them. And all this can crowd into one's mind with the clarity of a colored engraving, with the minute detail of a carefully told tale, but only as an aroma. All this is nothing more than an aroma at the door, an aroma that rushes at the person who has gone out to smell it, and then, desolate, goes back to the smell of lice in chicken feathers, to the smell of blood, to the smell of the pennies in the till, to the smell of the straw wrapping paper. Monotonous, certain, everyday smells with no memory . . .

'I was motioning for you to keep quiet, Araceli. I didn't want Doña Laura to hear you.'

'Oh, I didn't understand. But why? Because she has the flu?'

'No, that's not why. There's a very serious illness in the family. I'll tell you later. What is it you wanted?'

'Oh, I'm really sorry. Listen. It's not that I wanted to burden you with another job, no. I want you to take a look at what I thought of making with these old remnants. See? Don't you think I could wear this as an Egyptian at the Galician Center ball?'

'Of course, and the color is pretty. Red and black always go together.'

'I've made the stripes go horizontally because they shape the hips more.'

'Yes, they really do. But won't it make you look a bit too broad?'

'No, my waist is really tiny, with a very tight corset. I don't go for a straight corset. That's for those girls who have nothing here and nothing there.'

'Let's see. Try it on.'

'It's still just basted, but I'll put it on because I want you to help me with the neckline. I want it fairly deep, but I want to wear a camisole.'

'A camisole! How on earth do you propose to hide it?'

'I've taken the sleeves off an old one and, turning it in around the top, and holding it with pins . . .'

'All right, I'll come over and help you dress.'

'Oh, great! That's just what I wanted. But wait a minute, look, I copied the necklace from one that's in the museum, using some beads I had. And I don't want to cover my head with one of those cloths that hangs down on the sides. I want people to see my hair. You see? It looks really good when I wear it loose. I'll have to wash it, of course. I'd like to have that little snake that you see some of them wearing on their foreheads . . . do you think we could do it?'

'What couldn't we do?'

'Do you think we can, Isabel? You haven't said a word up 'til now. Don't you like the material?'

'A lot, I like it a lot. The red part is lovely, and with its black trim it'll be just right for you.'

'Well, it's stopped raining now. Bye-bye.'

'Hah, you've got the little snake on your shoulders now!' said Isabel. Yes, and not only the snake. And then it just burns me up for them to say – above all my grandmother who has a terrible opinion of me, and never tires of saying 'This girl is just dying to help everyone else.' 'She's the shoulder all the neighbors cry on.' 'She ought to become a Sister of Charity.' And it burns me up too because she says things like that thinking something else altogether. That's the question: the others don't say anything and they think that, they think what she says and she, the one who says it, doesn't think it . . . and neither do I. I haven't the slightest inclination to be a Sister of Charity. When Isabel said that Piedita seemed like my little sister, she also said it with ill will, because it made her angry; but there's absolutely no way to change that, just like everything else that she comes up with. If I end up acting like a big sister with everybody, it's not because I like to give orders: not even when I do it, when everybody is waiting for me to give orders, and I have to give them like it or not. I have to give orders because I see clearly what the others can't make out. That's the thing: if I end up being a big sister it's because ordinary big sisters or brothers exist by chance, but not me. In my case it's because I decide to be. It seems like that's what my grandmother is saying, but no, it's something completely different. It's not that I decide to consider myself everyone's sister, no; what happens is that I get near. At times I get too near: it's never too near in relation to how near I would like to get, because it's never too near to see what people are like. To see exactly what they do not see (I don't know who I mean by "them," everybody.) because that's the nice part – well, more than nice. Every one of them wanting . . . It's impossible to know what Piedita wants . . . The carnival: what things you hear people saying about the carnival. Some say What joy!, It's a festival of joy! Others just the opposite: that when it's all over . . . the vanity . . . the disappointment. Stupidities! The carnival is neither one: it's neither joyful nor sad. It's . . . I don't know . . . it's tremendous. What's hardest to understand are the ugly things, the clowns, the masks of the grim reapers, the grim reapers themselves, when what one wants is the crimson dye, the gauze, the things that we don't use every day, the things that seem a luxury but are really not. They are more than luxuries because the people who dress as princes or sultans are ancient princes or sultans, dead . . . almost saints. Anything so distant is almost holy: there must be something holy about it for one's memory to have preserved it with such luster. And what has no luster, the ugly, is also preserved by memory and must therefore be holy: no, it is sacred. Is the devil sacred, too? He must be. The ugly – can that be sacred? It must be because it never comes to an end. There are ugly things and ugly people everywhere, no matter how much we don't want to see them. It's not that I don't want to see them. It's not that I pretend not to see them: what I want is for them not to exist. But since they do exist and set themselves in front of me, I look at them in the same way as pretty things. Well, not the same, but as much as – I look at them maybe more because it's harder for me to understand them: it's difficult for me to approach them, but I get near. Because if there were nothing more than pretty things . . . There are things in the carnival which, even though they're pretty, are not brilliant or gay. And it's precisely those things which I like best, which I don't just *like*, but am attracted to. I'd have to say that those things make me fall in love with them because what I feel about those things, with those things, for those things, is the affection that they inspire, that they exude, that envelops one. My father says that the word melancholy does not have as nice a meaning as I think it does, but I don't care. It has for me the meaning I hear in its sound, that I see in its sound. Melancholy is what I see – and what everyone sees because I've read it a hundred times, but I don't see it because I've read it, but rather because it exists – Melancholy is like a paleness, like something becoming completely pale. It's Pierrot, all in white, with black buttons to set off even more his paleness: it's Pierrot's face with the paleness of the moon. And it's also the moon without Pierrot, the moon with cats on the roof. Those drawings you see in *Blanco y Negro*, silhouettes of bell towers against the moon and a cat or two with their backs arched. I love those silhouette drawings because they're like a portrait of the night, like night itself, like a portrait of silence, of melancholy. There's such a profound melancholy in the roof tops where the cats go that you feel you want to scream. No one dares to wail out of melancholy: only cats. Somebody might say – the idiots, the ones who always have something to say – that cats wail for other reasons. It's not that I know why cats wail, but I think it's stupidity to claim that it's *something else*. I hear them and I know they wail because I see it. Now, how can you say that what you hear and what you see are the same thing, but you can't describe what it is? Because it's not the same as that other stupidity that some people come out with regarding love. They're such idiots that they have no idea what's going on. I can't stand even the singing of *Voi che sapete che cosa è amor*. The music is divine, but Claudia singing it with that innocent face of hers . . . How is it possible not to know what love is? You learn that when you're three years old. Affection, hate, jealousy – these are things you know from birth. Because all these – affection, hate, jealousy – are things you feel for someone; and if you feel them regarding a person standing there before you, how can you possibly not know what you feel? It's not the same as that other thing, that paces along the rooftops, that is so overwhelming, that has to do with light or the lack of light, with certain places you pass through and you feel a sort of terror. People are so crude that they make all the important things into something like recipes. The dangers a girl meets as soon as she has 'crossed the Rubicon,' says my grandmother: 'she musn't show her legs, she must be very careful.' Yes, these things can pop into anyone's mind because it's natural to be afraid, but fear is one thing and terror is another. Terror is the desire to go up on the rooftops. But, of course, they don't allow you to do that. I don't know if I'd dare, if they were to let me, but to see the night, to walk along up there at night – would I dare go alone? No, I don't think so: I'd be afraid. If I stop and think, I can see that no matter how marvelous I think terror is, I would be afraid like any other girl. Would I really be afraid? Oh, how do I know? There's no way to find out, because they won't let me. Not Piedita or Araceli either, because they're pretty well grown up. Would Isabel's mother let her? No, she would never allow it. Isabel, since she hasn't crossed the Rubicon yet, can still wear socks. And it's precisely Isabel who never, ever makes me feel like an older sister. At times I shout at her and I even swear to look like I'm dominant, but I don't know, there are some things that she understands better than I. And on the other hand, she seems so innocent about other things that I almost don't dare to talk to her. I've never liked innocent girls, but when Isabel comes out with something she doesn't understand and it doesn't bother her at all – she's just indifferent, with no curiosity. I tell myself that either she doesn't know or she knows too much or she knows it in some other way. I just can't understand this, although I really do want to understand. This business of the carnival, for example, doesn't upset her the way it does me. It's not that she's lacking in curiosity, no; that's why it's plain that she knows: what she doesn't have is impatience, and that means she's sure of herself. But why? She has a lot less than I do; but, nonetheless, she doesn't hurl herself into everything the way I do. Those are my Sister of Charity qualities. On other occasions my grandmother says conclusively, without sarcasm, that I'm a perfect busybody. She must really think it makes me angry; but I agree, I agree: I need to butt in everywhere. What outrages me is that the others butt in so little. That's what I do with Piedita: try to make her butt in more. What is it that she brings to this undertaking? The desire to look beautiful, to hear everyone saying that she's gorgeous, that she's a real beauty. Yes, of course, but the beauty of everything else, of what she'll have all around her – what she's probably *not* going to have – because she'll get there right on time (if it turns out she does go) like she always does, and when it's over, she'll go back home – but it goes on interminably, this carnival beauty. I'm not talking now about the beauty of the people, of the beauties you see there, but of the things themselves, the carnival things that you don't see on other days of the year. The streamers, the confetti . . . You could almost get drunk on them! That's why people get drunk so much at carnival, because everything is so intoxicating. Watching a streamer unfurl and fall when you throw it from a balcony in a spiral: the corkscrew stretches and stretches to full length wherever the air might carry it, always shaking and weaving and intermingling with the others. Oh, how divine! Divine because it's inconceivable that a mere man could have invented such a thing. What was the inspiration for the inventor of the streamer? Perhaps the carpenter's wood shavings. Yes, but its way of unfurling as it falls and above all its way of intermingling with the others, all different colors and all the same, intermingling without escaping, all hanging from a balcony like locks of hair, tresses which not only fall of their own weight, but weigh hardly anything and blow in the wind without getting completely straightened out. Their ends stay curled, the corkscrew is not completely undone, there's a sort of hook at the end which extends like tendrils of grapevines but never clings; they seem to be demonstrating a desire to cling, the desire to hold onto something from whoever throws them and is stuck onto them, extended, protracted by them. And confetti – it's too much for words! Such an explosion! They throw a handful into your face and you feel a soft blow which becomes a multicolored cloud. That happens on any streetcorner – but at theater exits, at ballroom entrances in the bright lights, when the masked ladies in dominoes step into coaches and the men in their high silk hats . . . Of course, one has to have read about all this beauty, one has to have lived it before being able to live it, like something you've known since you were three, from birth, as though it were a thing you didn't need to learn. Because I don't know when I learned this: it's something I read before I knew how to read. It's not that I'm putting on airs about discernment, but it's always happened that I see more than what is apparent in things. I see an illustration in a book, a figure in a certain pose, a head with a particular expression around the mouth or in the gaze and I already know the complete story. At times I see things that grow as I remember them. I remember the color of an engraving that had no color, and I remember it with the most delicious of colors and even with movement. I swear! There's something I've recalled a thousand times – a page from *Blanco y Negro*, 'Leaving the Dance.' Rain was falling, falling at an angle in the glow of the streetlights, making splashes in the puddles, and she – the woman in the hooded cape – leapt into the coach, stepping onto the footboard with a golden slipper, and the coach moved forward. The horses' hooves and the wheels resounded on the uneven pavement, the coach started off with a rush. It didn't slip away, it rushed away. The woman in the cape and the top-hatted man didn't act as if they were leaving the theater because the play was over, but as if the night were young and they were going to another ball, another hall lit by crystal chandeliers. All these details together, without being jumbled, concurrent, implied in each other: the night, the lights, the music. Like that song: 'The waltz invites us to enjoy its delights, irresistible pleasure!' Delights that can only be conceived under the crystal prisms of the lamps, the light multiplied in the candelabra's tears . . . Tears of joy? No, tears of . . . I don't know, because all the words they use – delirium, frenzy – are too agitated; I see in all this something more like a bedazzlement, or a stupefaction, or an astonishment, which is how the song ends: 'And in the light of the gleams that make the soul tremble . . .' That's what I try to suggest to Piedita. I sing her the song and she says 'How lovely! How well you sing it. It seems almost as if I were watching them dance.' But she never gets swept away, she just goes on the way she was. Araceli . . . Of course, I don't talk to her as much as I do Piedita. And the odd thing is that I can see more clearly what she wants. And it's not that she's more forthcoming, that she shows more what she wants. Quite the contrary, she keeps it more inside her; her desires are deeper, and that's why I see them better. That's why I hardly ever talk with her. It never dawns on me to push her toward more dangerous waters because she, without saying a word, transmits to me her . . . I don't know: a sort of anxiety, an uneasiness. She gives off the smell of her anxiety. She doesn't dare to take off her camisole, as though she had never taken it off. The smell is in everything about her – even in her room, even in the clothes she takes off. She takes them off with an air of shame; but it's not modesty, it's anxiety, it's distrust of her body, even though she talks about her waist being tiny in her corset . . . When she undoes the corset and throws it on the chair, it gives off an odor that's not just the perfume she wears. It's like a lingering smell of some medicine, of some ointment or liniment you use for pain: it's the smell of pain. With her fear of the cold I can't imagine how she'll ever manage to wash that head of hair in a basin. When she undoes it there's a smell of brilliantine escaping the way steam does when you uncover a pot. At any rate, in this cloud of anxiety – because what she smells of is her anxiety, her unhappiness, her lack of confidence – amid all this there's more . . . more heat, more passion . . . I'm going to make the little serpent for her. Yes, I can do it very well with one of those heavy wires they use to make the frames of hats. The difficult part is to make it so it can be held securely with a ribbon, like a diadem, because if it twists around . . . My heavens! Why did that occur to me? Every time I set out to construct something in my mind, some part turns out twisted, there's a mistake, it breaks or I cut it where I shouldn't have and I can't repair it. I'm unable to imagine the thing fixed: the defect stays there no matter how much I try to forget it or correct it. I can't let this happen; I have to overcome it, I have to erase it. But how? The more I think about it, the clearer the defect seems, the more invincible and overwhelming the idea that the thing is going to twist around, fall off with its padding showing. No, I can't let it do that. I'll have to make it in the shape of a hook – that's it. A wire forty centimeters long, folded in half makes twenty, bent again at a right angle makes ten, that's right. Strong cotton could be wound around the part that's going to form the body and head, shaping it just right, and the two wires should be tied together tightly so they can be separated just after the right angle and be bent into two rings that can be sewed to the ribbon, that's it. Then, to give it some style, make a little curve . . . The hour just struck: I think it was four o'clock.

The old man, the concierge, Señor José, chewing on his cigar butt, said, 'How nice! Fondling the girl's hair with the same hands that you're going to be making pills with.'

'In the first place, this isn't hair, and in the second, I'm not fondling it.'

'Oh, so it's not hair. Then what is it, taffy?'

'I don't know, that's what I'm doing, trying to find out . . .'

'O.K., you've seen it, now let go,' shouts Isabel. 'Don't be stupid, Luis, you're hurting me: let go of my braid.'

'I won't.'

The old man, Señor José, went off with his eucalyptus. Isabel went on pulling at her braid, but couldn't get loose because Luis had said 'I won't.' He said it only once, but the negation still rang in her ears like furious affirmation. He had said 'I won't' so gravely, in a voice more captivating and more tactile than his hand. Isabel stopped pulling because she no longer felt that it was her braid that Luis held: she felt like a little bird caught in a hand – enveloped, oppressed, immobilized but not smothered, just surrounded by power, by a will which affirmed itself implacably in that 'I won't.' And they stayed like that awhile: Isabel pulling and Luis holding onto the braid. Isabel didn't pull strongly enough to get it out of his hand. She pulled just enough to keep it taut, and in this tension she felt herself held. She acted like she was trying to leave, pulling a little, to show that she was still there. Luis didn't let her go, but he felt as though he should. He thought about how he would release her: he wouldn't let the braid go all at once; he would lay it on the left-hand side. It was the braid hanging over her left shoulder, and it was in his right hand. He would lay it softly on the blue cassimere. (An unknown customer had said, 'Where did you buy that cassimere?' 'I don't know. My mother got it.' 'I'd like to know because I've been looking for one like that with little checks.' Isabel was wearing blue cassimere, and her left braid – so long, so soft – would rest upon a barely perceptible curve. He had to calculate exactly where to hold the braid so that when he deposited it, the back of his hand would graze the curve, the blue or white check – impossible to tell which one corresponded to the apex, the most sensitive spot that might, as his hand went by it, show that it was alive, might respond, might free itself from Isabel's cold, guarded will to give the response that she, with her blue eyes as clear as the hardest crystal, insisted on denying. Perhaps if his hand softly grazed . . .

'Are you going to give me my Socott Emulsion?'

'Yes, at once.'

'And the lithium salts, yes or no?'

'Lithium salts,' flinging the packet on the counter. 'The Emulsion? Yeah, right away.'

Isabel runs to the entrance and flies up the stairs with her braids over her shoulders and the lithium salts in her hand.

All the old ladies in the house – mothers, grandmother, teacher – all of them with flu, with pains everywhere, mixing lithium salts with water and Elena refusing to go down to buy them. Elena with her special cruel skill in leaving her defenseless. Elena, with the money in her hand in front of Doña Eulalia, 'Isabel, would you go down and get some lithium salts for my grandmother? I can't right now.'

And in front of Doña Laura and in front of her mother, 'You have to try some lithium salts, they're really extraordinary.'

The packets getting used up one right after the other, and Luis looking for the chance to get his hands on her. Braids, after all, as a joke, can be pulled in front of people: no one is shocked if you pull a girl's braids. Before, when she wore just one down her back, it wasn't as visible as the two she had now. And she wasn't about to put them back like before. The new way of braiding her hair had been a discovery, like a gift, like an inheritance from her ancestors, the Carreños. The desire to see them again, which she had felt for some time, was because she knew they were going to offer her something. It's like those stories you read when you're little: children go off to their grandparents' house and always come back loaded down with things; they always find old family junk in the closet or the loft . . . the junk and the closets and the lofts which she never had and would never be able to have. But it would be different with the Carreños. There in their home, the largest and grandest of houses, if she looked near them she was bound to find not a costume, no, not the cloak of a dead king, but something she could wear every day, wear when she had any old dress on to go out every day. To go out dressed as herself – to be herself, Isabel, something she had never been. In a vague way she knew that this business of wearing her hair in two braids was something she had conferred upon herself because it wasn't something you could transfer: it was something very much hers, of her very person. It had no determinate season like the dresses of Piedita and Araceli; it wasn't over at a specific time. And it wasn't that those tunics and those striped fabrics weren't lovely: they certainly were. They had been dazzling, they had been exciting even in the planning stage when they were threatened by everything; uncertainty, tragedy on the horizon but never arriving, using up energy, wearing out patience, wasting time away up to the final moment, when it seemed like it was already too late, when hope, worn away by tiredness, lost its appetite, its impetus and then, the liberating letter. Once the danger was over, activity had expanded time. Piedita, as always, fascinated. Elena like a shot putting things together, sewing, pinning up, combing light chestnut hair, fixing that Greek bun high above the slender, statuesque neck. Gathering up the tunic so that the hem wouldn't drag on the stairs, walking with her to Mrs. Smith's car which had come to fetch her, and seeing her off – all the neighbor women looking out their windows – at midday as if she were going to marry Leandro. The neighbor women, who knew nothing about Leandro, thinking God-knows-what. The carriage disappearing around the corner of Fuencarral . . . Then the afternoon along Recoletos . . .

A diplomatic conflict – undertaken by Elena, unknown to Isabel – had preceded that afternoon.

'Doña Laura, my mother says you should come with us. She wants to see Piedita on the float, so Isabel and I are going with the two of you . . .'

'Yes, naturally, of course.'

'Yes, of course, but . . .'

'Ah, now I understand what you're thinking. As far as I'm concerned there's no problem. Ask your mother.'

'You know very well that my mother never goes against what I want.'

'Then . . .'

Then it was only necessary to propose it to the party in question, and Elena felt funny about bringing it up so late, waiting until the last minute – there was scarcely time to dress. But nonetheless, with an effort to behave perfectly naturally, as though it were the most logical thing in the world, planned from the beginning – Isabel had gone down to the street – Elena seized the opportunity.

'Oh dear, I'd like so much to see her, she'll be so beautiful, but with this knee I can't go hobbling over there. No, Elena, no. Thank you very much for inviting me, but I can't go.'

'But your leg is hardly noticeable.'

'Yes, that's because I try to hide it when it doesn't hurt, but the last few days have been pretty bad. And I'm taking the lithium salts.'

'It's a shame you can't come, but keep using the salts.'

Isabel arrives, but not a word is said. Isabel does not ask: she understands at first glance. There is a long silence. Then, nothing more.

'Shall we go?'

'Let's go.'

The parade is slow: advertising floats from industry and others from sports clubs, or regional centers. Among them, the Chariot of Love, Mrs. Smith's creation, the whim of a rich woman, a traveler, an extravagant cosmopolite: a float worthy of Nice. The mountain of papier-mâché was well-executed, each of its rocky openings containing a pair of lovers, famous ones, of course, with the Weird Sisters in their grotto and Cupid aiming his bow. It was all very appropriate – the costumes, the postures, everything perfectly felt, perfectly interpreted.

The float had only one thing that was truly its own and that also had another property, the property of the natural, the true, that which imitates nothing, copies nothing, repeats nothing: something that repeated itself without knowing that it did so, being and remaining in its same age-old form: the white horses. The garlands of roses tied to their manes and flung across their flanks hung down heavily in curves that echoed the line of their necks, also heavy, but proud, meaty, muscular, ideal, so quintessential, so archetypal, so certain of their perfection in the serious and light movement with which they shook their manes. Mute and apparently deaf to the shouting and the applause, the horses were impassive, centered in their beauty, following the pace set by the little devils leading them. A lady exclaimed, 'Look, the Chariot of Love, and the devils are leading it!' The fauns in their goatskins reined them in when they got to the reviewing stand. Each raised a foreleg whose enormous hoof was accompanied by a wavy white fetlock, and then set it on the ground. They stood like statues, so still, only raising their heads from time to time, not out of impatience, but because they could not still the majesty of their movements.

The float took first prize and, when the thundering applause had subsided, it went on toward Cibeles and then toward Atocha. The crowds began to thin out, several lights along the route were extinguished; it was time to start heading home. There were still groups of students who tossed confetti and bold remarks at them, even though they were accompanied by older ladies. They laughed with the laughter that carnival permits as a costume that breaks everyday seriousness. Daily habit broken by corrosive, indiscreet laughter. There was something like ten centimeters of confetti in the street, pieces of streamers that had been stepped on without even being unfurled. They were like wigs or disheveled buns, or like nests; knots formed by the crisscrossing of countless spirals thrown by countless contrary and sudden impulses. It was pleasant – more than pleasant – it was spontaneously and mechanically voluptuous to stick your feet in, bury them or tangle them in it, to drag a bunch awhile and watch it break when the loop gets tangled between the left and right feet.

Then all this was left behind, hidden behind a neutral week during which there was scarcely a word about the brilliant outcome. Only Araceli described her Egyptian night, the elegance of her little golden serpent, gracefully rising above her black diadem. The striped tunic and the thick mane of hair were also gradually left in the past. Then suddenly, there was an early warm spell. The nettles by the dormer window began to suffer from drought. At midday the roof tiles broiled, and the light in the studio was unbearable in the morning. It was only when it began to get dark that Elena, with her implacable perseverance, put Isabel to work in front of the Ingres paper. And, indeed, Isabel drew. She had all the necessary qualities: she knew how to see, which isn't the same as simply seeing. It's not that she saw well: she saw intelligently, lovingly and rigorously. Elena had heard people say – because people talked about these things and, naturally, wrote about them, so Elena had *heard* it in some newspaper – that you shouldn't copy from prints or engravings; it was better to have natural models right from the beginning. So, she made Isabel draw pitchers or piles of books in different arrangements. She had to get in training so she could enroll in the School of Arts and Crafts when the school year began. Elena had already done one year according to the normal system, but she wanted Isabel to start already familiar with a more modern scheme. She wanted to give her a live model, a moving model, and Señor José provided it. Elena took it out of the mousetrap, transferring it to a cardboard box. She brought it upstairs very much on the sly because she wanted to surprise Isabel. She hid it in the kitchen, but the cardboard was too vulnerable to the rodent's little teeth. She put it into an empty fish bowl. It couldn't get out of that one, and it could be sketched right there. You could see it in all its funny, foreshortened positions. It could wait until the afternoon there in a corner beneath the bench. But before afternoon – she went out to buy paper and couldn't find it anywhere in the neighborhood – when she came back around midday, something happened.

'Hey, look, look at the fish we've got here.'

Sinfo, the maid, showed her the fish bowl almost filled with water. Not quite full, there were only about ten centimeters of water. The mouse, standing on his two hind legs, scarcely reached that height. The only thing above the surface was the tip of his nose. It had been like that for three hours. She tried to save it . . . it was alive but almost senseless, worn out, with no will to live. Comments – Isabel wound up finding out – 'These girls, so advanced and so know-it-all, still cry over a mouse.' They hadn't cried, they had turned pale, they had almost blasphemed, cursed like savages. Never – despite all her precocity, all her prodigiousness and book learning – had Elena felt more like a woman, like an adult. Never had she judged, assayed human characteristics, qualities, classes, so ruthlessly. It was as if that wave of pity that had struck her, stupified her and taken her breath away had turned its back, showed its other face, its denial of the various forms of human speech. Of all stupid, conventional words, in their stupidity betraying their corruption, impurity, emptiness, hypocrisy. In the face of all this there remained and persisted – like a spot of light that stings the retina and cannot be wiped away – the ineffaceable image of ten centimeters of life, of a little nose reaching the surface of the water. The afternoon light in the studio was not bad for drawing, but their spirits were terrible. They hardly spoke of the event – they scarcely spoke at all that afternoon, but single phrases did pop up.

'It's Saturday . . . remember?'

'Yes, already.'

'But tomorrow is Sunday, or don't you remember?'

'Of course, of course, I remember. Just now I didn't remember, but don't go thinking that I've forgotten.'

'Did you talk to Doña Laura about it again? Do you think maybe she's lost interest?'

'How could you think such a thing!'

Then, the project, the promise of returning, of recapturing the life-enhancing vision replaced the image of life recently lived, the face of abject, stupid evil. Everything was wiped away by twenty-four hours of hope.

First the smell, and you had to close your eyes to contemplate it. Then move ahead and feel the light as a contact, not exactly on the eye, but everywhere: on forehead, on cheeks. Feel the light as a climate, and then, asking its permission, excusing oneself for using it, forgetting it and looking at the things it uncovers, lays bare, caresses, tempers, shades or sets afire. Amid the light – looking out hospitably – faces, glances, radiant or pain-racked bodies, naked or dressed. Dressed in black, pale, wan and so noble, the Carreños, Carlos II, the nunlike Doña Mariana of Austria act as masters of the house, as early shoots who once were grandparents, like ancient fetuses from a dark world.

'But Isabel, didn't you just want to kill the person who thought of comparing you to them?'

'Why would I kill her? I like them a lot.'

'Come on! Don't be so eccentric.'

'I'm not eccentric, I'm grateful. I owe everything to them.'

'What exactly do you owe?'

'Everything, all of this. If it hadn't been for them . . .'

Everything, all of them there, waiting for us to come and greet them, to kiss them, to press our hearts on them like Veronica's shroud, and carry them with us forever. A meditation which nothing or no one can wipe away. Names like curtains drawn apart, like open windows, names that don't belong to a human being who walked along the street on a certain date nor to another who stood with a brush in hand. Names that belong to those structures that combine the two. That very lovely, pinkish, weightless woman putting on a glove is a Goya. That wan king with the bulging forehead and the most exquisite, noble, delicate blond hair is a Carreño. And that woman reclining on the bed with very small breasts and a rather broad waist . . . 'You see, Piedita, you think that's your defect.' 'It's true, and on her it's not bad at all.' That beauty is a Titian. That woman weaving: she and her work, the movement of her hand and the air that surrounds her is a Velázquez. Because they're not just faces, eyes that intimidate or fascinate or move us. They're also places, skies like lakes, lakes that fade into forests among blue mountains, among cypresses or velvet pines or amber rocks that shelter ascetics, that are a Patinir. Going downstairs, the large room is first, filled with the dreams of Ariadne. Here the maker disappears. There is nothing but Ariadne – she and the marble – as though the marble had transformed itself into her, as though she had flowed into the marble and had gone to sleep in it, trusting it, awaiting in it, in its immutable quietude, the arrival of the violent god. How can one imagine, before such quietude, faced with the innocence of that soft round arm that she holds up, forming an angle above her head, before the weightless breasts like hills upon the field of a torso stirred by no breath, how can one imagine that she loved and wept so? In the world, the sphere of marble, it seems as though silence were the maker, as though that hard material – by dint of being hard and everlasting – had received the condescension of form, had become a repository for its celestial and immortal word. Form – the word which names in marble the unanimous, stellar, auroral puberty of Castor and Pollux! There are fragmentary forms, too, which seem to stand on their own, pieces so individually whole that they wouldn't be surpassed even if somehow reunited with the whole to which they belong: the mystery of their meaning would remain, for their meaning is sculpted in absence. Perhaps the nymph's sloping back, perhaps her arms and youthful head . . . Would she smile? The smile, the youth, the lightness of a child of the air, the forest, the river . . . Perhaps from either of the orbs that can be divined in her hips, scarcely settled obliquely, as though she were going to rise or as if she had just come to rest. Such a quintessential rump, so finely wrought in its form that one cannot tell if it is a rump or a flower or an idea . . . And then go back up the stone staircase presided over by a tormented Titan chained to Ribera's chiaroscuro and enter some other less conspicuous rooms and . . .

'Elena, more Carreños!'

'No, I don't think they're Carreños. Let's see. They're by Mazo. Yes, they look like Carreños, but they're not. Do you see? Prince Baltasar Carlos is a baby in Velázquez. Here he's a boy . . .'

'But, this lady?'

'Ah yes, you can tell: it's Margarita of Austria.'

'Yes, I can tell. But don't you see more?'

'Of course I do. It can't be denied. Look, Doña Laura . . .'

'Well, in this one it's something else altogether. Although your nose is prettier.'

'Oh my nose . . . But what about everything else?'

'What do you mean, everything else? You're not going to tell me you like the dress? It looks like something a widow would wear. Are you going to imitate her?'

'No, Piedita, not her dress, because I'll never be a widow: I don't intend to get married. Don't look at me like that, Elena.'

'This poor woman was never a widow: her husband was the widower. I don't think she lived to be over twenty-five.'

'Oh, Doña Laura, is it possible? Then these people in the back kneeling down like they were in the bedroom praying for someone. For whom can they be praying?'

They're praying for her. She's dead there in her chambers, laid out on the bed. Not with this elegant black dress. She's in a simple white shroud, and while the rest pray, she is here, in this other room, thinking, saying good-bye to everything. To her son who would have that mouth – that some call pucker-lips – and who would also always wear black with that elegant, somber air. Her only jewels are jet: a little bracelet on the wrist of the hand holding her glove and something like a mantilla or a veil which hangs like a jet tassel between her braids. Her youthful braids, almost childlike, well-defined, singular, different from any other coiffure. What queen could we possibly find with such a hairdo? Two braids like two spikes of grain, one on either side, the part on the right side and the hair smoothly combed around the forehead; all the hair gathered back in those two braids that stay in two knotted curves on each side of the face, hiding their tips in the jet tassel. Two little braids that are completely out of style. The two braids may have been laid carefully upon the white shroud, but here in the portrait that Mazo painted . . . When? Before or after her death? Did she pose for the painter here in the lonely chamber where she came to say good-bye? In her other hand, the one she rests on the back of the large chair, she holds a handkerchief, a large white handkerchief, like something she might wave on her departure. Her look is very sad, as though she weren't prepared for death, as though this task of dying had taken her unawares and she feared she might not carry it off well. Perhaps without a will, but certainly not without a confession: it would simply not have been allowed. In that regard, seeing to this absolutely necessary requirement, she would have had the help of all, but in putting in order her . . . She must have had many more jewels besides those pieces of jet, and perhaps she wanted to leave them to some of her ladies-in-waiting, her maids or friends. But she really only left the legacy of the two braids, those two tight spikes, grains of the future, so to speak, because they were to quicken the youth of Isabel, who would transplant them from jet to blue cassimere . . . Quickly – back home now with the thick part of the comb smooth the hair over the forehead from the part on the right side. Slant the part carefully into the center of the back of the neck so the braids will have the same thickness; then, well tightened, the ends tied with thin silk strings, place one on each side, loose over the shoulders.

'Where did you get that hairdo? A German lady had a little girl who wore braids like that. But she was just little, and you're getting to be a pretty big kid. Go on, run down and get me some lithium salts.'

Luis looked at her in terror, shock, amazement, rage, as if he'd just discovered a rival. He saw the careful attention and the decision in those braids, the conscious femininity. He saw that it was something wrought; was it adopted or dedicated? That's what he wanted to know, what he wanted to ask her abruptly and violently, hiding his violence like a dagger up his sleeve.

'Who is that hairdo for?'

Isabel's hand grabs the package. She shrugs her shoulders, sticks out her tongue, turns her back and starts to run. His violence, the weapon used in such a minor attack, has not been satisfied and turns in on itself, recognizes itself, considers its own dimensions – and the more it does so, the more it grows. He studies the outbreak, the gush of violence caused by Isabel's presence, by her braids, which appeared and were disclosed as though she had taken off her dress, as though she had let him see something he hadn't seen before but showed it to him only to deny him, at the same time she showed it to him, she seemed to promise a negative response. That was the provocation: shrugging her shoulders, taking a half-turn and, before quite finishing it, before turning her back completely, sticking out her tongue, that forbidden fruit. That pink, mobile, living thing, even more tempting than the rocky carnality of pink coral, lying brilliant on the tense, polished lower lip that almost never spread into a smile. All this, the vision of all this so brief, so fleeting, but as permanent as a plant that takes root with roots like tentacles that dig in on purpose or with the purpose of taking over one's being, inflaming it, transforming it into a single entity of desire. Desire transformed into violence; or, on the contrary, violence flaming and desire guarding, protecting its intimate, silent and hidden source of tenderness from the blaze. And then the daily appearances among people with the increasingly infrequent presence of his father, every day less able to work, more defeated by his weak heart, condemned and transformed into a repository of condemnation – the one he feared, not the one he accepted – of separation, of departure. Interrupting with this threat of departure the life of his son, which should have been easy, joyful . . . And all this happening with overwhelming regularity: the pharmacy, the people dropping in with their halting requests for advice, with prescriptions written by quack healers. And studying at the same time, trying to finish up with good grades, hoping to get a doctorate, to be what one is in the fullest possible sense. And those appearances of Isabel, the subtle changes within her impassive and hermetic character. Her exquisite, childlike figure, her impregnable femininity, her intelligence, a blue spark in a gaze as open as that of a girl who's acting the fool. And the torrent of passions and of intentions, all impossible, until that day when lightly, childishly, disguising it as play – the empty pharmacy, midday, the old doorman asking for some herbs, and suddenly Isabel – like this, as if playing, sticking out his hand and grabbing the braid with his heart in his throat, but convincing himself he was no longer afraid – the braid so smooth that it's hard to keep it from slipping away. Squeezing it so tightly that he gets numb and it becomes almost inlaid in his hand, and not letting it go despite her protests.

'Don't be stupid, Luis. Let go of my braid.'

'I won't!'

'I'm sick of going down every single day for the lithium salts.'

'There's nothing to be done. People are getting more rheumatism every day.'

'What I'd like to know is if it does any good. The pain in my mother's knee hasn't let up. She should go to the doctor, but she doesn't want to.'

'Why not? She'll have to be talked into it. Leave her to me.'

'Can you at least tell me why?'

'No, Elena, it's not that I don't want to go to the doctor. It's just that I know what he's going to prescribe: the same thing as last time.'

'What did he prescribe?'

'Those injections.'

'And they didn't do any good?'

'How could they do any good if I didn't use them? Do you know how expensive they are?'

'They can't be all that expensive.'

'Not the injections, the fellow who administers them. It's either that or go to the hospital and lose the whole morning. Do you think I can spend the mornings sewing only every other day?'

'Of course, you're right. But still, you have to have them. Did you save the prescription?'

'Yes I saved it, but so what?'

'There's a syringe at home. I could give the injection. Would you dare to let me?'

'You! Would you dare?'

'Of course she would, Mama. She dares to do anything.'

'Not anything, but this, yes. The really important thing is the asepsis, you know? It means cleanliness, and I'll do it better than in a hospital. Luis will tell me all about it . . . Don't you go down, you upset him: now it's my turn to confer.'

Having to choose! It seems silly to have to choose when you like two things. I don't know, who can tell if it's two things or one single thing, or if it's two emerging from a third or who-knows-what! But nonetheless, a choice must be made because – not only because there's not enough time and energy to do both – there's so much criticism, so much ridicule of a 'painter among doctors and a doctor among painters.' I've heard that said about a very respectable gentleman, and it sounded like a spiteful statement, but maybe not, maybe it's the truth, the sad truth. Yes, that must be it; the truer it seems, the sadder it seems too. A choice must be made, but beforehand I need to understand, I need to know what is similar about the two things. No, it's not a case of similarity. What I want to know is what exactly is the same about them. There we are! What exactly is the same. I know what is the same, but I don't know why. I knock my brains out and I can't get it straight. I think the day I came closest to comprehending something was when I began to think about why I like sculpture more than painting. I wound up deciding that it's because there are a lot of other things involved in painting, other things are involved and I'm interested in only one thing: bodies – the human body. I'm not really interested in dresses or velvets . . . Well, it would be stupid to say that. Everything interests me. I like everything – everything meant to be liked. But it's not just that I like the other thing; it's the thing I like, the thing I want, the thing I want for me. If you are dedicated to something, does it mean you want the thing for yourself, or do you want yourself to be for the thing? You want to wed the thing, to merge yourself with it. But that's not exactly it either, because it's not that one wants to be deeply involved in as if it were a case of having a good time, no. You want to do something, something like adding what's missing, what the thing lacks: to make what is lacking. If I insist on this, I know where I'm heading, but I can't resign myself, I can't really decide because there's something else: that which needs nothing. In this case, I'm the one who needs it. But, my heavens! What is it I need if not even a grain of sand could be added to the thing I look at to the point of stupefaction? Claudina was singing a lovely romanza in French – my mother says her French was horrible – I can only remember one phrase about a patio where some men made of marble reached out their arms in the night and called to her. Isn't such a call enough to make you shudder? And it's so true to life! They call to me in the daytime – that's the difference. Because that terror would be marvelous on a large patio at night. It's not like in the museum or at school where the things connected with the craft, the smell of the clay and the pleasure of sinking your hands into it and seeing how the finished product turns out . . . Of course, you feel unhappy about how badly you do it. But even if it doesn't come out right, you don't give up because when you think about it, when you imagine what you might possibly produce in the future . . . No, I don't have false hopes, but I'm not prepared to do without the call or not respond to it. I'm not prepared to? I simply don't have any choice. I can't not respond to every single thing into which you can plunge your hands. And this isn't a desire to meddle, no; it's that I feel the emotion, the rapture that perfection – whether seen or imagined – produces in me, and I feel it for the most incredible things. And for such different things! And the emotion is the same. That's something I'm quite sure of – it's the same! It is as though that, perfection, could be, wants to be in all things, as if it were the peak of everything.

The peak is where confusion occurs, where things get jumbled in the happiness of having arrived. The difficult part is knowing just what the peak is – this is what Elena is struggling to understand – what that thing is that can seduce or subjugate a mind, a soul. That is, a creature in its original integrity subjugated by something that opens itself fully as an irresistible liberty, as if it were the only possible liberty, the only existing liberty, unintelligible, but as affirmative as a mandate, as a voice or a call, as a vocation. To understand the drama, the irrefutable fact of vocation is the crisis of puberty, because eros begins with life but advances silently, at life's own pace toward the season of genesis, the spring. The crisis consists of deciding to act, because the seductive image is veiled. Unlike love or an infatuation inflamed by a single glance, the response to vocation is a gaze in the dimness of one's own consciousness, a gaze that seeks the voice's shape. For the voice can be double in nature: it can call toward what cannot be doubted, what strikes the eye, and the eye delights in it; but it can also call toward a clouded, tormented region, a region where there is no voluptuousness, only anxiety. The anxiety to struggle, the desire to conquer, to be invincible in defending what is at the peak. This – Elena thinks, lives, feels, swears – is what is the same in the power of beauty and in the clamor of pain and in piety. Perhaps it is piety that is the same since that far-off time when piety was aggrandized in forms and found a mathematical shape that made bodies divine and humanized gods. Sublime forms that compensated man for being mortal, that ended up piercing him with anguish and terror, with the grief of being mortal and, finally, folding in on themselves, installed themselves in silence as a promise or a hope. And all this – duplicitous, provocative and elusive, ostentatious and shining but also concealed, hushed and modest – all this stirs in Elena's mind like a perplexity, nothing more than a perplexity. But in the mist, in the tangle, in the brambles of the perplexity, the voice is calling her to work.

'Do you think I'm going to be able to do the same thing I do at home here among so many people? In the middle of a bunch of probably unlikable girls and especially with the teacher standing over me?'

'Come on, get going. The teacher won't be standing over you. She assigns you your place, and that's all. As far as the other girls are concerned, don't pay any attention.'

'I am paying attention, and they're all looking at me. Why are they staring?'

'Because you're new. They'll get used to seeing you.'

'And the teacher! Can you see how that lady looks at a person? She has her spectacles on the tip of her nose. She glares like a man. It disconcerts me.'

'There's no reason to be disconcerted. She looks that way because she's very intelligent.'

'Yes, she looks it. But what does one thing have to do with the other? Just because she's very intelligent . . .'

'Yes, that's why. Go ahead with the ear: you've got very nice light now.'

I'm the one who chose it. She gave me a choice among three or four things in plaster – all with leaves or decorative things – and I preferred the ear. She said, 'You're one of those who leaps right in,' and gave it to me.

The ear emerged from a rectangle measuring no more than three centimeters in thickness. It was hung with a wire loop over the desk. The plaster rectangle looked like it had been cut with a knife, like it was a piece of something living. It wasn't flat. It had soft, fleshy undulations suggesting an enormous head to which it had been attached. It was an ear from a gigantic head which, judging from the soft undulations, must have been a benevolent head. It must have had a massive nose and a mouth that was not open, but not closed either – one of those mouths where the lips, independent, can be seen in all their roundness, in the perfection of their curves, made to adapt to one another. Isabel mentally reconstructed the head, just by studying the ear. She had scarcely touched the paper with the charcoal. With the stick in her hand, she imagined forms that seemed to her harmonious . . . A presence behind her brought her back to earth. She turned her head: the teacher was looking at her with her disturbing gaze, but she went on by, smiling imperceptibly. The porter called out: time was up.

'You haven't done much, but it doesn't matter: you've sketched well. Come on, your mother must be impatient to see if you were a success.'

'My mother couldn't conceive my not being a success.'

Now the voice orders a brief simmering; boil the syringe, prepare the cotton, break the ampoule with the little steel saw and skillfully, rapidly – without rushing, with the quickness of certainty – inject the liquid down to the last drop, all the while talking about the school year just begun and Isabel's certain, indisputable progress. As they share news on a hundred and one things, they comment on how splendid, benign, smiling the autumn has been and make plans for a winter of methodical work. The two things, the two phases of the voice seem to come together in possibility. The fact of encompassing them, of making them her own, achieves in Elena's mind the anticipated identity. More than anticipated – it was enjoyed, realized, lived as a love, as a contact. The desired object is in her, it is she, because she doesn't have to say that it is hers; possession is penetration, it is fusion. It is a property that has the delightful quality of being able to be forgotten; it can be surrendered to a dangerous existence, like that of one's own life.

'This makes four boxes now. At three ampoules a week, that's two dozen; and I think it's doing some good, no?'

'It certainly is. Let's finish up this box because, after all, it certainly isn't a sacrifice. I had to see it to believe it! Girl, you must be a regular witch!'

'Why?'

'Because I never feel a thing. You don't hurt me the slightest bit compared to how much it hurts when I prick myself sewing! Is it because you rub it first with alcohol?'

'No, that's not why. It's because that's the way it is when you do it right. And you remember that even the first one turned out fine, even though I'd never even done it before. Naturally, I had seen it done and I was sure I could do it right.'

'But it seems like you hardly even squeeze.'

'I hardly have to squeeze. The needle is extremely sharp and your skin is delicate. Since your arms are never bare, that very delicate skin is almost light pink. It looks like an arm of porcelain.'

'Of porcelain!'

'Yes, well, it's a way of putting things.'

'But . . . Well, we have to put things in order. Isabel is invited to Doña Laura's apartment today.'

'Yes, she already told me. I'll slip down a little later to see what they're up to.'

'The three of them are going to straighten up the classroom from top to bottom. They're going to take all the books out of the library – imagine! It's going to take some time . . . Why did you say that?'

'Say what?'

'About the porcelain.'

'Oh, you didn't like that?'

'As far as liking it goes . . .'

Even if they went on talking about downstairs, about the

whole neighborhood, the word would reappear. The word demanded all their attention. Elena's attention and the feelings, the whole mind of Antonia. Memory – not like remembrance but like imposition, like the presence of something which has never been the past, like the resolution of a plot – the intrigue, the scheme of concealment, the unavowable secret: the shamed silence covering a carefully hidden pride that suddenly protruded through the breach caused by an unintentional word, a word that's a 'way of putting things' and that now can be said no more, now that nothing else can be said because the most brilliant, the most truthful, the most painful word has been spoken.

'Did I like it? More than you might imagine.'

'Oh, that's just as well, because from the look on your face you'd have thought I had mentioned the devil.'

'Oh no, not the devil.'

'Well, who, then? Come on, tell me. Does it have something to do with Isabel?'

'I tell you you're a regular witch.'

'You don't have to be a witch to understand things as plain as the nose on your face.'

'What's so plain? What exactly did I say?'

'You didn't say anything because you were left speechless. And I know you. I know that for you to have your heart in your throat it must have something to do with the little daughter that God sent you.'

'Of course she was sent by God! Of course!'

'And the porcelain?'

The word again produces silence. The pieces of cotton are gathered up, the things are rinsed, the syringe and ampoules are put away. There are some shoe boxes on top of a trunk which would seem to make it difficult to open. There is a coffeepot filled with water on the gas which it would be better to turn off because it would just go up in steam during the conversation.

'I don't know, I don't know. You're very young to be talking about these things. Of course you know your way around – well, it's not that I think you know bad words, it's that you know everything. I don't know how you do it, but you know everything. All right, since you like Isabel so much, since right from the beginning you realized that she's not like the others . . .'

'I have every right to know about her past – isn't that it?'

'It's not that I don't want to tell you; it's that – I don't know. I just don't know where to begin.'

'You can begin with the porcelain.'

'There's the witchcraft working. How did you figure out that this was the beginning?'

'I didn't figure out that it was the beginning, I figured out that it was the key.'

'Well, whatever you want to call it, but it was the beginning. I began to notice it because I didn't understand . . . I thought it was like a nickname. The little lord and lady were on a table in the foyer; they were for calling cards. You're going to think I was silly, but I had just come to Madrid from my village less than six months before.' Everything from before the beginning came pressing in, rose like the mist or, rather, fell like a fog over everything else, wiping away everything else, past and present. Because to make all the past present in a simple tale, awkward because of the unusual nature of the thing and because of something even more inexplicable – the habit of retelling it to herself every day for the past twelve years. Recounting, going over the main points, but keeping in mind among the images surging forth with each idea and each memory, with each phase or tone of the total memory, the beginningless background of her own life, her childhood: what we call childhood when we know what name to give things. But the simple mind that preserves the image of the fields, the little fields where she hunted and hunted for fallen chestnuts and, with no transition, the fields, the very fields where she could see someone coming down the path. She could hardly see the figure, but she could tell if her eyes met someone else's eyes and it was all just a question of eyes. And at times not even that. Sometimes it was the field itself, the smell of hay that met her nostrils and quickened her breathing, as something sought or hoped for.

'And – you know? – I was very silly, a late bloomer. At sixteen I had never even had a boyfriend. Then came the following year with its sickness and misfortune. I was left an orphan, and I had to come as a servant.'

'And you left nobody back in your town?'

'Nobody . . .' The painful memory of the fatal push interrupts the tale momentarily, making recollection waver, as though the intention of confiding were withdrawing, intimidated – but only for an instant. And another tone, a decisive accent, emphasizes what there's no reason to speak about.

'Nobody! I didn't come here with small-town nostalgia, no. And I was treated rather well in the home of that lady and gentleman; they were quite considerate. I was like a housemaid, and I didn't have to do much. They struck my eye as soon as I got there . . .'

'Who?'

'The little lord and lady. I've already told you they were on a table in the foyer.'

'Ah, and they were porcelain. And why did they call them that?'

'But isn't that what they call them?'

'Well, if you want . . .'

'That's what she called them. She would say to be careful with the little lord, to clean the skirt of the little lady with a nail brush, that it was tulle, that I shouldn't let them fall. And they tell you you shouldn't believe in premonitions!'

'Did you let them fall?'

'Yes, but that's not the problem. That wasn't the premonition. It's that . . .'

The memory's impact produces another blank space. Dazzled by its own brilliance, swept away by its own scent, memory is dispelled by the contact, the nearness of a small porcelain face you could touch with your lips. Alone for long stretches in the foyer, one could touch that smoothness, as well as contemplate the elegance, the refinement of the form that bent slightly toward the tulle-skirted marquise. She was a hindrance, she had to be broken, but the premonition had come before anything else, when the little marquesses were nothing more than themselves, alone.

'When the lady of the house would say that her son went out with the young lord or that the young lord came to call, I thought they called him that because he looked like the figurine, just like it.'

'Just like it, of course, but a bit more dangerous. And you let yourself be seduced.'

'Seduced! Do you know what he called me? Ugly – that's right, ugly – as though it were my name. "Ugly, can you bring me a glass of water?" And if the young man wasn't in, "Ugly, tell him I'll be back around ten." I didn't like it. I wanted to act like it was a joke, but I didn't like it. Until one day . . .' The act of confiding, the kingdom, the universe of women, brings the one listening to maturity and takes the other back to her youth, to her naive girlhood, to the liberal exchange of secrets in the shared savoring of friendship's candies, its multicolored sweets. In the communication of mints and berries the secret's nuances are personified and achieve their strict and real truth, their deepest, most exquisite and labyrinthine truth through the elementary terms, the reticences and simplicities of common speech.

'But then one day he said to me, "You don't like people to call you ugly? You probably think you're pretty. Have you ever looked at yourself in the mirror?" I didn't answer. "Well, go on, have a look and you'll see." Then he went and took me by the shoulders and stuck me in front of the pier-table mirror. "Come on, look at that drooping hair and that dull complexion." And I didn't want to look at myself, but the sun was coming in at an angle, shining on my face. I looked, and I was pink – with anger. I was all rosy, with my hair, which was good and clean, all curly and shining like gold. I broke out laughing and went running down the hallway. He stayed behind saying, "Silly girl . . . she's not convinced." And he never said anything more.'

'All right, but if he never said anything more? . . .'

'No, he never said anything more because when it all happened he didn't say anything, it was impossible to speak. That's the part I don't know how I'm going to tell you. You're going to think I'm shameless.'

'Don't ever say that again as long as you live!'

'No, it's true. You never think the same as everybody else. But I don't know how to tell it to you and . . . Well, okay, since you say I shouldn't think I'm a . . . I said you were going to think that because I wasn't going to tell you that what happened happened even though I didn't want to. Do you understand? That's what they all say, but not me because I wanted to do it. You see how terrible it is?'

'Yes, I can see. I understood right from the beginning that you wanted it to happen.'

'Yes, I wanted it. I was dying for it . . .'

'I've never ever told anyone this. It was very hot. I thought I couldn't sleep because of the heat, but the fact is that I had heard them come in very quietly on other nights . . . and I had realized that the young gentleman wasn't alone. Of course he wasn't alone because he could hardly stand. Five minutes later I would hear the door open and someone leaving with hardly a sound. The person would go down in the elevator which had ended up on our floor. Do you understand? This had happened a number of times, and I couldn't sleep. When I heard them arrive I said to myself that now I would see what they're doing, and I slipped out into the hall. I just had a light robe on. It was all dark, and they weren't making a sound, but I heard him saying "Help me." I don't know how he dared to say it because if he had spoken a bit louder they would have heard him. But he said it so only I could hear him – "Help me." Sometimes I think I can still hear him. The two of us put the young gentleman to bed, and I took off his shoes. I was going to leave them under the bed, but he caught me by the arm and I let them drop. They didn't make a sound. I don't understand why, but they didn't make a sound . . .'

The cardboard boxes on the trunk had to be put elsewhere in order to open it. Turning her back on Elena, shaking her head and ducking it between her shoulders like a person who can't go on anymore, like someone who needs to hide in her thoughts, in a memory that in the process of being told, surrendered, grows larger and swells like a wave, enormous, threatening, overwhelming. The memory of the hand that pressed her arm, strong but soft. And falling to the rug and the painful act like something horrible lingering on like a sediment below the divine memory of the initial contact on her hands, on her cheeks. The contact with hands and cheeks of porcelain. The box tied with cord emerges from the trunk and the seals are broken. The little lord wrapped in silken paper and divorced from the skirt of tulle, free but with one leg missing. And beneath it papers, hospital documents – useless now – and Isabel's baptismal certificate. A page from a magazine with a large photo taken at a gala horse race: gentlemen in high silk hats, ladies in tight skirts. Beneath it names of counts and barons and their ladies.

'This one, can you see? This one that you can hardly make out if you don't know what he looks like. Do you see?'

'Well, I can hardly see him, but I can imagine him.'

Everything goes back to the bottom of the trunk, quickly because Isabel might pop in. On top of the papers, the little lord wrapped in those silken sheets.

'But he's lame. You weren't, back then, right?'

'Of course not! What a thought! But that's another story. The days and months I spent alone. Everyone had gone off for the summer. The cook and I stayed to take care of the aunt who was so old that she hardly ever left her room. I said alone, but the worst part was that the cook was a bad woman, stupid. And I thought she saw through me, I figured she had caught on to everything. Imagine! A full bottle of Carabaña purge water on the sly, and it didn't do a bit of good. I went around the lower-class neighborhoods and a woman who sold herbs in a market gave me rue and maidenhair fern, but it was still no use. One day I heard two people talking at the butcher's about a woman who had aborted. One of them said, "She fell flat on her back like a bag of potatoes." The other answered, "Ah, that'll do you in, flat on your back." This story can give you some idea of the facts but not of the anguish they inspire, of the determination with which you look for a solution to a problem which must be dealt with – it absolutely must be dealt with – feeling terror, repugnance and compunction about doing what you shouldn't do and the unhappiness of not wanting to do it but having to. And you try to find fatally certain methods. So guess what, I started cleaning windows. I propped up the ladder, climbed up to the top and pushed the top away from the balcony with my hand. Everything came crashing down with me, but I didn't fall on my back. I can't explain it, but I didn't fall on my back. I don't know what twists and turns I gave in the air, but I fell on my hands and knees like a cat that always lands feet first. Like any animal in danger making certain moves which rational beings cannot understand. But a rational being can, for the sake of the species, extemporize such a movement: leaping, changing the fall into a leap, turning in the middle of the leap and falling right, on hands and knees. Protecting the torso and the back, falling tense with arms fully extended. The ladder fell on top of me and gave me such a smack on the head that I was almost knocked silly, but the pain in my knee was worse and I had to hide it because if I acted like it was bad, they would have told the doctor, who came almost every day to see the aunt. I thought that if he examined my knee he would notice something and so I suffered in silence. I managed until I saw there there was no way to hide it, and then I left. I took my belongings – I'd saved a few pesetas – and I rented a room down by Atocha, near the hospital . . . I felt just fine! I'd resolved the double bind: I'd done what I should do and hadn't done what I shouldn't have done. But the not having done, in the middle of what I was doing, was the more difficult act because it didn't mean I'd changed my mind: the two acts were simultaneous. The initial decision to do what I must do – what I by necessity had to do – carried within it how it would be done. I had taken every precaution for carrying out the fatal solution. Nobody could say – nobody being someone deep in my conscience – that I hadn't done enough. Nobody seeing that fall – and who could see it except that someone? – could doubt the sudden turn, as kinesthetically perfect as if it had been planned. The mystery, or rather, the enigma of the double bind, reaching a climax in the simple mind's exaggerated idea of virtue, availed itself of the cat's agile irrationality. Don't think that my peace of mind lasted very long; the worst part began when I got out of the hospital.'

Steps are heard on the stair, the shoe boxes go back on top of the trunk. But it isn't Isabel, it's a customer's maid bringing more sewing. Elena decides to leave because it's about time to eat. She slowly descends the twenty stairs, first a flight of ten, then the landing, lit by the skylight so close above, then ten more steps.

Next, going to the door on the left and reaching a hand out for the doorbell. All this was eternal. Eternal means everything that has nothing to do with real time. Eternal means all levitation, all projecting of one's self into hypothetical worlds carrying the baggage of all that you are, of all that is real and commonplace. Isabel – the tremendous story of when Isabel did not exist, the story that was Isabel. What she didn't know, what could never exercise any logical power over her, turned into, became incarnate in her form, in the color of her eyes and her behavior, in her mystery. All that drama, all that risk, all that awfulness transubstantiated into a certain aloofness, into a certain passion alternating with a certain coldness. All this was Isabel. But Isabel was extraordinary by anyone's judgment, not like the foolish person who had lived that awfulness. The voice of a new pupil reached the landing, along with the sound of the piano and the teacher's interjections. Not at all like the humble creature endlessly sewing her percale on an old machine. Who would ever guess she was extraordinary if she herself adopted the commonplace view and reconciled herself to passing for nothing more than a fallen woman? Her rational being had scarcely awakened and she had no weapons with which to defend the glorious moment of her love. The lightning bolt stopped by force of will, persistent in its intention, dazzled Elena like a supernatural vision – the vortex and, at the same time, the source of all existence. But it was a hidden wellspring because one never thinks that, subsequently or prior to a creature's existence, its very being might have flashed brilliantly – what it is going to be – via a fatal conjunction, via a violent attaction which brought about the clash, the mutual understanding or, rather, the agreement.

The doorbell rings and someone opens the door. Elena goes to her room, and the voice of the pupil rings clearly throughout the house. Elena tries not to hear it. She wants to remain immersed in her meditation, in her emotions. But the voice insists, interrupted time and again by the teacher. If only the voice were to follow the melody to the very end, she might have accepted it as a companion for her ideas. But it halted regularly, it was cut off by the voice of Ariadne offering an interjection or a rap on the piano cover.

'No. Paulita, no! You sing but you *don't say* what the song cries out for.'

And then again two or three measures, and another interruption:

'No, Paulita, that's not the way it's *said*!'

And once more the rhythm of the habanera:

'Taran tan tan . . . , taran tan tan . . . taran tan tan taran tan tan . . . *io t'amo*.'

'Look, what we have to have is an ever-so-slight prolongation, a slight pause on this note to emphasize and strengthen the *io t'amo*.'

And a demonstration follows the explanation: the piano *says* '*io t'amo*.' Ariadne explains it like a mathematics problem and her hand spells it out on the keys. Elena sees the agility of that pudgy hand – pudgy, sedentary – which dominates the keys as though Ariadne were making them sound by a direct command of her thought. The keys *say* '*io t'amo*' because the hand thinks it, the dimpled hand that she, Elena, kissed and nibbled when she was a baby, the hand that knows how to say *io t'amo*. So she, Ariadne, had said it because, if not, she, Elena, would never have existed. But she certainly hadn't said it in a flash of madness, risking her life and respectability. She must have said it with music, and maybe even with verses. There were some verses which were like saying that, like demonstrating that on a moonlit night. No! – on a summer night. She, Ariadne, was the moon. No! – not that either! The moon, the glow of the moon, wafted out from the balcony in her music and filled the whole street. That is why she, Elena, had a mind with a moonlike clarity. Isabel had an inpregnable mystery, like mysteries that are consummated in the light of the sun, like a seed, like a blue flower growing from ocher earth. This also was in Elena's mind as a perplexity, only as a perplexity. The loves of the mothers, those defenseless daughters of destiny! Elena feels a good deal older than her mother, more filled with experience because what Ariadne might have experienced doesn't stay awake like that of Elena, who is prepared to be on the alert for eighty, one hundred, two hundred, five hundred years with eyes wide open. Elena, absorbed in her perplexity, hears the endlessly repeated habanera from *Carmen*, but not the shouts of newspaper vendors in the street. They're shouting like crazy. Something must have happened. Suddenly it's quiet in the study. And more extraordinary, her father leaves his room in his slippers and goes down the stairs. Her father makes his appearance on the scene. Elena feels that in her dramatic perplexity she had forgotten him. She had been thinking about her mother's loves and her father's verses. She had reflected on the transformation – or, more exactly, the alteration – that had filled out Ariadne's figure with the roundness of resignation, nostalgia or melancholy. She had even come to think that her mother ate chocolates to resist nostalgia. The chocolates were something like a vestige of what had not existed, of triumphs, of resounding applause. The alteration of all that – what had not been – became now a daily exercise, the struggle with the pupils – the majority of them inept – who aspired to a degree from the Conservatory, who were now launched or being dragged around the provinces as members of unknown companies and came to request her assistance in perfecting and refining their art. In the final analysis, all that was a continuation of the sacred fire now burned out, a standing guard before the ashes on the altar. Her father no longer stood guard. He had made no alteration; he had annulled himself, he had withdrawn into himself, occupying himself with piddling details which helped him hide as well as show off his lack of employment and his bitterness. The latter was aggressive at times, as though it came from a man who is perfectly right and does not care to excuse his misanthropy. Suddenly, carried away by the shouts in the street, he went down to the entrance and came back up with the extra. Everyone went into the dining room and her father read the news, to his mother-in-law mainly. The conversation was between him and Doña Eulalia.

HORRIFYING ATTACK

GOVERNMENT PRESIDENT ASSASSINATED

CRIMINAL COMMITS SUICIDE

'It was in the Puerta del Sol almost on the corner of Carretas, in front of the San Martín Bookshop window.'

'Mr. Canalejas had just left home and was on his way to the Ministry of the Interior.'

'That's all there was to it. Four shots, and the whole thing's over.'

'My God, you almost sound like you're happy!'

'No one could think I'm happy that they killed him. What I'm happy about is that everything is out in the open, that we can all see how far those who rule behind the scenes will go. Here we have it! It's in cases like this that it all comes out. A decent man, a man with courage, and they swat him down like a fly. Because he makes trouble, he wants to change things, and that just doesn't go over. Their dirty tricks have to go on. A person gets in who has a bit of honor and talent – that's the serious part, talent! – who has more talent than all the others put together, so they eliminate him and that's that. They don't care if he's the President or the porter, if he's . . .'

Sinfo puts the soup tureen on the table. They eat, one would have to say in silence because each one keeps silent about his or her impressions of the drama. Only the trivial comments between one course and another keep up a bombardment that involves rancor, unavowed meanings, as disguised as they are engraved, branded by fire. The domestic ritual ends, and Elena goes down to discuss it. Isabel opens the door, rather upset. Her voice is barely audible when she tells Elena to come in. Piedita is sobbing in the hallway. 'Magdalena is dead . . .'

In the afternoon people come to Doña Laura's house to offer condolences. Among them is Felisa, a pupil from some time back who hadn't visited recently. Elena remembered her from when they were little. Felisa was somewhat older. Banal conversations, difficult to sustain in a low voice – nostalgic memories or reference to the rosary, which wasn't pertinent in that house – with animation sufficient to distract the affected person. They murmured and whispered stories, news, minor gossip and, naturally, comments on the event which had affected all of them. When the topic came up, Luis's parents, who had come up to the apartment, became violently silent, made discreet excuses and left. Their desertion then became the topic of conversation. Doña Laura said 'Now they'll be killing each other on the way downstairs.' Elena started thinking about that statement. Felisa invited them to come by her house, only a couple of doors away on San Andrés; her father had a lot of records. Elena was thinking that some die, some are killed and some do the killing. How different! How different the death of Magdalena, anticipated for some time, mourned beforehand, feared for various reasons, some of them impure, selfish, unworthy of holding back the hurt that the plain news had caused. That pain suspended, as if perched on a fragile branch of joy – 'Thank God, the danger has passed!' And now there was no appeal. Magdalena is dead, rending the harmony of the clan, the harmony which exists at times but not always, mainly fraternal harmony, the camaraderie of blood, of time, more than anything. There's a rending – no, it's just the opposite! Grief tightens the knot from which something had escaped. Magdalena, so beautiful, dying in her bed, surrounded by love. How different! How different from the other event. A man shot to death in the middle of the street. A man like all men – not ugly nor handsome or old or young, with a turned-up moustache – limp in a pool of blood on the sidewalk. They would pick him up, of course, and take him to his home where he, in the same way, would be mourned. There would be cries and tears. Someone would remove his blood-stained clothing – a suit with a jacket like that of any other man. Someone might kiss him, perhaps. But besides this there would be people, many people, who would appear at the wake without a bit of grief. People who would only be thinking that the deed had been a disaster or that it was a good thing. The death of that man wouldn't stop you from having fun, but . . .

Mrs. Smith arrived with her daughter and her brother, her most effective collaborator, and conversation took a different tack at once. Mrs. Smith offered her sympathies to the mistress of the house, but soon the topic came up again. The new arrivals deeply lamented the assassination. Mrs. Smith said he was a great man and that it was all too frequent that great men died for an idea. The words of Mrs. Smith decked the man fallen in the street in antique vestments, or rather stripped him, not of his blood-soaked jacket, but of his very body, of his personal characteristics; she left him with his soul – personal as well – but reduced or purified or raised to its substantial idea. That gentleman, Don José Canalejas, a name without the slightest epic accent, which could not easily evoke a fall like that of the dying Gaul nor the drive or determination of Daoíz and Velarde – white, imperishable amid the foliage of Moncloa Square. No, it was a name which stirred ideas of family: for some he would remain Don José; for others he would be Señor Canalejas, the last four letters sounding like the slightly and tenderly pejorative diminutive used for things or insects or trifles, a name that belonged completely to the sphere of the familiar, of what is close, of what is humanly close, free from any idea, yet slave to an idea, the victim of an idea. The ideal. Ideas hovered around people. They were like something freestanding, enormous, removed from human love although human beings loved them to the point of death. And what's more, ideas, enormous, freestanding, did not struggle with one another high up in the heavens like those grand masses of clouds that shoot one another with their lightning bolts in their own sphere without complicating anyone's life. Ideas, in order to conquer one another, searched for and selected a man and, just by putting a bullet in his head, advanced and took control of the enemy for a good period of time. All this was far off, or seemed to be far off, but it was everywhere and it touched everyone. You had to stop playing games – love affairs, fancies, reflections – and grow up. Growing up meant in a certain sense a distancing, something akin to coming out of the shell, leaving the placenta, that carnal, bloody, hot, vital, oneiric, omnipotent, infinite climate. To relinquish frivolous pleasure, solitude and take into account . . . all the rest, the other, the unknown, the inconceivable, what you only guess at when its cry, its scream, its roar reaches you from afar. All this was just an infinite perplexity in Elena's mind as she said good-bye to Felisa, promising to go to her house with Isabel to listen to her records.

And once again the perplexity hovering over the stairway like an unrecognizable light: twilight or cloudy or perplexity, the mind clouded. Forty steps this time: twenty from the first floor to the second, twenty from the second to the third. A constellation of enigmas, heavy, difficult to transport, to carry to the everyday refuge, the study and the shared games. The facts, the two deaths whose disturbing reality had come from the street, from the shouts of the newsboys and from the sobbing of the two sisters, interrupting life – books lying on the floor and in the hall, the rows of desks crooked – the whole tragic disorder had served to . . . it was brutal to think it. But it was necessary to think brutally because the whole affair had served to distance Isabel from Elena. To distance Elena like someone stepping away to see better. Isabel had now the aura of her mystery. Elena was afraid that her eyes would give away the newness of her vision. She needed to get used to the new tone, not forget it but put it in its proper place, on its silent, secret, proper level where Isabel could never suspect its existence. Difficult, extremely difficult, to keep the secret, all the while wanting to share the change, the maturity imposed by the dramas lived through – dramas that couldn't be considered alien, they were so close at hand, so upsetting to the family sphere. Not, of course, to the actual families of either of the two girls, but rather to the whole climate they loved. These deaths were so unanimously lived that they served . . . Well, they had to be used, it wasn't necessary to say adopted: used was more exact because it was a case of the practical aspect, of how to put into practice the new vision, the new tendency, the voluntary tendency toward maturity. Because it wasn't a question of letting oneself progress step by step with the normality of something ripening on a tree; but of moving in a new direction: other aspects of life, even of books must be confronted. Now, thanks to all that, to the upheaval, books that weren't for study, books that were just for pleasure, appeared to be hiding something behind the pleasure. She had always read books, skipping the drier pages. Not that they had been skipped, really; they had just stayed in the background like something that you don't understand because you don't recognize it: it doesn't reach you, doesn't get incorporated because it cannot be grafted onto the branches which are already full of sprouts. It is something germinating in other regions that you have yet to get to.

I've got to go up those forty stairs and tell her good-bye until tomorrow. There's the danger that Isabel might notice the change and, with her suspicious nature! If Felisa hadn't appeared, there'd be no reason for her to interpret it wrong. But she has appeared and the most serious part is that, in fact, Felisa is – or is going to be – closely connected to the change. Isabel has noticed this: she was all the while looking at her with a particular expression. Isabel guesses, suspects, discovers things that happened a thousand years ago as well as things that haven't yet come to be – things that pass fleetingly through the imagination, things a name might suggest, for example. But this time she's wrong. It seems odd to me that she didn't see that right from the first I've tried to get them to be friends. There's no mystery of any sort in my friendship with Felisa. It's odd she hasn't noticed this, above all that she hasn't noticed it in me. Because when she used to bring up the names I mentioned – 'Oh, what's Pilarcita like? What's Encarnita like?' – I tore them apart with boundless cruelty, and handed them to her ripped to shreds: all their ridiculous simplemindedness, their obtuseness, their babylike innocence mixed with their ladylike circumspection and their old women's gossip. All this was elaborated and in many cases adorned in order to spark Isabel's cruelest laughter. But then, with a special sarcastic tone, she said suddenly, 'What about Adelina?' I answered that Adelina was fantastic. I gave no explanations, and she asked for none. That's the most amazing thing – she didn't ask. Well, luckily, Adelina is not in Madrid. Luckily? I love her dearly, but if I had to describe her for myself, I'd also have to say 'She's fantastic!' because I don't know how to describe the things she does. To me the things she does are just girls' things, pranks, saying bad words. I've always listened to them – and not just listened – as if they were kid stuff, like what you do when you're a little girl. Well, when you're a little kid, anyway, because of course boys do the same thing. I've never thought of these things as very serious, but still, I would never want to get Isabel involved in them. Why? The fact is I have no idea why. It's as if in her, in Isabel, all that . . . Is it that she doesn't know anything about that stuff? Perhaps it's just the opposite: she knows too much about it. But no, I think it's that I don't want to know how she knows about it. Because she must have found out the way people in general do. Her mother cannot have ever given her a different kind of explanation. Well, the serious part is that she certainly must have given her some explanation. My parents never gave me more than a few hints – so little that I never took it seriously. That's why the things Adelina was up to, the summer we spent together in El Puerto . . . We got to playing a lot – playing! – in that abandoned Moorish bath. The water had been cut off for centuries and it was all full of climbing vines and jasmine and heliotrope. We would play there for hours. Then we would play at night under the covers. The dark circles under Adelina's eyes! My aunt and uncle were always worried about Adelina's dark circles, and when they would mention them she would put on such an innocent face that it was worse than a confession. I asked her if she couldn't see that they were going to catch on. She said it was ridiculous, that they don't catch on to anything. She despised them, Adelina despised her parents because of their trust. No, because they didn't suspect her, which is different. The fact is that my aunt and uncle are complete fools and Adelina is not a fool, no; she twists them around her little finger. For me all that is a thousand miles away, far in the past like kid stuff. All I can remember is the Moorish bath beneath the heliotrope as something delightful, and our games – which were also delightful. But I would never invite Isabel to play one of those games. You have to put it behind you, you have to turn the corner. Let's see what Felisa brings . . .

'Okay, see you tomorrow.'

'Do you have paper?'

'Yes, I have some.'

'You have the charcoal and the tacks?'

'Yes, I've got everything.'

'You don't have to get up too early. Five minutes will be enough time to get there before class begins.'

'Yes, I know.'

'Until tomorrow, then.'

'Until tomorrow . . . Listen, have you noticed how Piedita looks? I find her a bit strange these days.'

'Yes, it's true. I mentioned it to her about a week ago and she told me it was because she was using Mlle Robin's hair style. Then I asked her where she had seen it, and she began to tell me about a film they were showing at the Prince Alfonso theater. That was several days ago, before the news came. She had gone with Mrs. Smith.'

'Right, right. Mrs. Smith must have suggested the hair style to her, too. It smacks of Mrs. Smith.'

'Wow, what a nose you have! It's true. It was the business of Mlle Robin that put me off the track. I began to want to see it! Since the Noviciado theater isn't there any more, it seems like a century since we've gone to a picture show. As soon as my mother has a free afternoon. The Prince Alfonso is really far.'

'Yes, the Mlle Robin thing must be true, but the fact is her hair looks like it's been done by a hairdresser.'

'You're getting warm! You're getting warm! We'll have to look into this.'

Dear, my very dear . . . no, I can't go on. It's useless. I've been trying for three days and I can't even write two lines because Piedita wants me to ask him if he's really set on coming and when. But in order to ask I have to tell him why I'm asking. Of course, I want to know – it's vitally important to me! But I have to tell him that I'm asking because of the other business. And the other business . . . what can I say about that? If I could tell him what I'd like to, I would say come as fast as you can, come and help me understand this affair, to see what this is all about, to see what side we should be on. Even though I think it's useless to choose sides. It's become inevitable. Would I have avoided it if it had been possible? Deep in my heart I feel more like I brought it on than tried to avoid it. Deep in my heart I have to admit that perhaps my intentions or my unconfessed desires brought it on. I'd have to believe – it's completely stupid, but I'd have to believe that I conjured up some evil spirit. But why evil? Why try to avoid it now? I especially have absolutely no right. It might seem that I do have because no one knows that I have no authority over myself. Nobody knows that I disauthorized myself by authorizing her . . . The only solution would be for Manolo to be here to give his opinion. And all things considered, it's doubtful that his opinion would be worth anything. The atrocious thing is that I should be so sure of his opinion: I pass the burden to him. I don't dare to have any opinions of my own; I hang on to the thought that Manolo would not approve. And I don't dare to ask him, I don't dare talk to him about it because he might perceive my . . . I don't know what to call it. Of course, if he were to come . . . That's another thing I don't dare to get into for the same reason, because I don't want him to perceive . . . Well, nobody – not him or anybody – could find it strange if I told him that I'm waiting impatiently for his arrival. No, no one could find it strange. But even in a letter you feel the accent, you feel the happiness of the arrival. It would be all right to say that his coming is a source of happiness for me, although happiness – for him especially – is something we won't feel for a long time. But no, my happiness is too great for me to mention, so I can't tell him about that or about the other business or about anything. Then there's Piedita asking me, 'Have you told Manolo? Have you told him we want him to come?' 'We want!'

It's absolutely crazy! How can I write something like that if I can't even say it to myself? 'We want!' And she says it perfectly naturally. Because, I'd swear with my hand on the Bible that nothing can have happened yet between the two of them. No, the way he presented himself, and in such a critical situation! In all this he showed his seriousness, he displayed the correctness of their relations. And her! That imbecile, that . . . I can't find insults strong enough because I've never used them with her, I've never had to scold her or criticize her seriously. When she was five sometimes I would give her a smack, I would threaten to make her bottom redder than a tomato – and she would laugh. She wouldn't laugh now if I were to tell her what I'm thinking. But as much as my insults might impress her – maybe I did wrong in not calling her on the carpet. I've tried to make her understand in a rational fashion. To do that I would have had to have been in possession of my own rational faculties, and whenever she came out with one of those . . . those . . . 'we's – I almost fainted. We! It's a bedroom, it's more tightly sealed than the blessing of the Holy Mother Church. It's a den, it's a clan. She says, 'We!' – and she is no longer one of us. There are many who would say I'm wrong, that this is how the clan branches out and enriches itself with new shoots. Of course, of course: that happens when it happens, and it is like that when it is like that. And . . . when it's not like that? When you don't know how it is and you feel, you divine, you sense a smell which has nothing to do with your own den? Once again many people would say – because very few people would understand that I put it in this dirt, I smear it with this mud precisely because it's not a question of mud, it's not a question of anything material – if we have to say it like that – it's not a question of anything that might tarnish our titles of nobility – something which we absolutely don't have. If we did have them, it would help us gild them, but it's not a question of that. It's not a case of anything that could be hurt or helped by a little bit – or a lot – of money, a whole pile of money, or by a good name, above reproach. And what can we say about Don Braulio Beltrán? 'It's he! It's he!' What nonsense! How stupid! The phonetic similarity! But no – my God! – I don't want to be the 'infamous accuser.' I don't want to slander him: what I'm accusing him of is his truth. There's nothing of the sort in this case: the only storm is the one brewing inside my head. Of course, in this case there *is* the business of 'I bear great treasures from the Indies.' That's it! Whether the thing is material or not material. That's it! Who would not agree that the pure love of the cabin boy should be blessed with wealth? Romanticism! We all swallow it whole as soon as they season it with a bit of love. That's it! I'd swallow it, too, whether or not there was love involved in the wealth itself, if there were something . . . beautiful? That's another illusion. 'Brazilian diamonds as pure as the sun.' And seeing the guy sweating to get them . . . 'My hand gathered them from the depths of the earth.' I have no idea where he got his diamonds – no, it has nothing to do with diamonds, it's fabrics, . . . or truck farms . . . who cares? I suppose the money's from something officially called decent and . . . sweatless. That's just what makes me sick! What a good time they have, how complacent, how sure of themselves, how moral they feel. How terrible! How terrible! My God! I'm trying to excuse myself by blaming them, and I was the first . . . that's it! Before all this happened I felt the storm brewing, I was afraid of the shipwreck. There is no excuse for fear. Insurmountable fear is usually attributed to those violent and sudden situations: situations that take you by surprise, like a rabbit. I don't know if everyday fear – of foundering in time – has more right to be called insurmountable. I've never seen Piedita threatened by any other enemy: that was the one that obsessed me . . . by comparison. That's the thing! Our times are so different, so opposite! They're only alike in being time. And when all is said and done, who cares? Who cares whether time eats you up with a fork or with a spoon? No, it's not the same, there are serious differences. For myself, I've never been afraid of time. How could I be afraid if I didn't even know it existed? I had too much on my mind, too many things to do. It only began to look like an ogre with its mouth wide open as soon as I saw that Piedita couldn't fill it, couldn't satisfy its hunger. How ridiculous! It's not a question of metaphors . . . or is it? Yes, yes it is. Because as soon as you begin thinking about time the past rises up gesticulating, scaring you with its grimaces. Time doesn't let you think about time, it permits no mutilations: time is the whole of time. And what is Piedita's past? An emptiness, a nonbeing. My God! Would I have allowed it to be something? Of course . . . if she had shown some qualities of superiority, of holiness even. I have to imagine that in order to laugh at myself because I wouldn't have prevented her even in that case. I've always thought that one must respect . . . What is it that I've respected? Did she go outside? To give her little lessons, of course, but only just so far. Did she take the risk of . . . ? I took risks by ignoring all restrictions because, of course, my intellectual ambitions gave me the right to everything. I seized all my rights but she didn't. And she – what rights could she seize? The right of displaying her looks? The right of being desired? 'Good cloth is best sold in the coffer.' Our grandmothers said this. But we, the granddaughters, no longer say it or do it or tolerate it. Nobody would ever keep me under lock and key – not even grandmothers or parents. And then when it came my turn to be the keeper of the keys . . . Watch out! Watch out! The sirocco or the lava might go rushing behind her and catch her. The lava and the sirocco of desire as I see now in horror hasn't followed her, only ne'er-do-wells on the street – Who knows, who knows what they might turn out to be? – But no, the coffer was well closed, and it was up to me to guard it. One can more easily take a chance of dishonoring one's ideals than of compromising common respectability. The blame is fully mine: not the blame of the magic spell – that's silliness – but blame for locking away the key to the coffer. I can't complain, because the cloth has fetched a high price. My God! Have we come to this? Come to this? No, we're just beginning. Beginning what? We're on a dead-end street. And the fact is that what makes me act foolishly is the notion that she is escaping. Because that's the issue – you escape from poverty and you end up in exigency. Can she possibly realize that that is exigency? No, she can't because here in our house, in her house, she only lived the poverty, she never swam in our abundance . . . That's what is most painful, that's what I see now: I see what she longed for – I can't say she sought, she wasn't conscious, she wasn't daring – she was . . . What was she, or rather what wasn't she? In any case, she didn't get carried away over Leander – poor guy! The curling iron had given him the look of a store clerk, but he was young, and he had a certain attractiveness. What was he, a young student? A young clerk? I don't know, but there was something of Leander about him. If it were I . . . Of course, I would never have gotten into that situation, but I could imagine myself in it. Yes, had I been in her place, I could have lived my Hellespont above the screaming masses which encircled them. I could have been intoxicated by all that, but I would never have lost my common sense, never would I have lost myself – muddied myself – in common sense. And what common sense that girl has had! That's what a lot of people would say. The blessing of Boaz. 'Blessed art thou of Jehovah, my daughter. Your final act has been better than the first because you have not aspired to any youth, poor or rich.' An exemplary woman, Ruth, the gleaner – and I always thought she was revolting. But it's even crueler because I have to tell myself once again that there's been no question of consciously seeking an advantage. Seduction was exercised. In this case Mother Celestina didn't come with a bit of thread, or anything ordinary or domestic, but with the trumpery of progress, with foreign ideas more brilliant than the ones we ourselves have. A horror of cut flowers, for example: how civilized! And the persuasive argument – directed at me because she knew I was just as eager for it as she was – 'She's the perfect match for my Leandro, because she couldn't say "for my Claudio." ' Braulio! Lord! What confusion, what stubbornness in associating those two names . . . She couldn't say it, but she could do it. The perfect mate for her total collaborator, for her comrade and companion in every sort of snobbishness – more sophisticated than Mr. Smith shut up in his factory, gayer, with the gaiety of one who shows off the need to be happy because he has lost a young wife. That's been going on for some time. At this point he's achieved happiness to the same degree as he has plumpness . . . Although his extreme cultivation does not allow for gluttony, but prompts him to boast of frugality. 'Ah, there's nothing like a good salad.' My God! how embarrassing. I'm feeling, tasting, experiencing shame for the first time in my life. This is chemically pure shame because whenever anyone feels shame – I or anyone – it's always in connection with one's neighbor. You go red in the face for any indiscretion, any slip that others might have seen. But now no one sees what I am ashamed of. I see myself degraded, lowered to the level of gossip, subjected by all this humanity crashing down upon me, with no pardon or mitigation. Considering, contemplating these dregs, scraping away their decent covering until I can see clearly and say, that's what they are, feces – shit would be too innocent a word – they are detritus, they're something worse, they are lies. That's it: that's what we find inside when we scrape, I can classify it thus without the slightest scruple. Because whenever I've been tempted to feel repugnance, I've always been able to hold myself back – sincerely, spontaneously, humanly, because it was my humanity that stopped short out of respect (with veneration!) when faced with the human. But not now. Now I can't. I don't want to! I can't say to myself like on other occasions, how can we know the pressures, the needs, the ignorance which brings things about? No, now I can't say anything like that and therefore I have to renounce all pity, I have to use up my blasphemies to get it out of my mind because it's shaming me. I have to let Manolo know about it. It's absolutely necessary! I'd like to avoid it, but it's impossible. And how can I bring all this down on his head, in his state of mind? But since he's never going to leave off this state of mind it's useless to wait a bit. It's also useless and even inconvenient to attenuate the seriousness. He could suppose that I don't think it's a catastrophe. He could also think I was sunk in the mud, and that for him would be too much. Could anything be – at this point! – too much for him? He didn't dare to write me or give me the news by telephone. I opened the door and I found his assistant, and I smiled at him, hoping for the latest news . . . and the poor fellow didn't know how to begin. Of course, as soon as I saw his face . . . The news was given in detail, the development of the illness up to the final moments, and Manolo's own condition . . . the definitive phrase. No, nothing can touch him now. Maybe what's waiting for me still is the spectacle of his indifference in the face of all these things. I've got to prepare myself for the worst. I have to write him immediately. My dear, my dearest Manolo . . .

'I think, Ariadne, that you should oblige your husband – well, yes, I know you can't oblige him. I think you should convince him that it would be a good thing for him to go and see that gentleman.'

'He doesn't want to, and when he says no, it's no.'

'Yes, yes, I know him. I know him all too well. But it's an opportunity he shouldn't miss.'

‘But that’s why I don’t go. That’s why exactly. I don’t want it to look like I’m taking advantage of the moment.’

‘Ah! You were there! I don’t care if you heard it. It wasn’t a question of conspiracy, it was a simple opinion: something that might occur to anybody with her head on her shoulders.’

‘Do you see? You’re telling me I’m right. You’re explaining that I shouldn’t go because Mr. Téllez has his head on his shoulders: I’ve seen it on a number of occasions and I know he normally uses it. He’s a well-known professor. As soon as he sees me nearing his office he’ll say, “here he is, coming to see if he’ll get a windfall.” ’

‘That’s how you think. Your way of arranging everything is thinking the worst of everybody.’

‘You’re wrong there. If I thought I could arrange everything by thinking the worst I would have put things in order already. I would have turned things inside out like a sock. But thinking the worst doesn’t solve anything, much less thinking the best.’

‘All right. All right. I know it’s like banging my head against a stone wall, but come on! If you don’t want to go to his office, you could send him a couple of words, a heartfelt letter – don’t tell me you don’t know how to write one. Because imagine if you ran into him somewhere. Saying nothing to him under these circumstances, with what this must have meant to him, with what it must mean to him and to the rest of his party, would simply be bad manners.’

‘If I were to run into him someplace, supposing that he recognized me, supposing that he ever was aware of my existence, who knows whether this gentleman would expect me to have good manners?’

‘Ah! Of course. Of course. Who’s to know? But if you demonstrate that you have no manners, then he’s informed.’

‘That’s true, and it’s no mean thing to be informed about something, about something certain via a demonstration.’ To know something beyond the shadow of a doubt is nothing to laugh at! Above all for an intelligent man like Mr. Téllez – a man who doesn't let a thing slip past him. He would come from time to time by the office and start in asking one and the other person questions. He took his notes and looked through files. He was pleasant with everyone, but suddenly he would stop and listen. He could tell the difference. Not just in what people were saying, but in their tone of voice and even their pronunciation. He wasn't one of those people who flatter the personnel in order to get good service. No, you could tell that in him it was something spontaneous. It was natural for him to have a different attitude – a way of listening, a way of addressing people, a way of asking a question or making an observation. He even looked at you differently when he was waiting for a response he knew would be satisfactory. It was a way of looking which inspired trust in the person in question, freedom to speak his mind clearly – without being too intimate, far from it. He never had anything to do with the jokes – usually dirty ones, really dirty – which is normal in an office, in the Bureau of Primary Education. That's the kind of atmosphere a lot of them delight in – some of the deputies, some of the professors, but not Téllez. Never Téllez. Whenever he appeared at one of those coffee breaks – a cigarette, some coffee brought up by the porter – everyone became silent. He imposed silence with his gaze, but it was absolutely not authoritarian: intelligent, just intelligent. He would just look around and all the idiots there would fall silent. Then he would address himself to someone he thought might understand what he wanted. His approach was deferential. It was as though, instead of asking a favor, he was rewarding the person by bringing the matter up, distinguishing the person, setting him apart from the others. A certain closeness would be established, but nothing more than a certain closeness. But with elegance, with the natural measure of a person who is a gentleman. That's what you see in him a mile off. That's what makes you respect him. It's not the same as the inhibition, discomfort, or stiffness produced by aristocratic airs, or by hierarchy, being in a higher position. That is what we mean today when we use the word "gentleman": that's what it means in these meaningless times. In these times when wearing a new shirt and sporting a couple of Havana cigars in your pocket makes you a gentleman. I've never noticed what kind of shirts Téllez wears, but I've never seen him with cigars. Maybe it's because he doesn't smoke. Oh, yes, he smokes a pipe. Now I remember that his pipe gives him a certain air of command, a respectability that has little to do with age: I don't even think he's fifty. It's a moral respectability . . . there's the difference. The one is respectability that inhibits, imposes, distances, but the other levels or attracts via the recognition of excellence, out of a sense of security . . .

'Dad! I've been calling you for an hour. Are you asleep?'

'No, I was just thinking.'

'Well, even though you're thinking, give me the dictionary.'

'Here you go.'

'No, I want the encyclopedia and you're leaning on it.'

'Oh, of course! I didn't realize. Why do you want it?'

'To see what period Dante lived in, the exact date of the *Divine Comedy*.'

'You don't need the dictionary. It's around thirteen hundred and something.'

'And the something?'

'It's not important. Why do you want to know?'

'Because we're going over to Felisa's and she's going to show us an edition that her father found in an old book store. I think it's damaged, but it's still got some wonderful engravings.'

'Yes, I can imagine what they're like. You'll like them.'

To look around secondhand bookstores with enough money

in your pocket to cover a find. People manage – who knows how – on a miserable salary! What kind of salary could he earn at the Telephone Company? Although maybe he's worked up to a fairly high position, though maybe he spent years stuck at a desk, or maybe at the beginning it might not have been a desk, but rather one of those boards with holes and pegs. And maybe not even that. Maybe it was a question of walking up and down the streets with telephone messages. At any rate, today Mr. Olmedo acquires old books, gramophones, records. He's an excellent father, he knocks himself out to enrich his daughter's cultural education. All right, we all do what we can. Am I clutching at this idea that 'If you do what you can, nobody can ask for more?' But, what exactly can one do? Does anyone know? You show movement by walking. Another demonstration! If you can do something you show it by doing it. But the man who can't, how does he show that he can't? Everybody wants you to put your shoulder to the wheel and show . . . , but no, they don't want you to show that you can't: they want you to be one of those who can do a little bit, badly, just enough to be one more fellow and never better than the rest. When you know that you're better without demonstrating it, then that shows you're worse. It doesn't matter much if they all think I'm worse; the thing is to figure out if the fact of not showing I'm better makes me worse. Because for myself it's not necessary . . . There they go: 'Mi mi sol, mi mi do, re re fa.' The A-B-C, the stammering of a little girl whose feet don't even reach the pedals. One more! Some play, some sing. None of them goes very far; some of them don't progress at all. It wasn't that! No, that wasn't the way . . . Back then, no one thought about demonstrating anything: one was superior, blind, visionary, idiotic, infallible – in a word, one was simply young. You didn't think about demonstrating anything – you wanted to dominate. Dominate? Shocking! No? Well, yes, that's what one wanted. She could have gone to the top! Why didn't she? We weakened, with a demonstrable power – a demonstrated power. With a . . . what's the point?

It almost makes you afraid to look at it close-up because if it were nothing more than a golden metal trumpet one might think that it could only go, 'Ta-ta-taaa!' But with that blue, a blue like bluebells, you get the impression that it's not something manufactured, that it's a flower: the flower of music.

'If you say that before even hearing it, what are you going to say when we put on something by Caruso? I know how to make it work, but we should wait until my father comes because, look, it's rather out of whack. My father put it back together with tape and you can't even tell, but you have to start it almost without touching it because the balance goes at the slightest contact. It's a little bit broken, but thanks to that he was able to buy it. Hardly a day goes by without him discovering something in the secondhand shops. You're going to see the engravings: they're his latest acquisition. Look, there's almost nothing left of this one.'

'How terrible! But this isn't from a woodborer. Woodborers just make little holes.'

'No, this is from mice. The book is a little over fifty years old, but it's been more than twenty in a cellar.'

'How do you know?'

'The antique dealer is a friend of my father's and he tells him the history of all his junk: the story behind this one is incredible. It was brought in by some young traveler and cursed by I-can't-remember-what old grandmother – maybe his mother, maybe not so old – because of those naked souls.'

'Oh, Felisa! Think about what you just said. Souls! The book doesn't speak about anything but souls, and what did the artist draw? Bodies, bodies. I don't know very well what happens in this book but I read a half-page résumé in a literary history book and my father explained a little bit more to me. I came to the conclusion that Dante wanted to write in his book about the pain, the torment of guilty souls. Listen, in this book you think they're going to talk about the punishment suffered by the souls of the people who sinned. Of course it's the same thing all our religious books tell us. We're tired of learning this from the time we learn to read, and even before . . . but reading is one thing, and seeing it is another. Do you get what I mean? Seeing it! And here the artist wanted to see it! If you see it, what do you see? Bodies, bodies, forms . . .' The human body in pain has its form, or rather, the sublime form of beauty, the body in its being, in its way of being, the way in which it is inscribed, that word which is the body: that harmony, that plenitude of world which the soul, the self, the subject, the who, the individual carries like a glorious and painful Atlas. That form, in pain, is the form of pain, without ceasing to be the form of beauty. Because we all know that pain deforms, but not in hell; that is, there where there are nothing but souls, where in order to be visible, comprehensible, audible, souls must speak in the form of their bodies. Naturally the illustrator doesn't show us the ugliness of the souls. He would have had to draw humpbacked, knock-kneed people and the like; but he didn't follow appearances because maybe humpbacks and knock-kneed people have very beautiful souls. Can the soul's ugliness be drawn? Of course it can, but only in faces. Neither the artist nor the poet have attempted to offer us the likeness of confession, denunciation, negligence or threat that is patent on the human face. The illustrator has looked upon them from farther off. He's shown them to us amid the shadows of condemnation, among the crags, the rocks, the difficulties of punishment, affliction. Tormented bodies, bearing their human form, their pain-wracked and writhing beauty, toward eternal darkness. Because the illustrator has seen nothing else. The same thing that Elena sees because Elena can't see anything else. She sees it, she contemplates it, she pursues it to the point of perplexity – that zone or sphere where her mind is lost without going astray, goes into ecstasy without stopping, plunges down headlong to reach what is in herself, in the final depths of her love. And she doesn't say a word. She sinks into silence because she is the most affected, the one fluctuating in perplexity, feeling as light, as vulnerable as a bubble that could burst from one moment to the next.

'My father is really taking a long time. He must be chatting with the old secondhand dealer. Right now he's crazy about something he's trying to buy cheap. He's been bargaining with him for a week, and they still haven't struck a deal. Ah, there he is! He never gets home this late. Dad, have you got it?'

'What do you mean, got it? That son of a gun is trying to get five *duros* out of me. Ah, I see you've got visitors. How are you, nymphs? You're waiting for me to put on the record player, I think.'

'Yes sir, of course.'

'Very well. Now you're going to see something really good. But have patience. We have to be very careful. First the record is cleaned with a soft brush. A silk brush cleans it perfectly well. Then we put the record on without upsetting the turntable. But what should we play first? Which one do you think these girls would like? They look like bluestockings. Of course – if they weren't, they wouldn't be friends of yours.'

'Dad, it looks like your hands are trembling.'

'Yes, they're shaking because I've had ten cups of coffee. He was just becoming convinced – the bastard – when a guy enters who I thought wanted what I was after because he looked at it as soon as he came in. It was within reach because I had taken it down from the shelf, and he put his hand on it. It got my bile stirring, I'll tell you. A little more patience, girls. Looks like this has come loose a bit. I'll fix it quick. But no, the guy had no idea what it was: it was just something comfortable to rest his hand on. If he comes up with those five *duros* I'll break him in half. I wouldn't have let it get away, now that I've gotten used to the idea that it should be up here. Ah, now it's tight; it's not wobbling. I stay up here at night reading and smoking, and it's almost like I can see it there on the bookcase, like it was always there.' *Correva il treno e nel vertiginoso* . . . listen! . . . *camin mi transportaba affranto e muto*. An immense, limpid, brilliant, deep, dark, masculine, extremely tender and aching voice. Once again the mysterious interplay of pain and beauty . . . Why, and how? Like that – simply – like that. You see and you live and you hear and you suffer and you take pleasure and – even better – you comprehend.

Because we can say in a trivial sense that we don't understand; and it's true, one doesn't understand via a logical explanation – but one comprehends, possesses, encompasses, reaches out. That sound, that accent, that timbre, that note . . . it clutches at the heart. The heart? If it were only the heart, anybody could understand it and that's not the point: it's a case of anyone comprehending it without understanding it because they comprehend it through the senses which never ever fail in the logic, in the harmony of contraries, in the tearing and fascinating dissonance of pain. *Il pensiero volava ad altro giorno cuando lieto, con te fecci la via*. Even that most extreme, most humanly inadmissible shrillness, the tearing separation that divides, leaving life tied, linked to a total absence nourished, held in suspense by memory, which stands paralyzed on the threshold of reality. *Ora, nella tristezza del ritorno, ero solo*. All this was said in a few notes, through a breath that was admirably free, that possessed – in the blood, in the tension of some vocal chords, in the accumulation of the data elements or notes that make up the structure of a person, of everything that lives and stirs silently between the chest and the back of a man – that possessed a high style, a law it must obey or die. Bursting forth next were 'Sorrento,' 'Santa Lucia' and all the rest, and it was all just the blue enamel, or rather, the blue satin background where love and time embroidered the whole inextricable pattern. And all of it contained in age-old melodies, told in the simple verbal forms of peasant or sailor dialect. And amid the silence of the interruptions – first aid with tape and makeshift splints to assure stability – the careful choice of something different, something requested by Felisa as a favorite: 'Si, Manon, o fato a punto, a punto un sogno.' The voice is very different. The background is no longer blue, but the white of the dresscoat of the noble Des Grieux. It's still masculine, but not with the same spirit, not with that open-sea feeling, but with an intimate, longing pining. Pining for what one longs for, not what one has had, but what perhaps one might come to have. 'Piccola casetta bianca, in fondo al bosco ner.' Each one has different features, but there is a certain sameness that throbs or resounds in what is spoken, though the gesture and the face might be different. The notes are not now directed or bestowed by the mouth that corresponds to the violent eyes. No, they escape sweetly from the lips painted above a little cleft chin – a bit chubby – which Felisa points to as she whispers a name, Anselmi, with love and with delight. And the pathetic story fills the room, a humble but learned study, packed with books, with scarcely room for the bottomless easy chair behind the table where Mr. Olmedo sits dreaming of the diety which will sooner or later appear upon his bookcase. Longing for what is desired, the presence of the lovely object, the beautiful thing that is not here yet but which will come because it always existed in desire . . . And now it's very late, time to put an end to what can never end, to what began as solidly as if it were a principle backed by an eternal longing. As if it were a fleeting taste of eternity.

From the entryway fragments of a feminine dialogue are

heard in the study. The head of Felisa's mother pops around the half-open door: blue eyes sunk deep in fleshless sockets that look, but don't want to come in. She speaks with a voice that doesn't want to make a sound. Through a mouth that doesn't want to open, she whispers,

'It's the mother of one of the girls. Isabel's, I think.'

'Tell her to come in.'

'She doesn't want to.'

'Have her come in. Jesus! Why can't she come in?'

So she does, and no attention is paid to the explanations . . .

'I asked Doña Ariadne and she told me . . .'

'Here, have a chair.'

'But, sir . . . I only came . . .'

'There in the chair. For heaven's sake!'

And Felisa's mother, who's only seen the girls in the entryway at the end of the dark hall, who's only said 'Hello!' enters as though it were her duty or an act of generosity, to accompany the cowed visitor, to act as the lady of the house, cowed as well, also an intruder. And the girls disconcerted. Everyone disconcerted, but performing a concert with each one playing her part, but not participating or participating without knowing it, just by being, taking refuge in herself. This with the exception of Mr. Olmedo who is the director – no, the accumulator and the contemplator of the glittering dissonances. Each one – each female, that is – sunk in her . . . contingency, situation, circumstances. Each one of them fearing or deploring or celebrating that this had happened. Hoping or fearing or bearing that it should go on or finish. And it doesn't finish because a male voice utters a hopeless lament and a female voice sighs for the one crashing on the rocks of despair. 'What a sad, dark melancholy his voice reveals in spite of itself!' And the sea is no longer blue, it's dark and gloomy. The tempest has led the sailor to the depths of disaffection. And she cries, 'Who was the ingrate, who was the merciless woman who could thus destroy his peace?' And then the two voices promising or beseeching destiny: 'From now on, smile. From now on, weep.' And perplexity, the zone that absorbs Elena due to her disproportionate ambition, to the giantism of her exceptional soul, now confuses and misleads the two mothers like abandoned children. Because that secret, that bloody crime that churns in the depths of everyday life, which never comes to the surface because around it has formed a very hard shell of trivial, vital, inescapable obligations so that life – no, living – can go on without crashing into the world, without provoking a rejection of work, of all that maintains civilized traffic through the suburbs of honor. But here, now, that secret – of passion, of insomnia's fever – screams, makes veins throb in the throat. But here, now, it's a lovely phrase, the cooing of a turtledove, very sad and beautiful. And decent! – respectable, accepted, sung in front of parents through a magic horn on a small round table in the corner – imposing the suggestion of forms and contacts sacredly concealed in Antonia's blood rather than in her soul. And that very thing, that foolish, invincible, ephemeral passion baring itself so cajolingly, showing itself with the deceitful smile of what has been and is no longer, with the improbability of what is no more, of what simply does not exist and tries to convince, to take credit for having been. But it fails because there's a rancor that denies it. No, no, no. It's there, obviously, tricking us with its captious accent, dazzling us with its glowing ruses that flicker, shining like water in a mirage, for a thirst which is never satiated but dies out as life itself dies out in Carmina's heart, in the depths of the circles under her eyes, caverns in whose depths gleam what were once blue eyes. And it is all like a foreign tongue. These hard-to-understand words were not like a foreign language to Elena and Isabel: they were so near, so crystalline, evident, believable, patent that they could swear by them, by their truth. The words, never before heard, revealed the world to those who on its threshold pawed the ground in their eagerness to take off at a gallop. And the bass, the experienced voice of the old drunk – 'It's been twenty years since we've had such a wild northeaster!' And the clock on the entryway wall – the sea dominating with its unexpected winds, terrible even when dreamed, when forged by alcohol, premonitions of shipwreck – always present in the dream, in the love, the life of the shipwrecked man, striking its conclusive ten chimes. And there's a movement, as if the concert were breaking up, but the law of concordance demands an ending . . . 'The helm and compass fell out of my hands and the ship rolled over!' . . . There are still a few more notes, some more words, then the record is finished and there's a scraping sound like a caption, or conclusion: 'That's it; it's over!' And the concert goes out to the hallway and says good-bye, feeling inseparable. The girls linked by their friendship, the mothers made sisters by their stupor, their not understanding and obeying what had happened, which nobody had set up or provoked but which, because of its singularity in the life of each of them, would remain indelible, would modify their lives in some way, its improbable presence standing out against the mechanics of daily life. For one, Antonia, it had the luxury of the superfluous; for the other, Carmina, it had the shrillness of the irregular. For both of them it was, finally, an impact, a collision, a caress, a powder flash.

'Well, I'll be goddamned! No, don't get hot under the collar. If you hadn't been in the room I would have said something else.'

'Thanks for the courtesy. It wouldn't be a bad idea to make it a habit.'

'You have to use strong language to mark unusual events. I'll bet you anything that if I were to read you this little letter you'd come out with a . . . under your breath, of course. You'd swallow it and hold back from saying it out loud, but you'd think it.'

'So what do you want? There are so few things out of the ordinary that ever happen! If there ever was one extraordinary enough to make me come out with a swear word I'd reserve front-row seats to see it.'

'It's not something that you can see. Sit down and listen. I was waiting for that girl to go, and she's still babbling in the entryway. All right, it looks like the door is closed. Listen, Ariadne. It's very brief, laconic. It must have been typed by some secretary, like an official notice. "Very Dear Sir: Thank you very much for your sincere letter. I am pleased that I can include you among those who have been touched by the dramatic events that have moved us all . . . My most cordial regards . . ." The signature doesn't follow directly. There's an extra part written by hand. "Your letter, my friend Morano, is among those which are truly consoling. The truth of the feelings lies in the refinement of the form. Please drop by to see me. We need people with talent. My very best. Téllez."'

'Well, I have to admit that you've won your bet. But the swear word which comes to my mind isn't out of amazement; it's one of the worst, and you deserve it. If I were to tell you all that I think you deserve you'd feel as small as a parsley flake. What a waste of opportunity! What complacency! What . . . Let's leave it at that!'

'Come on, Dad, let me see the letter. Who's it from? From that gentleman you knew in the Ministry? Didn't you say he was a very well-known professor? He must be a man who knows what he's talking about. Come on, show it to me.'

'Go on, take it: keep it among your valuable documents.'

'Of course! It's just something to joke about. Give it to the girl to play with, even though she's already too grown up. The way she's going, I think she'll continue playing until she's as old as her father.'

'It'll have to be useful for something. At least Elena can play with it.'

'The truth of the feelings lies in the refinement of the form.' Truly, Dad? When you wrote the letter, your feelings weren't as strong as that man's were. Mr. Téllez, when this horrible thing happened, certainly must have been a mess. All his plans, everything he hoped to do with the help or inspiration of his boss. It must be something so . . . satisfying, stimulating, calming as well as exciting to follow orders and feel full to the brim, satisfied, fulfilled by following orders. And then to see everything he hoped for come crashing down, all the trust, all the good fellowship and the sense of fraternity among those who work together. What Mr. Téllez felt then must have been something terrible. However, in my father's letter he finds revealed the truth of his feeling, and my father's feelings were a tiny fraction of what Mr. Téllez felt. No, that's not it, feelings can't be measured in fractions. What happened was that my father gave the quality of form to the feelings of Mr. Téllez and not his. But it's not that my father had no feelings: of course he did, just like me and anybody who's not an animal. But what he . . . the feelings to which he gave a form of very high quality, were not feelings he felt himself, but ones he thought about, or contemplated, we could say. Feelings he created – anyone hearing this might say that he pretended, but who has the right to think about these things? My father did not pretend, he created the feelings. No, that's not it either. He captured them, he caught them the way you catch birds with decoys. Or, also, copied them, echoed them like what happens in the air when a tuning fork vibrates . . . Oh, I don't know! The point is that one can see it's the truth. One can see that the truth is there. I've never read in any of the literary criticism that comes out in *El Liberal* a sentence that gives me a more exact idea of what is good in something you read. It's a sentence that I must keep. What a pile of newspaper pages I've kept! Sometimes whole pages from *Blanco y Negro*, because I didn't understand them. And I didn't want to ask . . . because I did understand them. That's it! I understood, but I knew that I didn't completely understand and so I kept them for later, for when I did understand. And when I did understand I didn't need to read them again because I had all of them by memory, whole and complete. Once I understood them I felt like I could throw them out, but I didn't do it. I just couldn't get rid of them, and I still can't. I remember every one of them, but this one is different. I'm certain that some day I'll find it framed, set off like an exceptional statement. In the excellence of form resides the truth and my father, who is capable of such perfection, does nothing with it. That's it! That's the horrible thing, the monstrous, idiotic, abject thing, as everybody says. Isn't it atrocious that something so mysterious, intricate and puzzling should happen, and that this something could be indicated, caricatured or – more serious than a caricature – could be blamed, and rightly so! Is this possible? Is it that I don't understand? Do I have to keep it for later? No, I don't have to find out about anything. I have to get straight in my own mind what I understand and what I don't understand. My father is capable of writing an excellent, an exceptional letter. What a pity I didn't read it! But I can't ask him if he has a rough draft, because he would be furious. That's something he despises. A rough draft of a letter? What are you talking about? You only do that if you want to compose a highfalutin missive. I can almost hear him. You write a letter the way you speak. My father wrote that letter as though he were talking to Mr. Téllez. Naturally, if he had really been talking to him, there would be something in it of what Mr. Téllez said and, since he was so surprised – pleasantly surprised – when he got it, it's clear he had nothing to do with it, it's clear that he found it a faithful reflection of what for him is the truth, which must be what he himself was feeling. And the fact is my father sees him only rarely; he never goes out with that gentleman. How could I imagine, reconstruct in my head, that letter? What relationship is there between them, what common characteristic, what similarity? None, nothing which comes to mind. From what my father says about this gentleman, he does a whole bunch of things, all of them brilliantly, and my father doesn't do anything. But it's not that he doesn't do anything because he can't, it's simply that he doesn't do anything. All his jobs have been failures, that's true; but why doesn't he do something he doesn't need a job for? Once he did, when he was young and my grandfather thought his poems were excellent. My father wrote those beautiful lines that were for the melodies of my grandfather, sort of like – I don't know – like their troops. They accompanied the melodies, but not as sound, not like accompaniment in music. They went hand in hand in the struggle, in the drama. Ariadne's laments were heartrending notes, but the verses . . . a single verse brought out, uncovered like someone unveiling a mystery, like someone unveiling the melody . . . Like when the sea says, 'Awake, abandoned one!' It's not the same as saying it just like that. It's another thing altogether, it's giving her that name, telling us that she is *the abandoned one*, that we must call her that because there's simply no other name for her. Did my grandfather sense that he would abandon her so soon? Did he know the measure of the chord left in her heart? He knew that he was the maestro, that if he didn't direct and conduct, everything would be over, the orchestra would fall silent, the treble would be left open-mouthed and the divine notes would fly away like a flock of birds, like when all the sparrows in the tree are all trilling at the same time and suddenly they fall silent because something frightens them, threatens them. It's the presence of death which cuts the trills short. And that's what happened, that's what happened to my father: he was left without a leader, without a captain. Will the same thing happen to Mr. Téllez? Is that what my father intuited, what moved him to write a letter that is truth, truth itself? To follow a captain, to serve, to obey. Another fact about Mr. Téllez: my father said once that he's a gentleman and that in this day and age no one knows what a gentleman is. What is a gentleman? Is my father a gentleman? Naturally I know what a gentleman used to be, but what I'd like to know is what is necessary now . . . no, what would make it possible now for one to continue being a gentleman. The question is silly because immediately you'll get everybody's opinion about what one should or shouldn't do. I see once in a while that my father is a gentleman just in the way he has of greeting people – and he certainly doesn't greet very many – in the way he takes off his hat, with no affectation or ceremony: with truth. That's just the word! With a sense of truth as though it were more than a gesture of politeness, more than courtesy, something like the special sign of those who've been sworn in. It's more, more still. It's his way of performing a simple everyday act in a way that is absolutely beyond everything. I once told my father that when he doffs his hat, it seems like the Holy Sacrament must be going by. He told me that was nothing but foolishness, but it's not so foolish. When one gentleman greets another, he is always saluting something holy, something existing in both of them. But what exists in them that's like the Holy Sacrament? But this is foolish because my father doesn't believe in anything holy. He wants nothing to do with saints. I suppose Mr. Téllez doesn't either. And my mother and my grandmother? Oh, who knows? But Doña Laura doesn't, and I don't think the people in Mr. Olmeda's house do either, nor do I, after all. I go less and less to church these days and I think I'll end up not going at all. But I'll be saying these things forever and thinking them too because there's no other way to think, no other way to express what one feels is very holy. I can't get anything straight. I rack my brains and I don't make any progress. Where am I going to end up with all this about gentlemen or holiness? I only wanted to know what was in that letter.

'Dad, tell me what you said in the letter to that gentleman.'

'You want me to tell you? You think I know it by memory like a multiplication table?'

'No . . . or maybe yes. You probably do know it.'

'Probably? Unfortunately, you're right. I remember every single word. I would never have imagined it would turn out like this. I tried so hard to avoid any line – even one single word! – that might sound like begging. And look what happened. I should drop by! Yes, sir, yes, I'll come by, and what? Just like always: promises and offers to help. Going back to all that rat race for nothing, just to end up the same four days later.

'It's brutal, Isabel. It's simply inhuman of us, but the fact is that we really don't miss her.'

'All right, it might be brutal but it's the truth and we have to face up to it. It's strange. Something so important happens and it's almost like we didn't even know it!'

'It's very, very strange! Just a few months ago we spent days and nights preoccupied with her whim. We didn't call it a whim then: we called it a hope: we thought of it as something lovely and even serious. It seemed to us like it was the most important thing that could happen to a girl. We were totally preoccupied with her, as if she were very ill and we couldn't leave her bedside. Remember? That presence of death, which couldn't be denied? We kept trying to hold it back with our wills so it wouldn't reach its destination too soon and take away in passing that hope, that illusion – that's what it was for us, an illusion like the tricks a magician makes you think are real – so that it wouldn't take away the littlest thing Piedita desired.'

'Do you think Piedita has desires?'

'And do you think so?'

'I think you stuffed some into her.'

'Don't come up with what any neighborhood kid might say. Don't start with that gabble about my inventing things, that I make people believe in what turns out to be no more than a soap bubble.'

'And it is nothing but a soap bubble. Or do you want to console yourself by saying that we're inhuman? No, I won't deny we might be, but I was just going to tell you about an impression I had the other day. It's a silly thing, but I think it means a lot. The other day when I was coming back I stopped on the corner and suddenly I was kind of sad because the sign had been taken down. I don't know how to explain it, but do you understand? It means something: the sign is gone and we feel sad, but Piedita is gone and we don't feel sad.'

'You do know how to explain it. It shouldn't suprise me in you, but you've understood that I feel the same as you. It's like she's evaporated. Why aren't we thinking about what she's doing now, on her honeymoon, in her house? It must be luxurious, and we're not even curious. No, of course we're not because if we went to see it it would be just like any old house. But, what would we say to her? How would we talk about it with her? I think we wouldn't be able to say anything to her – not about that or anything else. We couldn't talk to her. We wouldn't understand each other. It would be like talking to a person with whom we've never ever talked. And we've never really talked to her!'

'Well, you say that . . .'

'No, don't go back to what happened before. I'm telling you something that's worth thinking about. It's not that we loved Piedita so much before – you didn't love her, I know that: I loved her for the two of us – and now we don't love her because she seems different to us. No it's not that. If that were the case we'd be missing what it used to be like. We'd remember how much we loved her – I'm speaking in the plural even though that wasn't the case: think about it in the plural so you'll understand. We don't remember what it used to be like because there are things or developments or acts on the part of people that can wipe out the past. You say to yourself that the one we used to love is and was then the same person as now.'

'Okay, now I understand. Even though I really want to tease you about your disillusionment, I think there's a lot in what you're saying. It's true, talking about the sign again: We can feel a longing for it because we still think it was what it was and that it simply isn't there anymore, not because it's something else, but because it isn't there anymore.'

'And are we inhuman?'

'Heavens, I don't know!'

'Well, it's harder to figure out if her own sister is. Haven't you noticed how Doña Laura goes bustling about the apartment, not even missing her, without hesitating to dust away all traces, transforming and erasing the classroom and the piano room and Piedita's room? It's all changing into an apartment for a couple with a child. Yes, that's what it's going to be. Doña Laura is going to end up taking care of her brother and the boy who's been left without a mother. Does that mean she's inhuman?'

'Don't rack your brains: neither you nor I is going to come up with the answer. But what I can tell you is that things are going to happen. I don't know what, but I'm positive something's going to change. And don't think it's because my mother's insisted on letting down my skirts to the ankle. Ah, I didn't tell you! You can imagine who noticed it at once . . . 'Stockings, eh?' I figured he was going to come up with some naughty remark. But no, nothing of the sort. He looked at me with a certain serious expression, sort of sadly . . . no, sort of gravely. He looked as though he were going to congratulate me on something dangerous, on something – how can I say it? – something fatal.'

'You don't have to tell me anything: you know I know him like the back of my hand. You're the one who doesn't know him.'

'Well, you know him and that's enough. I won't argue with you: he's an angel from heaven.'

'He's not an angel. He's a wonderful guy, and he loves you like a fool.'

'What a way to love me! The other day he grabbed my hand and bit my finger. That means he loves me?'

'Of course. Why else would he bite you?'

'I'm fed up with this love business! You understand it all because you read novels that are full of it, and that's why I don't like them. I'm tired of reading. I'd rather draw, or paint when I can. When do you think I'll be able to go to the museum and copy?'

'I don't know. We have to find out what you have to do to get permission. What I can't understand is why you're fed up with love but you get carried away by what you see in the museum. You think any of that would be possible if it weren't for love? Naturally, if I tell you that all those paintings were painted for love I don't claim that the painters bit people's fingers. But you can be sure that all that world we love so much delights us because those people, among themselves, lived biting each other.'

'It must be true. You must be right. That's why it turns my stomach even in the movies. You like pictures with love affairs. I like adventure tales, horses galloping and cowboys with their lariats. I like detective films too, but you only like stuff with Francesca Bertini.'

'Not only her, but I have to say she's my favorite. She's so elegant! Not just her costumes, but in her movements and her poses. Felisa pointed something out to me. In the love scenes she always poses, not exactly arrogantly, but always placed so that her lover has to kind of rise up to her. It's always like that, when he comes to kiss her . . .'

'That business about kisses turns my stomach.'

'You're really something else! Why does it turn your stomach? Don't you ever feel like kissing people you love?'

'Yes, but in another way. It's kissing on the mouth that turns my stomach. I know they don't really kiss, but it looks like it. When somebody gives me a kiss and leaves my cheek a little wet, the only thing I think of is wiping it off. And what do you say about those verses I've read where they talk about how they want to kiss her lips? I can't imagine how anybody would like that.'

'I'm beginning to think that I'm more stupid than you are, and probably than everybody. You feel that aversion and you say so. If I stop and think about it, I feel the same. But I've read about it and what I've read says it's marvelous, so I'm incapable of thinking something different from what I've read. Is that stupidity or is it faith? I don't know . . . we'll see. Felisa says Francesca Bertini maintains a haughty or elevated stance; I'm a terrific fan of hers, but it's just never dawned on me to define her style so clearly.'

'Felisa is a little bit older than you.'

'Yes, but it's not just that. It's that she's more aware of what's happening in the world. She never comes out of her little corner, like us, but her father brings her more news because he's a man full of ambitions, little ambitions, and he passes them on to her. Felisa shares his whims and praises his discoveries. She's as determined as he is to get that deity he wants to put on top of the bookcase. What must it be like? Maybe the head of an ancient Venus or some lovely Pompadour, some courtesan. Felisa will call us as soon as he gets it. And you know what we should do? We could go by and go with her when she goes down for the milk. She says that every evening at seven sharp she runs into a poet who lives around here. She just knows him by sight, but she likes running into him and it makes her think they're friends.'

Autumn is already well advanced: dusk comes early – at six it's already getting dark. A biting wind from the sierra. It's wintry, but while there's light there's a luminous reminiscence, an opposition to darkness, or maybe the season's tendency to adorn itself with occasional, fortuitous gleams. The first stars, almost imperceptible in a limpid sky. Down below on the street the first lighting of shops and doorways. Each light with its own individual features, professional in character, doing its yellowish duty above taverns or small shops where old shoemakers squint. Strident bulbs with no shade lighting pieces of percale or satin. White and pale, as luminous as daylight, as something that could never go dark, seeming to announce the epitome of whiteness or virginity or maternity – the mantle of light, the breath, the vapor, of the neighborhood dairy. The neighborhood gossips, the housemaids, the whole collection of females joined by the camaraderie of the kitchen, all coming to commune with essential whiteness, as though no one among old people and adults, among housewives, military men, employees, workers, or ministers – no one at all could get by without his or her daily lactation. Bottles, jars and aluminum containers all lined up on the shelf to receive their just measure. The measuring devices made of tin – dark and heavy and stable in their tubular form, with a strong handle to go from one to the other and deposit the exact amount – dispense quickly and the neighborhood women leave. So do the housemaids. Felisa picks up her milk container and goes off with it – agile and not at all uncomfortable with the domestic, humble, necessary and prosaic look that she can so easily transcend and forget. It's a light weight she can carry without noticing, holding it with her left hand while thinking about something else. Thinking and talking because she has with her her friends, her cohorts, comrades who share neither her room nor her tasks, who come to her house to exchange and communicate via mutual confessions all their desires and help each other achieve them. Felisa, with a certain pride or rather with the pleasure of a hostess who offers decent hospitality, with the carefulness of someone bringing a tasty gift, describes or prepares the *mise-en-scène* appropriate to the Bohemian, who comes – or goes: He's from the neighborhood for sure, but no one knows where he lives – goes to a café, one of those famous cafés, the *Pombo* maybe or the *Zaragoza*, where there's music, and it's not scratched out by some two-bit, has-been, clumsy piano-mauler, but wafted from exquisite and mystical violins, and listened to quietly and very seriously by poets. The Bohemian, wrapped in his cape and wearing, slightly tipped to one side, a soft hat with a broadish brim, is going to show up at any moment along San Vicente. That's the route he takes and it's always more or less at seven. Then he's off, for it's not time to go home yet. He's probably going to have a couple of drinks, beer or vermouth, maybe something stronger, because they drink a lot. All poets drink a lot, everybody knows that. Sometimes wine, not to mention rum and not to mention something we never see in neighborhood taverns, but for sure is served in other places. It's absinthe, a kind of anise that turns your head into an irridescent cloud. It must be like some kind of aquarium with unbelievable visions floating about, divine and confused images . . .

'Yes, that's it. It doesn't seem possible for confusion to be divine, but it is. But it's the confusion you get from alcohol. The confusion you get when you first wake up is very irritating, but the confusion you get from being drunk is like a promise.'

'How do you know? Have you ever been drunk?'

'Yes, of course, just like everybody, like the rest of you. You're not going to tell me you've never felt anything like that. Everyone gets a bit tipsy at family parties, saints' days and birthdays. Christmas above all! Who hasn't drunk a little more than he or she should? Who hasn't sneaked a sip from parents' and relatives' glasses sitting half-empty on the sideboard or in the kitchen? And the reprimands and the comments. This girl's going to get drunk! Everything sounds far away in delicious confusion, in complete indifference to the strongest of reprimands. You want to clutch at the sensation; you don't want to let it go, you don't want to be interrupted.'

'You're right, Elena. We all did that when we were little, and we never thought twice about it. We never even realized that it's the same as – the same thing grownups do when nobody can stop them.'

'Well, they stop a lot of them, and maybe it's a good thing because their visions, their aquariums don't have those beings that float about . . .'

The Bohemian fails to appear. He's not punctual. If he is, not always. He has his habits, something many people might consider prosaic, but which can be quite endearing. His habits might also have an opaline lightness like something lived without feeling it because one feels one's thoughts living on their own. On their own, given over to the task of thinking, but not removed from, not oblivious or indifferent to what is scarcely felt, but rather impregnated with its aura, in tune with and colored by its climate. Every idea, every daily labor of thought bears with it the rain or the mist, the cool night dew or the blazing heat of the hour when the sought-for truth emerged, was felt or was reached. Thus, poets wrapped up in themselves under their rather wide-brimmed hats walk alongside urban pedestrians without bumping into them, without paying attention to them or ignoring them. Brushing against them perhaps, as though they were impervious bodies among which the poets' – opaline creatures – circulate or loiter, distant and present, foreign and familiar or rather, rapacious, thieves of aromas or tones or melodies or wails. The Bohemian appears at last. He walks steadily and he's in no hurry. He holds his cape over his face, but not because it's cold. It's because of the negligent armor provided by the cape, because of the self-embrace in which the man within the cape separates, affirms and accompanies himself. A soft touch of velvet on his cheek and a screen or wall that stops his breath and reflects its warmth back to his face. The Bohemian goes by. The girls look at him, timid, indiscreet. They almost stop. They'd like to stop him or go back to find him once again and see certain details they didn't notice before.

'He's ugly. There's no two ways about it.'

'I never told you he was good-looking. He's got character. He's different from any of the guys you see walking about here.'

'O.K., you're right. It's true: he's unmistakable. But what a shame he isn't a little bit more . . . oh, I don't know! One of his eyes, it seems to me, is . . .'

'Yes, I've noticed it too. One of his eyes is a little out of kilter.'

'Oh! You're so demanding, so meticulous. You've given him a once-over, and all I wanted was for you to look at him as a figure, a type.'

'Yes, Felisa, that's the way we looked at him. We paid attention to detail because we're fond of detail. We couldn't help it: we look at everything hair by hair. But above and beyond all the details is the figure that you created in our imagination. That's what will stay with us. That's what's true. A type, a special man, unmistakable.'

'A man, a poet, who has a civilian name: Emilio Carrere. His poems come out in magazines and in newspapers. He's published only a few books. I can remember some of the titles. Wait! Look! Can you see? Look! My father's just turning the corner carrying an enormous package. He told me for sure that he'd bring it today no matter what the price. Come on, let's run. We can still catch him on the stairway.'

On the table – the pieces of wrapping paper scattered on the floor – is the head. It is neither Venus-like nor Apollo-like nor hermaphrodite. It's a human head, anthropologically human. All the features are those of MAN: correct, with no beauty and no ugliness. They are not sculpted, but molded in some white material – porcelain perhaps. It's brilliant, as clean as a large bowl, as immaculate as the utensils demanded by hygiene. Its anonymous features come together in a face of surprising purity, impossible to imagine, such as one might find only in the world of absolute purity, in the sphere of the mind. And it has that purity without possessing it, without being someone who could say: this is mine. Its purity is to be all, to belong to everybody. The face, infinitely alien to itself, rises toward a naked skull that is likewise alien to identifying classifications. A skull that lets its shape be seen and that has inscriptions in blue ink – written below the enamel, incisions, given color before the work was sent to the kiln: columns didactically indicating subtle combinations, buried but regular, duly arranged in hierarchical order – all the functions of the human mind.

'It's the head of Gall.'

'Ah! I didn't imagine . . . Who's Gall?'

'He's the creator of phrenology. It's not studied very much. In fact there are campaigns against it.'

'Oh! So this isn't his portrait. This head is for studying, no?'

'Of course.'

'You're right, girls. That's what it's for, except that I'm not going to study it at all because I don't know enough about phrenology, but I like having it. If I had the head of Minerva up there on the shelf everybody looking at it would know it was a homage to wisdom. But this, on the other hand, nobody could guess why I have it, but to me it's the same: this is my Minerva. It's what men are racking their brains about nowadays.'

'All right, Dad. The fact is now you've got it.'

'That's right, now I have. Let's see if you can help me put it up there. I don't know if the bottom of the easy chair will fall out if I put my weight on it, but maybe if I put my feet right above the legs . . . I can't do it with the head in my arms and it weighs too much for you girls to lift. All right, all right, I see you're strong enough. Be careful! There we are. Can you see it from below? I didn't put it too far back?'

'No, Dad. From here, which is where you normally sit, you can see it perfectly well.'

'Then there's nothing more to be said.'

It wasn't the head of Venus. It wasn't an enchanting image inspiring sensual pleasure or tenderness. It was a correct human form: the presence of no one and of everyone. Now it was on top of the bookcase, and there it was an object. But before being placed there it was a subject because something was expected of it. It was expected. Its existence elsewhere was known and its fertile presence here was desired, so it could be possessed, spoken with, communicated with, enjoyed. Its promise was there before it was. Now the aura of its gifts, its incalculable possibilities, would flow from it. At night it would shine in the shadows, outside the light projected on the table by the lampshade. Little gleams would outline the nakedness of its skull, the straight line of the nose strictly balanced by the shape of the jaw: its schematic form was its mystery. And its Aphrodite lay in its mystery. Had it been the head of Minerva, it would have received homage for its clarity, for its proverbial, definitive venerability. Being what it was, it sketched what it was to be. Its pure and virginal pregnancy kindled hope. It was not a head of Venus, as Elena had imagined. It was a conjunction of all the goddesses –

a rare and also fatal conjunction – in which they, the powerful ones, hold sway. Athena added – new jewels, no, nothing external or ornamental. She added to the very body of the desirable one, what? Breasts, hair? Did she add to the abundance of the locks of hair gathered up on emerging from the shell? She enlarged the zones and places of pleasure, the areas of fecundation. Aphrodite gave power and warmth to the rigorous lineaments, the postulates, the equations, the infinite signs which without her would remain paralyzed in infinity, but which with her boiled, activated their nerves, the organic instruments of Man – of men, of any man seated at his work or study or meditation or dreaming table. The schematic head had Venus's most obvious virtue, the one most nobly rooted in human freedom: desire. The appetitive movement that leaps over necessity, following its own course, like the 'stubbornly enamored' lodestone of Quevedo's sonnet? That is the question. North, the necessary, obligatory course, and the hard, silent stone, loving it so much! Man, inconstant – and therefore mortal, subject to beginning and end – wanting to learn fidelity and firmness from the stone because, being mortal, knowing himself as finite and feeling within himself the bond through which his material being loves itself, maintains and defends itself, trusting and forgetting necessity's bonds, man leaps over them, leaps to what is beyond them, desiring to procreate in a beyond that he will never reach but will possess as an inalienable signature, the sign of his contribution . . . paternal . . . maternal perhaps because desire is long sheltered and nourished by one's own substance and entrusted to those made of the same material that loves itself. Entrusted, even though the contribution adds nothing to what is real, even though it is nothing more than a legacy of hope, a vision given or communicated, that has nothing positive but the tone, the harmonic composition of the being it will follow, or rather, the tension, the germ of desire for the beyond, loved and longed for at night, behind the table, lit by the green shade, piercing the darkness until it reaches and caresses the beloved numen. All this, this medley of finalities and essences swimming in the opaline inebriety of the imbiber of knowledge – or, in other words, of the person who savors it, barely touching it to his lips in humble taverns, because all this happens, takes place in the kingdom of humility. This antithesis is the enigma because *humility reigns there*. It reigns, quite in its place, upon its throne. It has no intention of abdicating or betraying its faithful for an upstart throne. It stays in its seat because it knows its treasure is there, its wellsprings of future possibilities where the prideful will water. Here in the neighborhood there are canteens for those who thirst.

'Didn't I tell you things were going to happen? They're already happening.'

'What's happened is winter, and we didn't even know it was going by. We've finished the school year with flying colors. Is that what you're trying to say?'

'No, I wouldn't say flying colors. I'd say decently, no more. I mean it wasn't anything really extraordinary. We each came home with our respective honors like the two serious girls that we are. I'm telling you that what's happening is that we're seeing people and going places that we didn't go to before.'

'Montero's appearance on the scene – providential – like you said.'

'And I'll say it again. He's a doer of good and not just for us. He decided to get his professor out of Zamora, and he did it. He must have some kind of connections, but I don't think he's a fellow with much family wealth.'

'He doesn't have a penny. What he does have is a position, an attitude that money doesn't exist. And, yet, no – no it's not that because I've heard him talking with Doña Laura about how it was good economically to get Don Manuel to move. He told her from A to Z about what he got out of the sale of the house. I guess it was he who saw to the whole affair. Money doesn't exist for him. He doesn't want or he doesn't need any for himself. He looks like someone who doesn't eat, but he does eat. I've heard him talking about where, how much and how he eats. How much it costs him, what the best and most satisfying things are, what's healthiest, what's tastiest: everything. He talks about everything and he understands everything.'

'And he judges everything. He's got the two of us classified.'

'Ah, but does he know we've got him classified too? I think he does and I think it doesn't bother him. But it's not something he takes lightly; it's not something he takes as a joke. He takes it as a game you play to see who wins.'

'Well, nobody's going to win because if someone were to win the game would be over and it's not going to be over. Don't you see? That's the difference between this game and the one Felisa plays, studying her poet but never saying a word to him. She sees him and she notices a new detail every day, unconnected things that don't hang together the way they do when people talk to you. Because if we looked at him the way you do things in shop windows, we'd be able to count every hair on his head, but we'd never be able to see the effect our discoveries might have on him.'

'That's it, that's it. He registers them: he acts as though he had studied them every night and brought the lesson all prepared the next day. Of course, we do the same thing. I think we do more because it's not just that we prepare the lesson to recite it to him the next day: we study it for ourselves, too. We take advantage of what he teaches us. He comes out with one of his typical remarks and we turn it over and over: either we incorporate it or we shake it off. It's difficult to shake them off because they're made just for us.'

'Everything he does is just right: he never praises us and he never struts about to make us admire his knowledge. Sometimes though, he hits the nail right on the head, almost without words, like the day we were talking about my prize – remember? I didn't think he would know much about ancient sculpture and when I told him I had won the prize because I liked the model, he looked at me like, sort of . . . agreeing. I said that if they'd given me the Slave, my copy would have been ridiculous, but they gave me Belvedere's torso and my copy turned out wonderfully. What an approving smile! As though he were telling me he would have reacted the same.'

'Of course, he knows that field well too. But when it's a question of something closer to his specialty, I mean his obsession with exactness – then little looks aren't enough. Then he's capable of coming out with something really sharp.'

'Do you think he's said something sharp to you at any point?'

'I don't know. Maybe it's that I make him more and more sharp. I have my reasons to sharpen him up. In the first place, I've got it coming for boasting about what one of my teachers said. I told him about it as though it were just an innocent observation. All right, wait a minute. I thought – and now we have to analyze if I did or didn't think – I was telling him about it so he could see what a funny thing my teacher had said. I told him word for word what the teacher had said when he saw me solve a geometry problem using strange procedures. 'Strange' was the word Don Joaquín used. And he added that if geometry did not exist I would invent it. Do you remember what Montero said?'

'No, I can't remember.'

'Well, it was something very different from what he said to you with that little smile that acknowledged your tastes and predilections as if you had spoken about them at length. He said, almost without looking at me, and shaking his head a bit the way you do in doubtful situations, that I should watch out for umbrellas.'

'What do you mean, umbrellas?'

'It's a saying that exists. You use it for someone who thinks he's invented something and it turns out that it's existed for centuries.'

'But, do you think that's what he meant?'

'Of course that's what it was. He said it very decisively because he saw that that was my danger – and my terror.

The witch passes through the marvelous garden and says 'This is a magnificent garden, but it doesn't have a tree that sings,' (many people have spoken about this) and that's all it takes. A mist rises in the garden, the leaves drip, crying because the garden wants to have what it does not have. However, this tendency to want to have is stimulating. But it's the contrary with an anguished longing, groping in the darkness, listening with the terror of hearing footsteps behind and not knowing whose they are. Not knowing if you have it and not wanting, perhaps, to have it. That facility, which can be like a gift from heaven, like a delectable morsel that, no . . . it doesn't turn out poisoned: it simply doesn't turn out at all, it simply doesn't exist. Because it's not Tantalus's torture, where things are there at a certain height and can't be reached. It's that they are reached, but after being reached, it turns out that they haven't been reached. Is there anything more horrible than betrayal? The most horrible thing in the panorama or arsenal or wealth of possible betrayals one can intuit is the possibility which seems impossible but which is really very possible: self-betrayal. An incalculable number of things slide down the inclined plane of this possibility: facility above all, small successes, flattery which at times is based on something pure and cordial but which nevertheless drips its balsamic oil and slips and makes you slip. Everything flattering and agreeable, even though it might not come from human voices but from events, from things themselves that allowed themselves to be done, which appear to have been done with conscious knowledge, but no: they just turned out like that, sprang up seductive, convincing and slippery because the atrocious thing is how pleasant it is to slide confidently . . . You slide and fall and come to your senses in mortal disappointment. Because disappointment is just that: to come with one's lived experience, with what one believed was his life or his living, and find it all dead, or rather, to discover not that it has died, but that it was never really alive, that we live the lie of what is apparently real. No, of what is really real, as illusion is real, it's really illusion. But it didn't exist where we thought it did. So then, what road to follow? Flee from the inclined plane, to undertake the uphill path and overcome difficulties. But the difficulties themselves can also be deceiving. They're not slippery, they're mazes, labyrinths of mirrors, in which will, the most tenacious determination, can get lost if you take the wrong turn. If you believe that the difficulty, that which you are living with passion – with a desire for possession – is the complex richness of the entanglement and that with infinite patience – because patience is among those things that seem infinite – you could untie the knot. But it cannot be untied because your fingernail – that tool nature gives to everyone – is not skillful enough or strong enough or sharp enough or subtle enough. It's not up to the challenge, not sufficiently effective or dexterous to keep time from being wasted, to keep from feeling here too the uselessness of the task, to keep from bumping into the edge of unbreathable nothingness . . .

'I think he said that about the umbrella to take a little bit of wind out of my sails.'

'No, don't be so suspicious. He said that, which is quite difficult to understand, knowing you would figure it out. Do you see? If he had thought that you'd never thought about it, he would have said it more explicitly. He would have said, "Be careful. Don't go inventing umbrellas." But he only said, "Watch out for the umbrellas," taking it for granted that you would know what he was getting at. Montero is incapable of an insidious remark. But why do we call him Montero? It's disagreeable to use the last name with a young fellow – he might be older than us, but he's still young – that we see so much of, but the fact is I don't know his first name.'

'I don't either, but it's not Michael or Gabriel or Raphael, no matter how angelic he seems to us. Montero is a very common surname that you hear a lot – Don So-and-so Montero, etc. But in his case more than a name, it seems like a position, an official title, maybe like *Montero Mayor*. As if a lot of sniffing dogs followed along behind him. But that's not why we call him Montero. It's because he's the first young man to use the polite form of address with us. When Doña Laura teased him about it, he thought she was belittling something worthy of merit. What's more, he felt that not addressing us formally deprived us of something we deserved.'

'That's it. He brought up the business of English, asserting that it was more correct. He was hoping – poor fellow! – that we would be speaking English with him in four days. Just as well that Felisa refused flat. She has an excuse since her father makes her study so much, but the two of us . . . The truth is that we're a little backward. Well, I'm pretty much ordinary, but you don't have to study because you know everything . . .'

'Come on! Go ahead and bring up the umbrella again!'

'Oh, stop being silly! That business has given you indigestion.'

'Don't you believe it: it's what I've digested best. Why has Montero come? Why was Montero born? To mention the umbrella to me. Do you remember the print we saw in the school bookstore? The Guardian Angel is watching over two children about to cross a little wooden bridge. The Angel is enormous and beautiful and shining, but you suppose it's invisible to the children. You don't just suppose, you can tell, because the two innocent children seem so happy and unworried. I'm not sure if this is in the picture or if it's something I'm adding to make it more perfect in my memory. But it's so realistic, so real! The smile, the bouquet of flowers that you see – or should see, the rotted planks, some held up by just a splinter. So why was Montero born? To tell me, watch out, don't act so innocent telling about your triumphs, you'd better look where you're going. Then on his way out he told me he was going to bring me a whole pile of books.'

'I'm going, Doña Laura. Right now on the five o'clock express. Ramón will arrive tommorrow.'

'You're going, Montero? You'll get to Zamora before Ramón leaves?'

An exchange of glances. When a dialogue is intelligent, when it's a rapid grasping of ideas and even a rapid argument and even a violent disagreement: when it has to do with ideas. Glances can be brilliant flashes like a ray you reflect with a mirror, fleeting and dazzling, but illuminating, when it has to do with ideas. When it's a case of acts, of dramas, of things one might do, that one might fear, it's also rapid and luminous, also dazzling – but like nautical lights, like signals sent out across nocturnal oceans. And the play or interchange is not an argument seeking logic and coherence, it is entreaty or corroboration. 'No, go, for the love of God! You must go at once.' 'I'm going. I'm off. You don't have to be upset. I'll be there. Nothing will happen.' And the glances are taken back after having discharged their duty. Almost ashamed of having said so much, almost fearful of not having said enough. And a soft clasping of hands, light although a bit prolonged amid questions and requests.

'The rooms are all arranged. I don't know why the boy has to come alone.'

'The boy! Wait till you see how big he's getting. Believe me, it's better he should come alone. I'm leaving the books here for Elena.' The pile of books was a single book: *The Insulted and Injured*.

A small privilege, the effect of a fortunate conjuncture. Nothing absurd like trying to pick apples from an orange tree. Quite the contrary! It was a case of a circumstantial blooming, but the flower in question corresponded to the nature of the tree. And happy circumstance was the only thing or situation or chance or accident that can produce happiness, in large or small doses. The only thing – of course, it's not a thing – which consists of an understanding, of an accurate perception, followed by a magnanimous response. To put it more simply, a state of affairs where one sees *how* or *who* another is and tries to see to it that he goes on being how he is and who he is. Precisely because this happy conjuncture had occurred, the morning trip toward Fuencarral was bearable, as was the overflowing tram, packed with fraternal tiredness: not the tiredness of after, but of before. The fatigue that comes before beginning the day. They were all day laborers, not for the stipulated day's work but the invariable task of seeing daylight begin – mist, frost or rosy dawn – and then midday with its smells, its hunger pangs and desire for the small pleasure of bread or wine or a fritter or the irresistible stimulus of sausage, the call of ancestral spices. And then it diminishes and the tiredness becomes almost a memory which might even fade away were it not for the threat – the certain, infallible threat – that the dawn would begin again. All of it was bearable because small privileges broke the monotony at times. Expected now every day – since the first encounter had happened – and charged, more than with hope, with memory, brightened, heightened by their meaning as the presence of the past.

'Hey, Morano, you're a music-lover. They've sent some box tickets to the office at Bellas Artes. Do you want one?'

'Oh, I'd really love one! Thanks a million.'

'They're in the second tier, but I think they're pretty good.'

'That's the best if you really want to hear.'

That was the first time. Afterward, it became a matter of stopping by her desk and, with a smile of filial roguishness, dropping on her notebook a slip of paper – pink or blue, depending on whether it was the Royal theater or *El Español*. And thus, things kept on happening. A new night filled with emotion for the girls – the three of them inseparable – something happening, an event. For Ariadne it was more than an evocation. It was a resurrection or a magic invocation, a repetition of the material facts: the lights, the red carpet of the box and the chocolates – above all, the chocolates. The familiar and the surprising creams enclosed in a hard chocolate shell, the white fondant, the yellowish vanilla and the pink raspberry. They were all words of love, like notes not heard, but felt: one received their flavor like a word and responded in the affirmative by tasting, relishing, dissolving even the final vestige of flavor until it is gone, consuming the final bit, pursuing with the tongue the flavor's trail throughout all the soft folds of the mouth until its extinction is confirmed. There remains the neutral taste of one's own tongue feeling at home and wanting still another, longing to break once again that bitter chocolate shell and dissolve in new cream and hear those notes, like a child's lullaby. Those classic venerable harmonies were voices from childhood which had grown with her till she was old enought to wear her first long dress, till she wore a bride's orange blossoms . . . Of course, till she had worn a veil of mourning as well, but this – for now – must be put aside. The memories must be checked and not allowed to bring back that misfortune that now seemed laid to rest. That misfortune seemed absolutely vanquished there in the box, minimized amid the dramatic exuberance of Verdi. The one who didn't believe in the things that were happening was back at home. No, the slight improvement of position, rendered even more pleasant by the cordial privileges . . . No, no, no . . . there was no serious prospect ahead, like being a regular employee, having a bit of security in the face of the shifting sands – unpredictable, incomprehensible – of politics. No, no, no. A position supported by congeniality, by the vanity of a well-written letter: perhaps by the knowledge of those old verses which seduced the master, the brilliant husband who left everything up in the air so it could go straight to hell . . .

Things that happen take unexpected turns. Felisa doesn't want to go down any more for the milk at seven. She's given up the evening hour which was like her palace, a mansion where she reigned with her own particular authority. With the special air she gave to her short coat made of ordinary corduroy, her black cotton stockings not always intact at the heel. To this extremely modest outfit, she gave the bearing of a young lady – a yound lady among the neighborhood women, the maids, peasant girls in an urban setting – which inspired a respectful sympathy because her authority lay in her indifference to poverty, her elegance in poverty. And suddenly Felisa skipped her seven o'clocks, abandoned the San Vicente sidewalk – the more dingy stretch with its miserable shops, wine merchants, tinsmiths – where she used to run into the Bohemian. The Bohemian sank into oblivion, replaced by her interest in another more interesting figure – or perhaps a figure contemplated, waited for, spied upon in a more interested way.

'Oh, my heavens! She's gone silly over that little German fellow.'

'What do you mean silly? She likes him, she's in love. I don't know if it's a lot or a little, but she's in love for sure.'

'Well, that means going silly. Always forgetting things, mooning over the little neighbor who plays the violin. Don't you think that's corny?'

'No, I don't think so.'

'Oh, of course, it's very serious. Now Felisa has a suitor, right?'

'Yes, that's it.'

Men come onto the scene, playing very different roles. The neighbor isn't acting. He plays his violin on returning home from work. Because of the timing of his return, because at seven he stepped into the focus of the milky light that showed the perhaps-not-intact stockings and shone on the aluminum milk can, because he broke into the evening atmosphere with the hard inexorable light of reality, he had chased away all the phantoms, he had eliminated all ideal reveries with a stroke – uncertain but all-conquering – of future.

The other men are closer. They come to the house from Zamora. And they hadn't won it, but lost it, in less than an hour: in a lightning flash, the decision. If we can conceive of a time below the surface of time; that is, an intention – the action of a will, like a running motor that doesn't move – an intention that is set and at the same time propelling, pushing in a given direction until it provokes or achieves the word that sets in motion the time of actions, of what must be done: Well then, let's go! And that active will carries away objects and subjects. The boy, above all, deposited in his new home and there in Zamora what no one will ever know taking place because knowing would mean knowing who Montero and Manuel were – Laura knew who Manuel was, but maybe not even Montero himself knew who he was. But nonetheless, his impossible filiation made all distrust superfluous. Montero was his presence. It was a presence so efficient that it could be sent away, entrusted with something. 'Go, then, for heaven's sake! Go at once.' Because it's clear that with him present nothing bad will happen. You don't know what could happen, you know that something must happen, but you have no idea of what it might be because you scarcely know the place. You haven't seen life's imprint sketched on . . . A house on a slope with a garden in front; a tiny garden overflowing with ivy, and then a bit of earth with plants sacrificed to the kitchen every day. Small animals running around there unaware that they will share the same fate as the plants. And something must happen there because what had taken place was an uprooting which doesn't lend itself in the least to sweet melancholy but which is ratified by radical corroborating destruction, terrifying the hens on their roosts. The implacable devouring force which grows from what it devours, which destroys and only exists so long as it goes on devouring, because it is not mere appearance: it is something – no one can catch it in his hand. It exists vibrating, shining as it changes, growing luminous, intense and dense at the moment it embraces and possesses, possesses without preserving, being only the substance of possession and languishing as the thing is consumed, consuming itself if it is given no further nourishment. Omnivorous, sputtering sparks according to the material devoured – wood that crackles when it's bitten, cloth, blankets that add black smoke to the glow and dyed muslins and flesh-colored or rose or ivory satins that offer a quick intense flash of light and disappear. Something had to happen there. The ephemeral, definitive monument to that which passes had to be erected. Because the intolerable had taken place, that which is unacceptable to the mind – to being itself because it's about how that which exists, exists – to the human being, who is ephemeral and doesn't want to be. And this not wanting is so strong that it changes to wanting, to thinking one exists differently, that one exists, exists and won't cease to exist. But what had happened was that something – someone – had ceased to exist. And it was not a matter of putting slowly dying flowers on a grave. It was necessary to grow something upon the altar – the earth that knew her footstep, that had received lightly sprinkled water from her hands, and had repaid the debt with little green hearts climbing the lattices – to kindle the ephemeral mane of destruction that looks so much like life, rising, palpitating, languishing and then disappearing . . . They came to the house and their presence was felt. There was the odd brief visit which went unrepeated as unnecessary, though it was accepted with courtesy. There remained only the usual assiduous disciples, the habitual family, what was born there and not established by anything conventional.

'Oh, we just can't get it out of our minds, Doña Laura. If you could only see how wonderful Guerrero was. What a shame you can't go!'

'Why can't she?'

'Well, because she's in mourning.'

'And what does mourning have to do with it? Is going to the theater like going out partying?'

'No, of course not.'

'In the first place, even if it were like going partying, if she felt like doing it she wouldn't have to stop feeling like it just because of the mourning. You can feel like partying because you can't stand the mourning – the mourning inside your heart – but not because the neighbors . . .'

'No, Manuel, it has nothing to with the neighbors. I really don't feel like going.'

'Well, you should. The theater is something that can fill your imagination or your mind or whatever you want to call it for a couple of hours just the way a mathematical or a philosophical problem can. For someone really able to work out problems it's very entertaining.'

'But I don't want to, Manuel. Montero told me the same thing the other day. He always says the same thing as you. And it's not because you've said anything to him; it's because you have the same point of view.'

'It seems to me, Doña Laura, that Montero says things not as though someone had told them to him, but as though they were so clear and certain that it's not even necessary to say them.'

'You've got a sharp eye, girl.'

'Ah! If you, Don Manuel, think I hit the nail on the head, then I did.'

'You certainly did. Before long it won't be necessary to tell you anything.'

'Then it seems all right to you for Ramón to come with us?'

'No, if he feels like it, I don't think it's good or bad.'

'I would like to go, but then getting up at seven to study is going to be hard.'

'Think it over, then. You can't afford to lose one more year.'

'Montero told me he was going to invite me one of these evenings to see *Juan José*.'

'*Juan José*? Ah yes, I read about in the papers, but I can't imagine . . .'

'It's something very different from the things you see. It has nothing to do with kings or raised swords . . . it's something else, something else altogether.'

The things Montero has are secret things. It's as though he were the trustee of everyone's secrets and you could ask him about some of them, knowing he would never tell or betray them, but that he would breathe their mystery to you as mystery. Even his presence or his absence is mysterious, unpredictable: he appears or disappears without explaining why. His lack of explanation serves, in a certain way, as an affirmation of any possible case. He disappears when he's not necessary, and he appears infallibly when he's needed. He appears as well to dispel or corroborate intrusive apparitions, the ones that trouble Laura's mind, which disproportionately fantasizes the dramatic events. In the provinces, each small group or clan – here clan has nothing to do with ties of blood, but with social, economic and hierarchical convention – each neighborhood has its gossip – always a woman – who divulges family secrets, but not as secrets per se. Building on intimate facts, on the private laws, the irreducibly personal matters of a person, she constructs commonplace stories. There in sacred Castile, in the land plowed by the faith of old, the weeds of vice sprouted like parsley, the condiment of exportable gossip – candied egg yolk made by the nuns, Benedictine liqueur – a stinging, biting paprika with which they season the acts of the dissident, the impious: they spy, they catch out, they tear to pieces mercilessly. In the glow of the fire a legend had emerged. There was no cross on the grave, not even a stone. There was, therefore, no dead man – in this case a woman – buried there. The fire had devoured the body whose beauty had amazed, whose beauty defied those who felt unloved.

'No, Laura dear – I agree to do away with the Doña because it creates distance, I'll address you the way you want me to – no, Laura, don't imagine your brother subjecting himself to that anguish on top of the real anguish he already felt. No, Laura, I put her in the ground. I put a wall of stones around it, not in a circle but making a rectangle, and I took the ivy there. I dug it up from the garden; that really made me sweat! I had to dig deep to get out the oldest roots – who knows how old they are. I planted it inside the rectangle. He didn't let me use fertilizer so it wouldn't look for easy nourishment on the surface. He didn't let me put a headstone and, of course, a cross was out of the question. He told me a cross is something he'll have to bear now or that it was something he had been nailed to, or that . . . Just touching on the subject made him rant and as far as I'm concerned, you well know that what my professor says is sacred, eternal, something more eternal than a stone. He wanted the grave to be like a sort of well where nobody could come with stupid condolences. The only thing there is the ivy. That ivy will fill the area quickly. Once it takes root, it never lets go.'

'Yes, I believe everything you're saying. That's my brother all right. It was all to be expected. But still you know – servants and nurses commenting on the phrase he kept saying in his desperation.'

'Ah, that's damnable! Of course those women can't understand. They don't know or understand anything more than what they're taught. They have no way of knowing it's a sacrilege even to repeat what he said.'

'We have to read *Juan José* before seeing it. We can find it in one of those bookstores on Ancha Street.'

'Do you think we'll like it? You're the one I think won't like it.'

'That's because I can't stand popular plays. And don't even talk to me about *zarzuelas*! They're for riff-raff! But this must be something else altogether. Ramón already warned us so we'd be on our guard. He said, "The two of you won't like it, but I do," and he added, "it doesn't have any kings or raised swords." He could have saved his breath, because I really sense something very different here.'

'What is it you sense? I don't sense anything.'

'You don't sense it, but you'll understand it. Listen, the people who think about these things talk about justice and injustice: they defend the people, who always had a hard time of it. It would seem that this question would stay in the hands of those who make the laws – well, those who impose them and those who put up with them or refuse to. But you see? These are the themes they use for plays, to say nothing of novels.'

'Why do they write novels if it's not so that the others can make the laws?'

'Well, no, it's not just for that reason; although that's part of it. They write them because they like to. Because they like to and because everybody likes them, except, of course, those who don't like them. No, no, I'm not talking about that sort of beauty some people find by painting ugly things. You know I can't stand Goya's *Caprichos* or those midgets of Velázquez. Because, let's see, what did he get out of painting *El Bobo de Coria*? Putting him there for a very long time so that we can see that the people back then were entertained by looking at that pus, at that pair of rotting eyes . . . What we're talking about now is very different. In these things that seem ugly there is a beauty – a beauty that you don't see, although it might be written about or painted.'

'And if it can't be seen, what you get out of it? Well, wait a minute. I think I'm beginning to understand.'

'Of course, you have to understand it, of necessity. There's a beauty in all this which doesn't appear right off to the naked eye. It's like within, in the depths of what you see, there might be something better. For example, if they give you scenes of poor and hungry people, it's not to move you – well, yes, it's to move you, but it's also to do something else. It's so you will feel or know that among these characters – not because they're characters, not because they're having a very tough time – but because they form or belong to . . . something like a genre. And in addition, it's not that they are what they are, it's that they, among themselves are doing something . . .'

'But, what are they doing?'

'Gosh! How can I put it? Everything, they're doing everything. Of course, other people do some of the things. What I'm trying to say is that there's a beauty in what they do, but not that they do things in a beautiful way. It's the fact that they do them . . . That's what has beauty, their work.'

'Well, that's what you might think, but work was always considered some sort of punishment. That's what they teach you in school, and later they tell you to work, that it's good to work.'

'Naturally, they have to say that so that the punishment will be carried out. But as to whether it's good or bad . . . And speaking of work, you haven't done anything in a couple of days.'

'It's true. I can't work. I can't give myself over to this idea of beauty, although my work has to do with that. I can't because I can't get out of my head something horrible, something atrocious – I don't know what to call it.'

'Yes, I figured that something unpleasant had happened to you.'

'No, nothing happened. It was a dream, a nightmare. You can't imagine.'

'Ah, a dream. Tell me about it!'

'I can tell you in two sentences. I didn't tell you before because it seemed almost stupid to say that something as simple as this was so horrible. I'm walking along a dark street and suddenly I feel a man grabbing me from behind. That's all. Nothing else, he didn't do anything to me.'

'Well, if he didn't do anything to you, it's not so horrible.'

'Yes, but something did happen, even if he didn't do anything to me. It's so atrocious exactly because I don't know what he did to me. I don't know what he looked like. I don't know what the street looked like. I think there was a church. There were no shops or doorways – everything was dark. But I think I remember that there was a street light that hurt your eyes to look at, but everything all around was black. You couldn't see a thing.

And I felt him coming up on me. I have no idea why I was walking along that street. I think that before I heard him coming I hadn't realized he was lurking about. Then suddenly I felt him grab me by the arms, and I couldn't move. He grabbed me from behind, but then – I don't know how – not then, but immediately – he was in front of me. He was so close that I couldn't see him.'

'Well, and then . . . ?'

'That's it. Nothing more happened: nothing happened at all . . .'

'Yes, of course, it's frightening.'

'No, that's not the frightening part. The part I've told you about is really nothing. What you can't describe . . . Hasn't something like that ever happened to you?'

'What? Tell me what you mean.'

'I'm telling you that it can't be explained. The man was in front of me, so close that I couldn't see him, and I didn't know what he was doing to me. All right, he didn't do anything with his hands. I don't know where he had his hands, but he squeezed me so tight that I couldn't even breathe. But don't imagine that it lasted hours on end: it was like a bolt of lightning: the man appeared, he grabbed me, he squeezed me . . . against the wall? I don't know if it was against the wall, but he squeezed me so hard I was about to suffocate. And in that same second, I'm thinking, my heart will burst! And something happens that is not exactly bursting and not just in my heart, but everywhere . . . Something like when lightning strikes you. Hasn't this ever happened to you?'

'Yes, of course, a lot of times. Do you know why this happened to you now? It's because you've crossed the Rubicon. Before that it never happens.'

'Yes, I know, because I'm a woman now. That's what my mother said to me when she put on my stockings: "You can't wear socks any more because you're a woman now." It turned my stomach! I thought it was absurd to wear stockings so that everyone would know, instead of hiding it. What they call "women's things" have always turned my stomach. Of course, they're always mixed up with "men's things." '

'I don't know where you got this business of it making you sick. It's crazy. But the point is, as you now see, you'll never be free from these things.'

'Hey, you can't imagine what I'm thinking now. I'm trying to recall all this and I remember that I didn't defend myself. Isn't that fantastic? I didn't defend myself.'

'And did it turn your stomach?'

'No, it made me afraid. More than being afraid, it was like I felt or I knew that I was about to die . . . And I didn't defend myself.'

'Let's see, try to remember what the man looked like.'

'I don't have to try because I remember everything perfectly. I recall that I couldn't see him, that he didn't look like anybody, like anybody you know. I remember that it wasn't something you could see, only feel.'

'Well, if you feel it and you've felt it inside yourself and you know that this is what happens between men and women, there's no reason why it should turn your stomach. I think it happened to you like that, in such a frightening way, to cure you of pride. That's the thing about you: you've got so much pride it won't fit in your body. So then your conscience tries to cure you with a dream.'

'Conscience – maybe so, because I do have something on my conscience. But why are you bringing this up now? Has somebody told you?'

'Nobody's told me anything. Who could tell it to me?'

'Maybe your Luisito, for example.'

'In the first place, Luisito isn't my private property, and probably not even yours. In the second place, he hasn't told me one word.'

'He could have told you about how I insulted him the other day.'

'Why? Why? How can you insult that boy and come out smelling like a rose?'

'Smelling like a rose! Didn't I tell you I have something on my conscience? Besides, I really didn't intend to hurt him. In fact, I was really trying to behave well.'

'So what happened? Come on, tell me the whole story.'

'What happened was that he was wrapping my parcel like he always does, like he was wrapping birds' eggs, to make it last an hour, then suddenly he told me he had a helper. It's the boy they found because Don Luis can't come in any more. He said that in the evening he could go out for a while and that maybe we could take a walk together. "Why don't you come down when it gets dark and we'll take a stroll around the plaza – I've been wanting to have a long talk with you." Now don't think I insulted him then, just like that. I told him something that couldn't possibly upset him. I assure you that what I decided to say was nothing like "I don't want to." I told him that as far as I was concerned, all right, but if my mother finds out she'll raise the devil. And what do you think he answered? "No your mother won't mind because I'll talk to her. I'll go up and tell her that . . ." I didn't let him go on. You? Talk to my mother! Don't even think of it! Don't let it enter your mind! And he didn't answer back, I thought he was going to try to argue, to try to convince me, but he didn't say a single word. He just looked at me. His eyes got very big, and then he blinked and turned his back. He went quickly into the back room. He lifted the beaded curtains – or rather, he shoved them aside. And I heard the beads knock against each other and make a certain sound. I don't know what they're made of . . . something heavy, but that's not all. I heard him start to cry. I heard a sob when he went into the back room. I was so surprised that I stood there like an idiot without moving a muscle. And then the helper came out – the kid, they call him – and he looked at me like you can't imagine. That pest looked at me with contempt!'

'You see? It's something you can also call "men's things." And you're going to tell me it turns your stomach?'

'No, it doesn't turn my stomach but it sort of bewilders me. I don't know what to think. I don't understand it. I don't want to understand it.'

'Tell me why you don't want to. I would never think of asking you to explain what you don't understand. You don't understand it and that's that. But if you say you don't want to understand it, it means you understand it. The fact is you don't like what you understand.'

'Maybe that's so: you make everything clear and I have to say you're right. I don't like what I understand.'

'Okay, now I'm the one who doesn't understand. Tell me what it is you don't understand and what you don't like.'

'Are you playing the fool or do you just not feel like understanding?'

'I'm not playing the fool. This whole mess leaves me feeling like a fool.'

'That's not true. You're acting the fool because you have to be on top of what's happening in the street. What do you want – for him to come upstairs to talk with my mother like a serious boyfriend? And then, what do I do? Do you think I could visit that witch of a mommy he has? Do you think that's possible? Do you think I could bear what would happen at his house when they found out? He can come up if he wants to, but do you think my mother could go down?'

'You're right. It's a problem. But I don't think Luis will give up.'

'If he doesn't give up it's because he doesn't see the problem, and that's not possible because he doesn't seem like an idiot. What he wants to do is find out whether I act like I do with him because I don't love him.'

'And do you love him or not?'

'Me? What do you mean, love him? Not him or anybody else!'

'Not anybody else? You've had that decided since before you could walk. But you never know what might happen some day . . .'

'Well, maybe somebody from China – perhaps. But this guy! This guy who wants to come running up the stairs . . .'

'He doesn't go to the theater, like the neighbors say, to enjoy himself. He goes to take his sister because literature is her profession and because he needs to think about something different from what keeps going through his head all day long.'

'And what he wants is to get it out of his head, that's what. Because he can't accept adversity. He thinks it's an injustice that something like that has happened to him – that this has been done to him, that's how he talks. It's a case of egotism – a really big one.'

'A case of egotism! As soon as somebody doesn't act like everyone else, like the whole gang, it's a case of something insulting. What would you like him to have said, that he was waiting patiently to be reunited with her in the portals of heaven?'

'I couldn't care less what he might say, but everybody who heard him thought it was scandalous. Don't tell me it's not absurd, for a serious man in this situation to break out shouting, "They've killed me! They've killed me!" He wasn't crying for her: He was crying for himself. Can you imagine anything more egotistical?'

'It doesn't matter whether it was egotism or not. You have to make some sense out of what he said. I mean, saying that would be permissible if it's true.'

'What do you mean, if it's true? Isn't it obvious that she's dead and he's alive?'

'No it's not obvious. What he said is fine. He has every right to say he's been killed if the fact is that he's been killed.'

'Okay, keep playing the same tune.'

'I'm not playing anything. He has every right to say he's been killed if the fact is that he's dead.'

'Really dead?'

'No one but him can know that. No, don't try to get me to accept your arguments. Egotism! Juliet calls Romeo an egotist when she sees he's taken all the poison. Mmm . . . No, I think egotist is not what she calls him. I think she calls him ungrateful or greedy. Both are stupid. A woman who finds her lover dead doesn't reproach him, as if they were having a spat. Well, whatever it is she says to him, we're convinced, we've been convinced for a long time because when she sees that he didn't leave her a little bit of poison she sticks a dagger in herself and that's the end of the story.'

'And what did this guy stick in himself?'

'He considers himself knifed. And I'm going to tell you again: he and only he knows if it's true or not. He doesn't need to satisfy any spectators.' Above all, his audience isn't like the audience of Romeo and Juliet, an audience that goes to see a love story and comes away happy because it isn't one of those love stories that ends in some filthy way. With that kind everybody leaves sick to their stomachs saying, 'I told you so, that's what happens when you try to glorify sex.' But when the couple ends up with a dagger and poison, love comes out as a good thing. Of course, in this case there isn't anything like that. It's not an impossible love, but a fulfilled love. That's the kind that usually result in more pedestrian tragedies – or don't result in a tragedy at all, and who knows if that's not a tremendous tragedy. In this case, it's a question of knowing – of comprehending because as far as knowing goes, nobody can know. It's a question of comprehending, from the point of view of a neighbor . . . To what extent can there be any other point of view? How can a person consider himself, with regard to somebody else, anything but a neighbor? Because neighbor in the biblical sense is what we call anyone on the face of the whole earth. A neighbor's point of view would have to be that of a person who sees something from close by, but from his own floor: not someone who looks on from upstairs or downstairs, but from his room. Without leaving his room. Without prying. Without peeping about like the gossips in any old apartment house. Naturally, if it weren't for the gossips, I wouldn't know about that remark – that shout – I don't think he said it shouting. More likely, it was sort of muffled – a kind of rattle in the throat. It's the gossips that cheapen everything, especially when it's something that one shouldn't ever dare to repeat. But what happens is that it keeps repeating itself inside your head and there's no way not to want to figure it out. You want to know – no, you want to see – what truth is really there: what exactly there is dead, really dead, in a living man. Because – and this is the thing – a tragedy between two young lovers, very young, as clumsy as babies, feeding on love like milk from their mother's breast – that's it – ignorant of any other form of nourishment: they hang on, clutch at love, hanging from it as if from a cord and they have to end up crashing to the ground when the cord breaks, or else they stretch. Stretch out the self's elastic – what's it called? Oh, yes, the instinct of self-preservation, which is a blind sense of survival . . . blind? Well, blind because it doesn't select, it scrapes together and protects even the sediments of life. The truth is, it defends life and that's that. And it's elastic, it falls of its own weight. Now I've got it: it's stupid to think of it as a fall. Life's elastic doesn't stretch from zenith to nadir: it expands, it doesn't waste away – well, obviously, it can waste away, and when it does, it becomes impalpable, numb. Something like your own skin, that grows with you and you don't feel it, but if you get a cut you feel it and your skin tends to close itself again. These things happen at the beginning of your life, when you're completely idiotic, as if life had caught you by suprise. Later, in maturity, you can't be so blind. Of course, you get blinded by bewilderment, the excess of things, not knowing what to think . . . There, too, there are two ways out – that is to say, there's a way out and a blind alley. There's wanting to embrace everything and there's hesitating, fearing . . . the effort involved? Not only or exactly the effort, but something like the disillusionment involved. But, what disillusionment? The fear of having illusions about yourself. Because illusions about an ideal aren't the ones to be feared: the ideal never disappoints – unless it's a cretin's ideal. The illusions that must be avoided are the ones that could give a false measure, a flattering notion of your own ability to climb up the greased pole. You get dazed from all the lights beaming at you, confusing you in the middle of the road – may the cliché 'be praised for its impeccable ancestry,' as that little Latin American fellow says. And the lights aren't what we used to call splendor: natural light, the splendor of Nature. The many lights of maturity are . . . Well, they must be: I'm not going to start thinking now that I know what they are. No, I don't know; but I know a lot more than those who think they know. This man who is dead, unquestionably dead because of and for the sake of that which killed him, has come here like a *revenant* – a word we should have. Because 'apparition' means something that has appeared to someone, while *revenant* designates only something – someone – who returns, and only he knows where from. We don't know where this man has come back from or why: from a neighbor's point of view, that's about all one can gather.

And, no matter the gender or number, the neighbor's point of view is based on gossip. It can also be based on human interest if the neighbor in question is a humanitarian, but . . . if he's a misanthrope? Misanthrope! A commonplace which doesn't have such impeccable credentials now. Misanthrope is a reproach hurled by the plebians among civilized men at someone who refuses to adapt to their plebianness, against someone who has dared to reject – who has given two or three justified kicks in the ass. And they single him out as someone from whom you can expect nothing but kicks. There's a misanthropic point of view, one from which you see not what stands out, but what sinks down, with more pride than that which rises up. There is a molehill of sympathies where the blind meet and recognize one another. But they don't talk: they converse in silence as though they were smelling each other from a distance. What would I have to talk about with that gentleman – a writer, a professor, a thinker, they say he is. I don't know if there's a title for it. I have nothing to say and he doesn't have a desire to say anything. Because as far as knowing goes, he knows a lot. He knows ancient philosophy like the back of his hand – or so they say – not to mention current thinkers. He spends his time reading Tolstoy and Ibsen and all that.

A *revenant* can come back because it didn't break its ties with earth, it didn't wholly detach itself, but stayed stuck in the birdlime like a soul in torment. If it's a soul, it goes on existing, but it cannot communicate its suffering to living beings. Whomever it appears to sees it as an apparition rather than as an appearance. Its apparition is a reflection, an optical effect of something which is elsewhere, suffering, but existing. A person who does not go away because he cannot find a place in which to suffer cannot be a *revenant*. A person who does not go away because he's attached to suffering, repelled by the lack of suffering, by lack itself. Because he knows that what is missing has become a part of the sum total of lack, of nothingness, and cannot tolerate the nonexistence of what he misses. Because, of course, staying – rather than coming back – isn't a way of substituting what exists for what is lacking. It is a way of living in hostility to lack, to all absence – something completely meaningless although you can feel it violently. Why be hostile to nothingness? It is true that we cannot conceive it and that with a bit of common sense, no one could imagine that nothingness might be something but, above or below common sense, there throbs or buzzes the perception of nothingness as someone . . . and you hate it, you make war with it, you block its path. As if nothingness could have a path! It cannot. Let's be sensible. It can't, yet it advances and gains ground. No, it doesn't gain anything, but ground gets lost in it. Not the ground that stays in place, but ground that flows. Water flows more than earth; air more than water; time . . . Everything goes toward nothingness, and it is stupid to try and stop it. It's not stupid – or yes, it is, but it's necessary, because at least it exists. And all this because of our lineage, rather than ancestry, because of certain biological laws which are rooted in being, which are sworn in, chained by their fidelity to being. So, then, life can be accepted as punishment or affliction, even though it assaults one's sense of shame to live it, as though living it were enjoying it, as though it were an escape hatch from hell – from the hole, the grave or the abyss. A person who thinks there's no hell in the abyss bears the burden of temporal suffering the whole of the way – one step, another step, a pound, an instant, a second, a minute – and doesn't want to unload that burden because unloading, finding relief would be giving in, and resentment is as inextinguishable as passion. Whoever associates with nothingness – a fallacious association – is weak and deserves to belong to it. He wears its name, because a name is all it has, and spreads barrenness. He spreads hate, with no fear of being hated. Indeed, he passes as respectable, as a partisan or a henchman of the abyss: they call him a negator. No, it's not a question of names, even though names have tremendous power. It's not a question of names because some have adopted it – pretending to be adopted children of nothingness, as though it could adopt since it can't give birth – adopted the title of negators, of defenders of nothingness: Make way for it! Don't try to oppose it! And as they shouted this, the very shout was rejecting it, their words, syllables, breath filled mental space with enigmas, filled all the air invaded by that pollen with beauty, with seduction . . . Time! Time, the riverbed of reality! Riverbed, or flow? It goes with reality, or reality goes with time. Time – a time, an imponderable quantity, since it does not have distinct contours. But it does have a being, a way of being – a whole bulk of time fertilized by a beautiful word that appears to be blasphemy and is really a plea.

'You have to admit it: we're going through an enormous slump. Although it may be optimistic to think we're getting through it. Are we even protesting about it? All right, all right, I know that some are protesting: the few that you go around with or you defend. Not me, I don't defend. I accuse. *J'accuse* those who protest without any success. You know that for years I've wanted to copy that title, and I'll do it. I'd do it if I thought it could possibly do any good. Although probably I'll do it knowing that it won't do any good. And then I'll have to accuse myself. And I do accuse myself. I begin by accusing myself for not having done it when I had no excuses. Now you'll probably imagine that I'll use the excuses I have. No, I accuse the good guys, and I count myself among them – or I don't – because in our times we have first-rate bad guys, really "good" ones. What I mean to say is men who are ethical, irreproachable, devoted to the best of causes. Yes, there are a handful, but you tell me: what have they accomplished up to now? What accent, what note, what siren's call have they made us hear? . . . No, don't try to tell me that we have to put aesthetics aside. Put it aside and stomp on it if you want to: do it and you've done nothing more than show bad temper. Evil genius – bad angel – but neither angel nor genius. That's what our little corner of earth suffers from. They've emaciated us. I don't know what kind of knock-kneed rickets, what kind of shameful scrofula has infected us . . . Look, we don't have to look further: this trivia you're going to applaud unanimously – would it survive even a few kilometers beyond the border? Don't try to tell me that it could, because it simply couldn't. It just wouldn't go over. On the other hand, you can see the efficient and daring things that come to us from the North. I don't know where they stand with regard to aesthetics, but the fact is that they're not indigestible like our own productions . . . No, no, no . . . Don't start in with the business about being ingenuous, about the merit of struggling amid ignorance to succeed. In the first place, there isn't so much ignorance because people know how to read and there are piles of books at a penny apiece. They can read! Just imagine! And there you have a problem, a national wound that really hurts. You can tell it because it's given as the *vox populi*, but you and I know that those who propagate it have had their primary and even their secondary schooling – in fact, they make their living by writing. But what I want to make you understand is that they touch on this theme, and by the very fact . . . No, I'm not going to pause now to take up the business of "Is there anything more insolent than a fact?" A marvelous statement! – but let's leave it for later. By the very fact that it's something true and painful, the modest writer – who certainly is not modest – achieves a "literary effect." I don't know if I'm managing to give you a clear idea of the conundrum . . . The wound, already pointed out by the distinguished bearded gentleman who died recently and who worked tirelessly to heal it, the wound cried out in a woman's voice – movingly, tenderly, cleverly in the letter from Pilara. And, what does it all turn into? Into the fantasies of a young girl whose boyfriend is away. "What would he say?" And then she goes on to suppose such things as . . . Well, the dregs of corniness. And then all of a sudden, in this case, just because it touches on a real source of pain, it's given literary value. Does it have technical value? Perfection, precision, intensity, are they technical values? Literary quality goes up like a thermometer in boiling water. And your *Juan José*, which started out in humble hemp sandals, so to speak – the author did: the character is supposed to wear them – that is, he started out getting us used to the tavern, to the hiccups in the john and all. When the dramatic moment comes, the letter that will swamp him in the evidence of his betrayal, he finds that – no, it's the author who finds that his character does not know how to read, and it's at that point that he gets inside his character: he penetrates him, he explores him, he establishes his dimensions. If I were to tell you that his most intimate worries are less compelling, it would seem like I'm taking away a part of his humanity. But no, I'm not taking away anything: I'm adding . . . It's difficult to know whether something – something without adjectives, not external, not strange, but just something in all its abstract dimension – it's difficult to know whether *something* added to the intimate pain of the suffering individual could be a deflection, a variance that could cloud the glow of pain . . . Perhaps, if it's not that this *something* is like an extension of pity. As if all around the man hungering for pity there vibrated an atmosphere swollen with it, as if . . . More, much more than the lament appropriate for the situation, "The terrible misfortune of those born as I was! We don't even learn how to read!" I've read, as you can see, the complete script, very carefully. That's how I discovered the hidden nectar of intelligence: the essential nectar. It's not that Juan José, a wretched being, links his wretchedness to that of those who were born, as he was, dispossessed. It's not like he's standing with the paper in his hand crying out on behalf of those who have been deprived . . . He's crying out for all men who without Man, without intelligence, are slaves. He has the paper in his hand, but he doesn't go mad over the betrayal. The betrayal poisons him with resentment, but the paper, what the paper represents as a decipherable mystery, as an *Open Sesame* that could be opened by a specific spring, drives him crazy because he sees something, what he calls "goddamned hen-scratchings," and it's as though he didn't see it. He looks at it, but he doesn't see it: he sees the hen-scratching but not the law that makes it a sign. He knows he's holding the outline of his misfortune – he knows this because he's been told, but what if it was a lie? There's no reason at all why it might be. But there's something there that's intolerable because it's inaccessible to reason: that the same scribbles, apparently the same, should contain "the signature of his friend and the betrayal by his wife." This, you have to admit, is significant. A writer – let's say a second-rate writer, and that's being kind – this is what you need to see – the mere fact of having bumped into the truth turns him into a lightning rod for it. He's placed at the magnetic center and receives the flash of intelligence. Of course, that flash is hidden behind clouds of commonplaces – "What a terrible misfortune," etc. And I'm not saying that this commonplace has no right to assert itself, that it's not – in the final analysis – the heart of the matter. The writers we call "natural" or naturalists serve it to us very raw – they're capable of convincing anyone. But I prefer something more powerful than convincing . . . A contradiction? Do I have the right to prefer something to logical conviction? No, I don't have the right. I would be wrong, I'd fall into an obvious contradiction if I preferred something illogical. But what I prefer is logic itself. I'd rather that reasoning convinced in its season – that it create a season, a climate.

There you have it – what I call knock-kneed rickets, scrofula, or rather, a lack of wind, a lack of senses – a lack of logic because the senses are logical. "Sweet candy never tastes bitter to anyone." A commonplace! All the sounds responding to, affirming, giving themselves over to the proposed springtimes. Those Russians that promote flowering – watch out for aesthetics! – that sow grain for all hungers. For all of them: that's what we must never forget. Because we all become spokesmen for the virtuous things that they propagate. Christians, very very Christian, those little monks with their three kisses. But the power, the Eros that flows from their naïve princes, from their mysterious beauties – diabolical! – apparently chaste and perhaps chaste in fact, but capable of turning on half the world. Yes, I know we're in agreement here. But you love them for their virtues, and I, let me confess that without their sins they would bore me . . . That's what I'm trying to hammer into your head: don't bring the people of your generation toward your asceticism. Don't deny it. Your climate is asceticism, and we've had enough of that. What's needed here is something to heat people up, but without the smell of onions . . . and without excessive refinement, God forbid. We need it. Well, in popular fiction there is or there's beginning to appear an explorer of the jungle. The jungle of the senses, to be exact, the jungle of sex: Felipe Trigo.'

'Manolo!'

'What's the matter? What are you afraid of, little teacher? These girls are already old enough to be mothers. There's no reason for them to be in a hurry, but they have to learn not to be useless.'

'Could they learn from Felipe Trigo?'

'Of course they could; and it might surprise you, but without a doubt they already are. Am I right or wrong? Answer me, Elena – haven't you read him?'

'Yes, sir, of course I've read him.'

'And why haven't you ever talked to me about it? It's very difficult, if not impossible, not to get the idea of sin into your heads. And it wouldn't be because anybody has ever seen me trying to put it there . . .'

'No, I never talked to you about him because I thought he wouldn't be your type of writer. But I've talked a lot with Montero, right?'

'Oh, yes, a lot. We talked about it one day for exactly three hours in Retiro Park, as I recall. If it hadn't started to rain we would have gone on. And it was about sin, precisely, or at least its detestable ghost – "the irreparable."'

'How atrocious!'

Piedita! Piedita had been away. Now she was back and she continued not to exist. That was the conclusion reached some time ago, but while she was away it was easy to think such a thing. Now with her before your eyes it was no longer a question of thinking. Without thinking about anything, what you wanted to say was, 'Do you remember Piedita? What a shame you didn't see her when she was here! I wish you could have known her . . .' But Piedita wasn't the least bit sorry not to have known her. She was fully satisfied to see herself now, in the present, like a glossy cat. Although she didn't have what is most characteristic of a cat, what is most endearing, seductive and contagious, what is most communicative of its well-being – its purr. No, Piedita didn't lick herself with satisfaction at her good fortune: she grew rich passively, naturally, without astonishment. She brought . . . no, she didn't even bear the weight of her shiny Kodak. That was brought by her husband or by her bustling, radiant and tireless sister-in-law, Mrs. Smith. They brought a marvelous array of photographic documents of the seven wonders. Piedita hadn't transformed them into documents in her memory. She had just opened her chestnut eyes wide before the sights in question, and now she opened them at whatever was put in front of her with her usual serenity: her eyes were never startled by amazement or fright. Piedita had returned and there was no way of keeping her from appearing. No one ever even thought of preventing it, and she appeared – infrequently, but she appeared. And when she wasn't around, they talked about her from time to time. Now that you could feel her nearby, the talk was sparing and somewhat difficult because there was no point in evoking the past – now even the most trivial memories were impossible. Now just observations, predictions, approval or laments. Her beauty continued to be just as impassive as her serenity.

'She's looking beautiful!'

'Maybe even a bit too beautiful.'

'Could it be a temporary beauty?'

'No, it seems that's not what he wants: he prefers to keep her idle.'

'Just as well! This way we won't have a Beltranejo.'

'You're terrible! You're cruel!'

'I'm sorry about being cruel to you, not to her. But don't think you're the only victim of my cruelty. Sarcasm is a stiletto that cuts with the handle as well as the blade.'

'Oh, what a *cinquecento* expression you've come up with!'

Piedita has returned, and her absence and her nonexistence allow for no further commentary. They had been discussed so much that it was like a drawing you correct a hundred times, where you can't tell the mistaken lines from the good ones. There was no reason to remember Piedita, because she had come back. But if it was easy to shake off her memory, it was impossible – being so facile and so imperceptible – to deny or ignore her presence. It was impossible to reject her influence, because her influence consisted of accepting everything and rejecting nothing. Piedita lavished her naturalness. Her invitations, her gifts, were nothing like repaying the former affection – so freely given, so deserving of faithfulness. They were more like a habit, like a way of behaving that wasn't the least bit different from before. Piedita didn't make a debut of her well-being, and she didn't make a debut of her generosity. It's just that – without this being any cause for surprise – she doubled it, or rather extended it to one or two other generous persons. Her house was filled with delicacies. The very house was one of them, but not tempting enough for her brother and sister, who always found an excuse – sadness or a little complaint – not to visit it. The girls went, as sparrows come when you scatter bread crumbs into the air. But not for the novelty of having tea – hot pastries with butter – or for the desserts with frostings, whipped cream or frosted cherries. They went because the house was an unexpected world. Elena said – she said it to Isabel when they decided to go, she said it to Doña Laura when she noticed that she was a bit put off by their visiting rather regularly – 'Let's go see the crane.' And it was true that this is what they went to see, although everything else went along with it. The crane was at the far end of the garden. The garden was small, but it did have a far end. Higher buildings had gradually surrounded it, and it was sort of boxed in; but the trees, the bushes – lilacs, celandines which had still not lost their leaves in the fall – gave shade that masked the cement walls . . . A mossy shadiness that framed the pool, or rather, the puddle where you could see the crane. The gray bird was as silent as a princess in exile. It would stand on one foot and extend the other in a rather tentative fashion, as though it were deciding upon something worthy of its taste. But it never reached out with that little, skinny hand. When something tasty moved in the water, it would stretch out its neck – its bristly corona would quiver – and snap up the prey in its beak – a precision-tooled tweezer –

and the delectable morsel was swallowed. The morsel wasn't a thing. It was generally a tender, graceful, undulating polliwog recently separated from the umbilical cord. Hidden in the aquatic grasses lay a gelatinous necklace deposited by the frog or the large toad from which there emerged, as they matured, the pollywog larvae. The tiny toads – the truest subjects of the pond, little creatures of this watery world with their soft bellies and their throbbing throats and their bulging eyes – were the clear-throated singers of the night or the masters of the evening croak. They fed the gray, elegant, impassive and implacable crane. It was horrible, and at the same time fascinating. Why go on watching such a thing? Why not hate that ferocious animal so secure in its kingdom, well-served and well-fed thanks to special products placed in its food dish and at the same time surrounded by natural delicacies so easy to catch, so fresh, newborn, dripping with water, so liquid that they could hardly be felt? But how could we hate it? Its kingdom was a refuge of depth, intensity, darkness, silence, vegetal dampness, hungry life being born and being devoured. The far end of the garden, the crane's haven, was something sacred. Sacred because it brought salvation: its depth offered the only elevation possible above the trivial level of the brilliant house. That house and its things. Things filled that perimeter. And the things renewed themselves as well, but they weren't born, they never looked tender and larval. They appeared, round and full, one substituting for another. They changed places, and though they didn't quarrel about their positions, they did occupy them according to a hierarchy of newness. New things arrived, and were put in the spotlight. They received attention's homage for a number of days and then were supplanted by other things that relegated them to oblivion. The crane's haven was sacred because it was untouched by the invasion of things – though not by their existence, not by the fact that there were things in the house, because things were everywhere. The city was filled with them. The most humble homes had things, humble things. So humble that they didn't even seem like things! It wasn't that. It was that the field of things in question was directed, organized and inhabited by four beings – plus two, plus two more, plus one or two more – six or seven in all: servants who, like six or seven things, attended the four human beings who, like four things surrounded by their troops of other things, filled it up, imposed the trivially obvious, the apparent, though it was real: these appearances overflowed with reality. Saying 'Let's go see the crane,' was like saying, 'Don't worry that we'll get lost, shipwrecked among the things.' With that security, counting on that refuge, it was possible to cruise among the things. It was possible, of course, to enjoy their landscapes, their shores and their fruits. Because things were lavish there and, sheathing oneself in a very discreet disdain, they could be gobbled up without leaving a crumb. The adolescent, so conscious, judgmental, at times biting or mocking, was taken over by the child's greediness, its purity of ignorance – by its innocence, in the real and amoral sense of inexperience. The child's hunger took over, as insatiable as the crane's, as animal, as capable of digesting the hardest objects, and, arousing the organ of curiosity, it coldly passed things under review. Things were looked at with authority as they passed, they were all considered equally, with no suspicion that there might be one that could stop the judge short . . .

'And what about this folder, Mrs. Smith?'

'Oh, those are things from London. Who knows what's in there. You can put it on the table in the study and sort the prints. Oh! Look what we have here – the Pre-Raphaelites.'

The classification went unheard. The names that appeared in the margins of the prints – oleographs, color reproductions – were exotic, some of them difficult to pronounce. The images were impossible to sort. They bore no relationship to anything known. Could they have been seen in the Prado Museum? Never. The forms, the colors, were as correct and well-finished as those of the greatest paintings, but the beings represented – equally beautiful – were in another world. Were they from another world? They looked at other spaces, they belonged to a sphere where no one had been. They were impenetrable creatures, inhabitants of a hermetic world. But they didn't put you off. Quite the contrary! They invited you . . . More than inviting you, they absorbed you, tangled you in tentacles – like the cuttlefish in the depths of the sea in its amber cloud, like the boa in the desert of solitude, snagging you like the wild bramble that entangles you if you go off the path. They held your gaze – your mind – not in the paralysis of contemplation, but in a suspension of breath. To enter them, you had to leave – like taking off your sandals in oriental temples – or forget about your other life at the threshold . . . Although, how could there be so much beauty foreign to life? No, life did not stay behind, forgotten. You could say rather that it was there and present, but not with the presence – with the obviousness – of form. It was like, for example, a wail. Can we explain why a wail, a voice, is painful, anguishing, frightening? It is nothing more than a voice, it's not even a complaint. It is not a shout – direct news of pain – it's a doleful voice, a premonition of something that hasn't been hurt yet. The life being lived in the world of those beings was life in danger. And in what? In what can the wail be seen? In the eyes, perhaps? There are admirable eyes in faces that no one can forget because they have looked at us. We stand before them and they look at us. They seem admirable not because we see them, but because we think they see us. Someone has said all this already. These eyes do not look at us, and what we see are not eyes, they are gazes. These wailing gazes – with the pain a wail has, but with nothing of its protest, its call for help: pain with no possible help, with no longing for help. These gazes are also like incense, like something balsamic emerging from a funeral pyre: a surrender, a giving, a wasting away.

'We're off, Piedita, it's getting late. We were absolutely amazed by the prints, Mrs. Smith.'

'I knew you were going to like them. Do you want to take a book, Elena? Look, you can have these: Maeterlinck's *The Intruder*, *The King's Mailman*. They're absolutely tops – works one must read.'

'Here, take these brioches for my brother and sister, for breakfast.'

'Oh, so many!'

'So much the better. They'll have some for the afternoon.'

'I think you two worry too much about Elena's nerves. She's as strong as a horse.'

'She's healthy, so she manages; but she reads too much.'

'The problem is not how much, but what she reads. That's something you don't seem to care about.'

'No, Mama, we don't care because it's not important. She's used to reading whatever she wants. I'm not afraid it will corrupt her mind.'

'Ah, of course, you think your little daughter is as pure as ermine.'

'Exactly! You couldn't be more right. I'm surprised that you, madam, are precisely the one to come up with such an appropriate simile.'

'You're surprised because you don't have an especially high opinion of my intelligence.'

'Ah, if it were only a question of intelligence . . . What's needed besides is a good ear – for good music, for good verse, and for many other good things.'

'My heavens! I certainly think I'm as good as anybody in music.'

'Oh! Yes, that's true – you've a well-trained ear for music, but as far as other things are concerned . . .'

The difficult part is having a good ear for harmonies which have not been established on scored paper . . . nor in hendecasyllables or Alexandrines or anything else: the things that have not been written. And it's not even a question of 'There's nothing written down about tastes.' Because a lot has been, even if there were nothing established – as there obviously has been – stipulated by other people's opinions, by the concern with what other people might say, which is what everybody worries about. But there's something more difficult, more complicated, more obscure – that's right, much more obscure than tastes, because it's a question of something you can't choose or decide: you can't even think about it. How could someone have a good ear for what doesn't yet exist but is going to? It's possible, of course, it's possible . . . and, of course, something's been established about this. One wants certain things that don't yet exist to be the way one wants. There's a way of establishing it, of forcing the thing to take the shape one wants. Of course, forming or shaping cannot be called forcing. It can be something like nurturing or sowing. Quite a lot has already been said about this: this business of sowing or planting a tree. No, the tough part, the devilish part, what makes you really angry is not knowing how what's going to be will be. Because why do we think we know how it will turn out when we're sure that we haven't forced or deformed anything? With the experience we've had of coincidences and flukes! You get something by a fluke, but it's ruined by coincidence . . . That's right, and, nonetheless – what do I know? – There's a feeling, a presentiment they call it. But no, I don't say presentiment: I say feeling. It's probable that when a person talks about presentiment there's nothing 'pre-' about it. Because where is the beginning of things that are to be? It's possible that there's a law as certain as the law of the carom in billiards, where a person knows why he does it and how he does it. But what I'd like to know is how what is done by itself is done and this is all connected to what I'm saying about feeling and not having presentiments. Because you can feel that something is going to be done with things that are already made, and these are the ones that you feel . . . It's not that it's going to be done like a jigsaw puzzle, with the model or the pattern already known . . . No, it's that they're known . . . It's enough to drive you crazy! There are exactly seven notes, and their combinations are infinite. Yes, yes, yes, but we say that there are seven if we look at their elemental nature. In the human soul, in the human being that walks around in the world, there is nothing elementary. As soon as we see him walking on two feet, he becomes a combination of combinations. Because who can possibly know how one person's blood will mix with another's? Any country bumpkin knows about 'a chip off the old block,' but – what can we learn from that? The block can be splintered into fifty thousand chips, some so tiny that you can't even see them, and sometimes they're not completely separated from the others. This is a little idiotic, but it's good food for thought. There are chips that have little chips, fibers, threads all mixed up and combined. That's it! There are visible combinations, and that's why you think you perceive the invisible ones, with all their opposites: their flukes, their billiard caroms. The business of opposites is the most puzzling because there could be a case in which something looks the opposite of what it's combined with, absolutely opposite –

antagonistic, as we say. Could we even say antithetical? I don't know why, when it's a question of beings which is what you have to think about if you want to understand anything about this business of combinations. Are they perfectly squared or does each one hold its own secret, its particular meaning? It's enough to scramble your brain! Every time I think about it – and I do so continually – I want to come to some conclusion, but I get carried off into something else when what I should do is examine the probabilities . . . and the probabilities are something you can't even imagine if you don't take certain proven things into account. That's what you can feel, what you can see from the moment the object starts walking on two feet through the world. It walks and comes toward you – plants itself in front of you – and demonstrates, shows you one of its chips. A tone of voice, a gesture, a way of doing things, a sally. We say sally, as in sally forth, because it seems like it's a remark that gets away from you, and those are the things that can surprise and even frighten. Depending on what they might suggest. If they are cherished things, or at least cordial, things that are familiar to us in their cordiality – which not all family things are – things we comprehend because they've been handled, touched, and measured with our very fingertips, then we think we're understanding them, and suddenly, the opposite, the contradiction, pops up! Up pops the thing that bothers us, the thing we argue with – argue with to avoid a gunfight – something we consider inadmissible, for example: toughness, a despotic and impenetrable force. And it turns out that in this new, extremely new, combination in which it reveals itself to us, this same force immediately elicits from us the adjective 'incoercible.' Now it's not toughness – being the very same force – and we recognize it and don't reject it: we hold it in high esteem, put our trust in it and don't worry about a thing: armored in it, the ermine can go through mud, through fire. The force which we find antagonistic is not antithetical. On the contrary, it's what will protect our consciousness. There is even a certain satisfaction in finding it on our side, as though it were a weapon rather than a banner, . . . though – yes – also a banner taken from the enemy. A banner too because it has a color, a tone that is the very same, but yet different. The seven colors combine infinitely: we know it only too well, but what a pleasure it is to be surprised by something you know only too well. How secure, how restful it is to feel what is going to be. Above all when you recall having felt – with the same certainty – what was not going to be . . . when its nonbeing was emerging. There are very few who can feel these things, but those who know what we call impotence are not few at all . . . The horrific struggle of the black beetle turned on his back, to say nothing of the turtle. Hours and even days struggling to grasp something that simply isn't within its reach. Twisting and turning, bracing itself on any grain of sand, which offers no resistance, which doesn't make things any better, which seemed like something solid for a moment but incalculable energy was expended in grabbing it and holding on: the support failed, time passed, and it stayed, feet up, on a tile floor and wasn't even stepped on by a passerby. And it spent the night like that, waving its legs without giving up the fight . . . Impotence is the most horrible thing. Yes, it's the most horrible, there's no doubt about it. But there's also another horrible thing – which is more horrible: kicking violently or not kicking at all? – a third horrible possibility: giving in without kicking. Worse than horrible: it's stupid, easy, abject, but easy. The second horrible thing – as much as or more than impotence – is knowing: with no struggle but without giving in, without resignation, without making an effort, without protesting, without hope, without . . . with certainty, conviction, feeling – that above all! With the sure sense that what never had more being than its inability to be will never exist. Can one feel what will never come to be? I can't imagine myself racking my brains like this in such a puzzle if I hadn't begun thinking that one can feel how what will be is going be. To feel, it now turns out, as if I were given a second chance, a rematch. The first time it couldn't be; the second time it will be. Exactly how it will be, I don't know, but it will be. And if it turns out that it's something very different from what one would like? No, that's impossible because the only thing that one cannot desire is that it shouldn't be . . . And from there to infinity. Isn't this the same as spending the night on your back on a tile floor? It's not completely the same because one knows that there's nothing to hang onto: you pull in your legs and wait for dawn to come.

'The poems, yes; they're very good. I liked some of them a lot, but the room! I assure you that sometimes I didn't even understand what they were saying because I was looking around that room. The gilded palms, that goddess or muse presiding at the lecturn . . . the portraits of all those learned men . . .'

'Yes, that's true. The most fantastic thing about the room is that anything said there – and they certainly said a variety of things – seems like something that could only be said there.'

'You're right, because the thing I liked so much – about the storks in the bell tower and the swallows and the pines – that was lovely; and it's as though it came to life exactly there, amid that silence.'

'The one about the storks really wasn't the best. It wasn't bad, no, but there were other things. There was one that I praised a lot and Montero smiled and called me decadent. He said he knew where all this was coming from. It's because the other night when we returned he was looking through the books. Not a thing gets by him!'

'Not only Montero. Don Manuel was looking them over too while you were putting the brioches on the sideboard. It looked to me like he was raising his eyebrows.'

'That's really strange! The books are magnificent, very impressive. It's possible that if I had heard the poem before seeing the engravings and reading the books, I wouldn't have been so impressed, because it seems like the engravings are illustrations of it. I've spent the whole night reconstructing it in my mind and I remember almost all of it.'

'You remember it? That's crazy! You only heard it once.'

'I've had the same experience with songs, walking down the street, hearing just a stanza – it's the first time I hear the tune, not just the stanza – and I never forget it.'

'If you can do that, why don't you study? Everybody's telling you all the time that you have to make a decision. And if you didn't like to, that would be one thing, but you like it a lot.'

'It's something else, something else entirely. My memory is useless when it comes to studying. My memory is something like what they call inspiration. Because, besides, what stays in my memory never sticks there all alone. For example, this stanza I'm talking about stuck in my head along with the whole street. Along with someone who was walking by and also stopped to listen. And we looked at each other as though we were promising to remember, or as though we were betting who might remember it best . . . knowing that we'd never find out who won, but we looked at one another, and I was wearing my red dress. It was very hot!'

'All right, that poem – do you remember it along with the room or . . . ?

'No, it's not in the room that I remember it. Of course, I was hearing it there but seeing it in another place. It was in that engraving, *Love amid the ruins* – do you remember that couple? The arch which sheltered them seemed like a wing. It was like they were angels, as though angels had love affairs. In the poem they weren't angels, but they were also in a place . . . It didn't say they were in it, it said they wanted to be in it. Listen: it's not description, it's not evocation, its . . .

I want a house with windows open wide
With a sleepy garden silent and sad,
To live a life full of things that died
With the vague aroma of nothing more to be had.'

'Incredible! Phenomenal! The first time you heard it!'

'Oh, I know a lot more. I've got a system for reconstructing things. Above all, you have to remember the images well, some of the rhymes: then, going over and over it, you can fill out the lines and complete them with the rhyming words. In this one, apart from the image of the ruins, there was a bit that made me think of another one of the engravings. It was by a German, I think, something like Boeklin. Two lines, most of all:

Oh, we shall love in a distant garden soon
Amid tall cypresses, silent as the tomb.

'What do you think about that? To feel like the prisoners of those cypresses. Well, this is all about the setting, but the image of the woman, as he presents her . . .

Your dress will be of soft and cream white
As pale as all our lofty dreams
And upon your brow a poem I'll write:
A crown of white chrysanthemums.'

'It's really, really lovely. And what's the name of the poet?'*

'Now that's the strange part. I can't remember! Right from the beginning I forgot it. On the way out I asked Montero and he told me. When he said it, he made sort of an evasive movement with his hand. Not quite negative, no; but like someone saying "he'll be gone with the wind." Montero is very cultured and has very good taste, but he's obsessed with something else: he lives for something else. I always feel like he's doing you a favor to listen to you, like he's coming out of some deep place. I feel like

*Gonzalo Morenas de Tejada

he's always unhappy because he can't take you there with him. But he doesn't try to, no: he seems to feel you wouldn't follow him.'

'Do you think Montero has been in love, or that maybe he might be interested in some girl?'

'I've asked myself that a lot of times and I don't know. I just don't know. He might have a lover. That's occurred to me, because he couldn't possibly have a fiancee. Could you imagine him in church with a proper young lady in a white veil!'

'We'd die laughing. But why?'

'Well, I don't know exactly. Because he isn't one of those fellows who don't like women. No, he isn't one of those. And it's not like they say of some people, that they're incapable of loving. I think it's just the opposite. You've seen how much he absolutely adores his professor. And it's clear he felt the same about Magdalena. When he talks about what that house was like you get the impression that he's talking about something far off, but not in kilometers. It's like he's going to end up saying such-and-such a century before Christ.'

'And Montero's eyes – are they blue or green?'

'I don't know. They're so wide-open, so clear. They're too clear. They're kind of a colorless shade, like certain marbles. Not like the ones with streaks of color, but like the others, the cheap ones. They're like the glass for bottles of white wine.'

'Empty.'

'Of course. The color of the bottles, not the wine.'

'But it's not just the color. It's the business of being empty, a little empty.'

'All right, I was going to ask you something; but it's probably useless. At any rate, listen. Imagine that I'm asking a question, but not asking you . . . imagine I'm asking the morning star. Do you think anyone could fall in love with Montero?'

'You might be surprised, but I've asked myself the same question. Of course, I've never asked myself as such. I've asked myself sometimes if you could fall in love with him, if you had fallen in love.'

'And what was your answer?'

'It was no. But I also asked myself why not and I also had an answer . . . Something very different from what you might imagine.'

'Come on, come on!'

'I began with the first question: yes, one could fall in love with Montero. Someone could, anyone at all, but not you. The reason why seems ridiculous: because you love him too much. We love him, I love him too. He's too close, and you always fall in love with some "Shooting Star" – another little poem you know by heart.'

'You're getting warm! Very warm!'

'You don't fall in love with the ones who more or less fall in love with you, the ones who look at you or say something to you. Do you remember that guy at the Prince Alfonso theater? You fell for him because of the hat he wore or because of the way he wore the hat.'

'No, don't get carried away: it was because of the hat itself. It was the latest style, a soft hat. That was last year, and some men are still wearing it. The crown has a split in it like the two sides were coming together in the center. Remember? And the shape it gave men's figures when combined with the cut of the jacket and those wide pants, the American kind. All that was so new, so in fashion. Well, I don't have to explain this to you, because we talked it into the ground. We don't talk about it any more, but don't think I've forgotten. I remember sometimes and I say to myself that it's not the fashion now but I recall the flair and charm it had. It was like you were being told something enchanting and you were hanging on every word, wanting it to go on.'

'I certainly do remember. You spent your whole life waiting for him to pop up, and he never ever appeared.'

'No, he didn't turn up. I only saw him once. Once, for sure, is all I actually saw he. But then I seemed to see him everywhere, but I was mistaken. It just wasn't exactly he. Do you understand? It was the hat, the air, but not he: not something quite so perfect.'

Love and friendship wrestle for space. They struggle, but without aggressivity, pushing against each other as though they were impenetrable bodies. Are they impenetrable? Are they bodies? If one insists on seeing them as concepts, they must be delimited and assigned a place. But when no one tries to see them and everyone – more or less, but everyone – concurs in experiencing them or hating them or avowing them, fearing them, hiding from them – there's concurrence here too – then they get tangled up. Not tangled, no: because two heterogeneous materials can also get tangled. It's like they grow from one another, because either of them can separate itself from the other or – on the contrary – give way to the other, transforming itself, becoming more intense or weakening, backing one another up or blocking one another, not only disputing but in essential opposition to each other's goals. The dispute, more than space, has to do with potential, really. Because if it were a question of space, it would have to do with the amount of time dedicated to each thing – one takes precedence now, the other later. No, but it's not that. It's that when love predominates, the background is blurred, the landscape loses its color . . . You can argue the exact opposite. It's common to say that love renders everything beautiful. And, very well, it makes things beautiful! But what it beautifies is precisely what is alien to it, what surrounds it, what frames it, what reflects it or receives its light. What shares in its very energy, what usurps rights for itself – what has rights by its very nature – what once vibrated in plenitude now languishes or gets smaller or withdraws with a certain courtesy, almost abnegation . . . These are categories that in this case – in the case of love, not a personal or unique case – in this case the withdrawal affects attachments and predilections which, rather than declining, are transformed in order to serve love by offering themselves . . . The notes like bouquets – rich chords, fleeting scales – so pure that no concession could stain them abandoned the marine blue, the barcarole, the serenade. They no longer suggested Mediterranean visions, but clung to dark and cloudy dramas: gloomy heroes casting away their lives like someone tearing up a hateful letter or pledging himself in a pact with the devil. A storming hurricane bending the forest's trees. But still – clinging to the notes, following their measure and rhythm, linked in accent or expression – the words still preserved their pristine Latin sonority. Musicians from the Levant linked them around dramas from the North. With clear melodies they sketched the stormy heroes, pulling them from their native mists. Latin voices too were heard – at more reasonable prices than the Germanic counterparts. The recordings with familiar trademarks twirled beneath the careful needle, emanated from the sky-blue horn in the study presided over by the rational and positivist goddess. And friendship defended its rights. With no grudges, with no jealousy, it welcomed the new melodies; it assented to the dramatic or melancholy gestures. '*Ah! non mi ridestar, o soffio dell'April.*' The soul that wants to escape shuns the seductions of life, of April. On the other hand, the soul that is now completely free, that has taken the journey of no return, caresses, licks with contemplative pleasure – '*Salve dimora, casta e pura . . .*' – the virginal body that is going to be delivered to it. And rising from the mist, helmet and armor plating shining bright – the fraternal leave-taking of the swan . . . '*Adio, adio, cigno canor.*' And the white form flees and draws away, sliding off like an ice floe of feathers, and sets out on an incalculable voyage '*Valica ancora l'amplio ocean.*' The sea where it's impossible for the shipwreck to carry you into the abyss: it carries you to the safe, the infinite kingdom of the spirits that will welcome you '*Nel santo asil, in cui non penetra lo sguardo uman.*' It all goes on singing there, surging in words and notes, until one day . . .

'But, what happened?'

'Nothing, nothing. Don't be upset. It's my father's swapping habits. He took it, but he's promised me on a stack of bibles that he'll bring a nice new one this very day.'

'You've moved the table.'

'Yes. I've put it closer to the balcony, so that I can share . . .'

'Well, it looks like things are going well. And what does your father say?'

'Nothing. He looks the other way for two reasons: first, because he doesn't think it's a bad idea. Second, because he understands that it's nothing more than an innocent game.'

'Ah, but aren't you getting beyond games?'

'Who knows? He does some strange things at times. Charming things, but it's hard to understand them.'

'Do you speak to each other in German yet?'

'No, we don't talk. He speaks Spanish perfectly. And how he writes it! But don't go thinking he writes me love letters. He writes to me on a blackboard like children have and shows it to me. One day he prints, "If you look at me." Then he erases it and writes, "I can't study." He erases that and then writes, "Go away from the balcony." I get angry, but I stay where I am. Once again he erases and writes, "I'm going to throw a stone at you." Then I get even more angry. I want to kill him with a look, but I see him hiding something behind his back in his right hand and waving at me with the other the way you shoo birds away, telling me to go inside. You can see that the balconies are face to face. I step back, and the stone falls in the middle of the room. The stone is wrapped in a paper, and there's a rose tied to it. On the paper, in his usual printed hand, "The rose couldn't reach you without the stone." Isn't that divine?'

'Well yes, he must be an amazing guy.'

'He must have already been here a long time to do something so funny and delightful.'

'I don't know. He moved in across the street a couple of months ago. Maybe three or four – in January, I think. All the balcony windows were closed, and I began to hear music. I didn't know where it was coming from, so I began to try to find out. I figured it out finally because I noticed that the music came only at the end of the afternoons. I would go down for the milk, and when I came running back up it would already have begun. So then I decided not to go up, to stay in the entrance and see who was going in across the street at just that time. Do you remember, Elena? Do you remember those short books about Nick Carter?'

'That's just what I was thinking about. You hated them.'

'You're right, and I couldn't understand why you were so crazy about them and now . . . Don't think it wasn't until now that I connected them to my spying. No, I remembered them the very day I decided how to do it. I said to myself, with good detective work I can find out, so I made a plan. It was to go down a half-hour early for the milk and then stand guard in the entrance to watch the guys who went in. I put the plan into action immediately. So as not to be fooled by appearances, I kept constantly in my head that sonata by Schubert he played every day, I kept repeating it, keeping it in my head like – I don't know: it was my tuning fork. A guy would go in and I would say to myself, "No, he doesn't sound like that." One day a rather acceptable suspect went in, and I went running upstairs. Nothing: the balcony was dark, there was no music. I stayed there waiting for about fifteen minutes, and then the light in the room went on and I heard Schubert. He's there! But, what if he came in after I ran up? What if a more likely one had come in when I wasn't there? Waiting until the next day made me desperate. Being certain that he was there in the room behind the shade, and not being able to go in! Not having a detective's I.D. so I could go in and find out . . . and with my heart in my throat . . .'

'That's it. That's what makes the whole thing attractive and exciting. Nick Carter didn't have clues like Schubert – he had other clues.'

'Exactly! The clues are what make you imagine how what you're looking for will be. Having Schubert as a sort of point of reference and not letting yourself be tric . . . hush, hush. It's my father, and he's not alone.'

This one was not blue, it was pink. The color was faded here and there as well. It became almost red in several places, a wine-colored red. The horn by itself put – or rather, sunk – on the broken bottom of the armchair while the box was installed on the table, adjusted, leveled and everything about how it worked was checked: the felt turntable where the record went round and round, the crank. Everything was checked, brushed and polished piece by piece. And the horn waiting: its trumpet form focusing, watching and hushed. More than hushed! It didn't sing or even breathe. It had neither the scent of a flower nor the breath of a trumpet. It lay there abandoned like a head that's been cut off. The air of the room went down its throat, without a throat, passed through its funnel, and there was no resonance. Finally, when the countless operations were finished, it was installed, reintegrated in its organism. It was firmly fitted and screwed together with no need for patchwork. All its brilliant joints fit together so well that you couldn't tell it was made of different pieces. It seemed like one single piece, like a flower and its plant. And then, emerging from its brand-new envelope –

made of waterproof material, intact – the new record. Held lightly by its edges, placed on the turntable. And then the extremely careful operation of inserting the needle at the perfect point, of looking with a magnifying glass to make sure there was no lint, not a single speck of dust. And then bringing it near the record cautiously, as though fearing some involuntary movement, and placing the point, finally, exactly in the first groove. Seeing it peck like a bird feeding on its ration of notes. But the notes weren't softly picked up and transformed into the voice of Philomela. They burst forth in a torrent, they shook, they vibrated wildly, too vast for the limited cubic space of the room. They irrupted like an army in disarray, rushing with all its weapons into a narrow pass: an army that could have spread over steppes. On the table the waterproof envelope, sealed with a respected trademark, with letters that give away the name of the recorded piece: *Tannhäuser*, Overture.

May lavishly anticipating the mighty blaze – scorching every blade of grass, frying the very birds in the air. the ovenlike atmosphere, the smell of overheated roof tiles and the shimmering light, the glare of the sun, high noon: all were present in the study. They didn't come like a new spring, but like an eternal, sempiternal, obstinate genius of heat, cloaked in memories. Perhaps one or another rootlet of hedge mustard might have survived by taking refuge beneath a roof tile or in the shade of a dormer which at certain hours projects to the left. Maybe it had succumbed because of its nearness to the rain gutter, which threatened to become red-hot. The end of the school year, with its predictable prizes, was coming on. The rolled-up drawings were piled in a corner, to keep them from getting hands dirty with charcoal, to get out of sight the errors, the modest achievements, that weren't disheartening, but caused discontent or maybe just impatience – the impatience that said, 'still not right.' It was necessary to face that truce which is called vacation, but to vacation in everyday spaces. The family summers are long gone: the port, the sea, Adelina's garden. To vacation at home, crossing the street, going from one corner to another ten times a day. Along with the academic year, the poetry readings at the Ateneo were over. The meeting room dozed, closed afternoons and evenings. The golden palms would barely shine in that crepuscular light. There was only one great attraction, but it was far away – there was nothing in the neighborhood! – and costly: the Prince Alfonso cinema where the stylish girls went, and the boys too, who fluctuated in their tastes. The cowboys were too juvenile; Max Linder was too top-hat . . . Those Italian beauties, irresistible, intimate, above all so near. Proximity! A proximity so certain that it's already possession. The beauty of a human being and the beauty of his or her gestures, of his or her situation, of what in real life is always far away, inaccessible at times and yet there it is so close, so caressing. Because it's the caress itself that one contemplates, near, as it never can be seen. Or else so frightening, so brutal, so ignoble – what you shrink from on the street and want to ignore or destroy. All stopped in time, exposed to everyone's consideration. And the things far off in time: the Roman chariots, the circus, the gladiators. In short, the infinitely possible – but unfortunately the cinema is a long way off, made farther because of being a luxury, the necessity of going with someone else compounding the difficulty. The final result: infrequency. Merely visiting when what you desire is to go and stay there, to stay every day with all that, with the nearness, with the possession. Salvation, unexpectedly, in the discovery of another place . . . Piedita's neighborhood was 'the end of the world!' according to her sister. However, it was, in fact, the beginning of a world waiting to be conquered, explored and possessed. It was still nothing more than a route you could travel swiftly. Walking swiftly was the safeguard of good girls' behavior. Good girls: a comic, contemptible caricature, and, at the same time, an exemplary model, an unavoidable model, which they followed without deviating an inch. They had gone over this route for months, but so quickly that they weren't even aware of the things going on under their noses. The route was divided in detail and in proportion. The first half belonged to Montero. Or rather, the first half of the second stretch, although it was Montero who had showed them how to follow the whole route in all its topographical complexity. He had laid it out for them one day on paper to show how easy it was. He had made such an elementary map that it excluded the rest of Madrid. You only had to go on until you reached that turn, change trams at the Puerta del Sol and get to the Retiro Park. He had been allowed to accompany the girls along this elementary trajectory a number of times. Although allowed is a term that always implies concession, and Montero was a man who needed no concessions. He had a right to go anywhere: he was admitted on the first floor as well as the third floor, and on the top floor where there wasn't even an apartment, he was always received with fanfare. And in the entrance, in the poultry shop and in the other house as well. Felisa too had had him listen to her barcaroles, but when they got onto the terrain of Schubert – with the concomitances it entailed – a certain chill had cut off the dialogue. You could always expect that in Montero's company there would be moments of silence or cold gusts. It always seemed like you were going to hear a door slam. Like someone had carelessly left a door open and a current of air came in, blowing out the candle – in a place where there weren't any candles. In the Retiro Park, too, one had been blown out. And the day had been radiant. May wasn't scorching yet: it was magically drawing legions of lilies from the earth. They fluttered amid their sword-like leaves – the lightness of their petals so sensitive to the air – and spread their violet color along the edges of all the paths.

Darker in the shady places but everywhere fragrant, sharing their aroma which is scarcely an aroma.

'Why don't they manufacture essence of lily, Montero? I've never seen it advertised anywhere.'

'I don't know. I suppose because it isn't strong enough; or rather, dense enough.'

'That must be because what's normally called perfume really isn't. It's like a breath or a spirit. It's the spirit of the elves, of the wood nymphs. I can smell it and I don't need to close my eyes. I see them passing above that purple gust . . .'

'Right – painted by Dante Gabriel Rosetti, no?'

'Yes, why not? I prefer Burne-Jones, but I like Rosetti a lot too.'

'Rosetti is even more spiritual . . .'

'It's not that I like the other one more because he's less spiritual. It's that I just like him more, that's all.'

'Well, if we hang around here until the discussion is finished we're not going to get to see the animals.'

'You're right, Isabel. Let's go see them. They have a breath or spirit that's very different and, by Jove! – A rather archaic interjection was needed here because there's another decadent who's taken delight in the breath or spirit of the animals.'

'Another one – as decadent as I?'

'More or less. But the heroine of the one who likes animals is more Isabel's type.'

'Who is his heroine?'

'Herodiade. Cold, untouchable. The lions looked down at her feet which could calm the seas.'

'What imagination!'

The lions, those ancient kings, dozed stretched out upon their manes, which were not very thick, as if they were going bald. There was nothing to get them caught on in their very limited exercise, but they were still pretty sparse. They abanoned themselves to their lack of care and slept with an air of neglect, yawning from time to time. They would extend their lower jaws in a mechanical movement – the effect of an apathy without weariness – and show their canine teeth – of the feline variety – almost in silence, exhaling only a rough sigh. Their breath reached you mixed with emanations of everything else they exuded, secreted or excreted. Hygienic liquids were sprinkled around the outside of the cages, but they didn't stop the fetid vapors from reaching the garden. The best they could do was form a sort of curtain, but it was . . . incomprehensible – that's the only thing it could be for the lions: incomprehensible, like something you can't experience. Depressed, they abandoned themselves to that vital perplexity. Because they didn't manage to die, they were not like the birds – the hoopoes, the hummingbirds – who can't tolerate captivity and die at once. Not the lions. They woke up from time to time, when the keeper approached. Well before he got close, when he was just coming out of the food storage area or larder carrying the bucket with the daily rations. From far off the gust that chases sleep away, that perks up wakefulness, alert, keeping a sharp lookout for what you understand from the moment it reaches your nasal passages and spreads throughout your whole body with such evidence that it's like a memory of living. Memory in the lions is like a repetition, being reinstalled in the distant, habitual function of tearing tissue apart, thirsting for blood, dominating a more fragile life which defends itself hopelessly. Living again above the cold, chopped-up ration. Living again as a convincing, mechanical affirmation, because life understands that its ends are served by this cold chunk smelling of death. The tiger is the same way, less sleepy, parading through his reedy landscape around the cage, and the black panther, staring from behind its own shadow. Only the hyena is comfortable in the stench . . . And then the small and friendly animals: the fragile flamingos, the antelope, the she-goats with their ancient beauty, submissive toward the males with their great horns, their great beards, as sculptural, as in possession of their form as archetypes, carrying out the functions entrusted to them – no more than to any other animal, but certainly with more paradigmatic rigor: they cover the females – an efficient pastoral, or rather livestock, usage which indicates the act of sheltering as well as possessing. They are academic in their copulation, which is as noble as the execution of the law. Only doves emulate them in this – divine forms – perfect, perfect, perfect. It's trivial to repeat the word, but there's no other way of dragging it out of the mud of common usage. Doves are perfect, made – made how, why? – as infinite, prehistoric secular repetitions, as dazzling, flashing, resplendent and pure as a thunderbolt. Doves with their rounded cooing, with their unanimous fluttering, are free, free to relish the food of the captives, gliding and perching on the prison of this one or that. The monkeys also enjoy a certain freedom, but to a lesser extent. They're free in a bare tree surrounded by a pit. Free, with the defect of their ugliness, naked, incapable of saying, 'I was afraid, because I was naked; and I hid myself.' Inept, ugly, obscene because they're on the verge of saying it but they can't. They can't! They can't! This is another phrase that must be repeated and repeated and repeated until it can be understood, . . . Or else it must be understood in silence before their ugliness, as an explanation of their ugliness. Finally leaving the animal house, taking a turn around the park and the flower garden and, near the exit, pointing out the Casón Portico on the other side of the street. This took up a full day; or rather, a full morning, with its light intact and not threatening to go dim. After the animals, after that difficult and always positive viewing, we had to go toward the tram, walking fast to cross the garden which was getting shady now. In an especially shady spot, 'The House of the Poor and the Rich.' More absorbing than a witch's den, more irresistible than the most promising paradise. The sick old man is stretched out on his cot, and the old woman is taking care of him. And rigidly, with a brief creaking of wood, he sits up in the bed. His eyes are fixed, without blinking, and then, immediately, he falls backward. That's the extent of his action: that's all the poor old man does. The stairs are beside the bed. Above, yellow satin covers the sofa and is pleated into two curtains, pulled back on either side of the window. A window that's like a painting hung on the wall, looking out on a path amid willows. Yellow satin also covers a tiny dressing table that has a mirror with a mahogany frame, and there are bronze wall candelabra, Empire style, and small vases of opal.

'My God! The coziness of that room is so charming. The sofa's only for two people. Imagine everything that could have happened there!'

'It was without a doubt a love nest. Duchesses, candidates for the guillotine, hid their love affairs here, disguised by the presence of the miserable slaves downstairs. The old woman would stand guard. The old man must not have been really paralytic, but if anyone came near, he would throw himself on the bed and start emitting weak, rheumatic moans. All this to serve their mistress, their lovely duchess, who would leave them the scent of her perfume as she left.'

'In this country we didn't guillotine any duchesses.'

'Right – that's the way we are!'

'I don't know whether we should be happy or sad about it. But it's not something to stop and think about now, while we're in this room, this silence, with this color . . .'

'The color of gold. Everything is golden here. The spirit, the god of gold is represented by that yellow satin.'

'Well, if that's what's represented, it's quite divine. How welcoming! How intimate!'

'Okay, let's go.'

The open door let the cold draft come in and the candles of the twilight went out. The silence was no longer the silence perceived and taken up by Elena: it was a consequence of that silence because it wanted to be something else and couldn't. It wanted to be a hostile and definitive silence, but it still had a soft, melancholy tinge. It wasn't possible to keep it aggressive. It wasn't possible, above all, to color it with a touch of harshness or disdain. On the contrary, it came out as reserve, hiding an unconfessable admiration, a certain envious feeling, maybe a bit of peevishness.

'*Alouette, gentille alouette . . .*'

'What's that?'

'A French song.'

'And how does it go? Is there any more to it?'

'Yes, a lot more, but the rest isn't so nice.'

'Is it indecent?'

'Very indecent. Frankly immoral.'

'So indecent that you shouldn't sing it?'

'The boys sing it at school; but it's immoral, violently immoral.'

With this, they had covered half the second stretch. Returning to the Puerta del Sol, changing trams and going on home in silence. Only the part of the song not sung refused to be silent; it expressed itself in the humming of five notes: 'Ta ta ta, ta ta. Ta ta ta, ta ta.' Those five notes enclosed something terribly immoral, that much was clear, but it wasn't obscene. It was something cruel, something rejected for being too much desired: something impossible, in short. Then from the corner of Fuencarral on home, in silence, along the everyday route.

Along the route known now as the way to Piedita's house, to the garden and the crane. The eagerness with which they started out made them oblivious to their trajectory. Besides, the route itself had stages which must be religiously observed. An offering of admiration – two minutes of wonder, an idealization of the present – had to be made in front of the House with the Balls. Right there, ten meters before it, was the tram stop. There they got off and were thrilled once again by the house. Its singularity was a luxury which gave it imponderable worth. Its singularity consisted in something that seemed arbitrary, but it was the arbitrariness generated by beauty, grace, whim, suggestive tenderness . . . This house, made of brick, had rounded corners that recalled fortified towers, and in them gleamed metallic green, red, and yellow balls. Christmas balls, that's all. They were incrusted there, high enough so that no contact with the urban comings and goings could threaten them, only time. And they faced time day and night, in rain, in sun, in snow. After kissing the house piously they took the street leading to Piedita's house. By some vague coincidence – you can also coincide with the imperceptible – their attention had never been drawn away from a certain building. It was a school surrounded by a large lot and an iron fence. In the center there was a tower with a sort of observatory which made you think that from time to time a school prize offered the children would be the privilege of climbing up there. Thinking about this, they always focused on the school as they walked along. Then a sort of music you couldn't quite classify – the hum of a hand organ and the ringing of small cymbals – pulled their attention to the opposite side of the street. A multicolored organ, pink and blue, with a nymph or a directing deity, baton in hand and pages on either side moving their heads at her command. There was gold in their robes, copper in the instruments. Above, in ornamental letters: PALAIS DE L'ÉLECTRICITÉ. The news, brought home like the discovery of a mother lode, inspired a number of very different responses. The most delighted was Ariadne. For her it's really a lode or vein of rest, evasion, something rescuing her from the sedentary solfeggio. A place to go! And the length of the route was its principal charm. The hot nights of June could be made bearable by long, leisurely strolls. On their way there, they were impatient to taste the delights of exulting sights – landscapes as sweet as faces, faces as inexhaustively interesting as whole worlds. On the way back, there would be a brief stroll along Velázquez Boulevard. Now that the acacia blossoms had fallen, some beer gardens had chairs and tables outside, and sitting at them were nightwalkers, ecstatic beneath the Milky Way. From these nocturnal walks came knowledge of another movie house, more modest – and, of course – cheaper: El Pardiñas. It had a canvas roof like a circus, wooden benches, but on the screen was the same splendor. The same beloved faces, the same horizons. Everything came together to make a happy summer. She could put up with the hours of work in the sweaty quiet of the studio, dripping out like a leaky faucet the elementary exercises, the beginners' scales. She could tolerate it all, waiting for the night that not even summer rains – be they light drizzle or heavy shower – could disturb. Calm and happy nights would stretch on throughout June, July . . . And not only that: these frequent escapades created between mother and daughter a certain camaraderie, a certain complicity which went beyond habitual benevolence. In this game, Ariadne was not the limitlessly benign spirit – lax, careless, blind, improvident in her mother's opinion – but an active participant in the new universe. Indentified with the girls – since her duty to accompany them could not be challenged – she created or professed with them a reticence about those secret hours. There was no reason to speak: they kept quiet about it, affecting a kind of shame about being 'regulars at the Pardiñas' – a nickname assigned them by parental scorn. Yet what the secret kept safe was the solitude, the intimacy created by the confluence of fancies, pleasures, emotions, convictions, intentions – more than simply feelings – into a whole and unanimous agreement. The cinema's magic visions, the nocturnal silence of the boulevard, the harmonious face of the world – all this infused Ariadne with a briskness that was like a liberation. The nights – increasingly shorter between the two twilight zones which marked them – offered more and more space to the daytime desert of idleness. No escape was possible; it was better to face it, give in to it, going straight to the heart of fire, taking refuge in Apollo's light. They knew the path well: it had been shown to them, that world had been disclosed to them, and it wasn't a place for sightseers. It was open to all and, besides, there was good reason to get to know it. September would come. Unlike the school on Palma Street, you didn't get into the Academy of San Fernando with a simple ten-*céntimo* stamp: an entrance exam awaited them. But that wasn't frightening: what was hard, what was difficult to bear was the rumpus it stirred up. To aspire to that purity, that loftiness. To make it her profession, to take it so seriously as to . . . It was too much! Because besides doing that, the unheard-of thing was not doing anything else, not thinking about the future, not considering the times, which were becoming more difficult every day. The storm raged, but not with the wind along a road, with dry leaves and sand. It whirled in the breeze of all the kitchen fans, lifting the sour parings from the corners, producing hurricanes of bad auguries, upsetting the ignorant mother – so trusting, so submissive, courageous and loving beyond any fear. Unleashing quarrels on the third floor and arguments on the first: probabilities, aptitudes and vocations were weighed and measured. The rumpus stayed behind in the house. Then, it was a long way, but there was a bit of shade beneath the trees and you could run along Alfonso XII, go up the stairs and enter the portico. *The Lady of Elche* alone: two horses' heads to the left. *Victory* in the central room, and around it, Apollo's people: the people of light, of truth, of purity. You had only to sit there in the chair rented by the beadle, set the drawing board on any plinth and then . . . always the cherished, pleasurable contact with the utensils: the sound of the charcoals in the box, the velvety touch on the paper, tracing, then tracing again, insisting on getting just the right line for the shoulder or belly of that Diadumens or Apoxiomeno or robust Canon or Policletes or the very tender Anadiomena. All of them surrendered, defenseless, to your eyes and, at the same time, protective of the meaning or secret that was their being so open to view. Their nakedness was the mystery. It was as though their silence were an endless explanation, as though by looking at them you could succeed in comprehending a sign, in reading a clear writing that had left a formula in twisted lines, an indisputable mandate: 'Thus is Man.' The light of midday was fading and there was almost no strength left to go on, but you didn't have the will to tear yourself away. The power of those images . . . no, those creatures, forms endowed with . . . forms that were the shape of life or perhaps life itself, and therefore its power wasn't bewitchment. It was like a pact required because there was an understanding with them. To look at them until you could see . . . until you didn't see them as volumes in plaster of Paris, until you didn't see the plaster, but only the forms. As if you'd closed your eyes and could hear only what they ordered, the obedience they demanded, feeling the compensatory mystical pleasure . . . a response, a corroborating echo rising from the depths, the final depth. Because it was as though your feet and hands, the pulsing in your chest, the stab of hunger, the soft, tense bellow or the incalculably extended stretching of limbs, came from . . . not exactly from the sexual organs, but from the rootage – that immensity which can be estimated well when looking at an elm: innumerable buried branches, tender little rootlets advancing, penetrating hard earth – and the awakening Eros spreads out . . . through the veins? Yes, through the veins too, but it penetrates, moves and shakes the diamantine realms of thought, as pity, as tenderness. An echo similar to a vow, to indissoluable nuptials . . . And all this becomes an everyday affair, something taken on and shared fraternally: the work place and the home.

'Have you noticed how from time to time Montero comes to keep an eye on our work, to check our progress? But I don't think that's the only reason he comes.'

'Yes, I've noticed. Who are the guys he goes around with?'

'You see that pale, very skinny guy and the other one who's always carrying books and packages of sandwiches? Later he goes to the Parterre to eat them: I saw him one day. Those are the regulars, the ones who really come to sketch. But sometimes others pop up, as if they just stopped in. You can tell they show up only to meet him.'

'When those guys come, the conclave gathers behind the *Lady of Elche*. I've seen this. They stay awhile talking in whispers, and right away the group dissolves.'

'This heat is so brutal that it would dissolve anyone.'

'No, not them. They don't even notice it. They belong to the world Montero comes from.'

'But I've asked Doña Laura, and she assures me he's from Zamora.'

'Well, wherever; but that air of a foreigner is something I'm sure he carries everywhere. It's not that you think he's not from here, it's that you think he's from an imaginary country: a country that doesn't exist yet.'

'Today's the plenum. I went by there around five minutes ago, making believe I was looking at a faun, and they looked extremely upset: they weren't talking in low voices, they were almost shouting.'

'Good-bye: I have to go now. Someone's waiting for me.'

'Oh, all right. Good-bye, then. See you later.'

'See you later.'

'You see? They've got something going on.'

'Politics. Could they be conspirators? Could Montero be carrying a bomb in his pocket?'

'Yes, of course he could. But that's the thing! Do you think anyone could carry a bomb in his pocket without its being noticed?'

'No, impossible. You can carry one without it being obvious, without anyone knowing what you're carrying, but it must smell. It must emanate terror.'

'So then how do you figure that at the same time, if he was always carrying a bomb and we smelled it, we're not afraid of him? Haven't we always called him our guardian angel?'

'That's true. I hadn't ever thought clearly like this about the business of a bomb. But I certainly have noted the smell of danger. It's just that I always felt that he was the one who was in danger, the one who could . . . Listen, I never thought he was going to commit suicide, but I did think he was capable of throwing himself head first into who knows what . . .'

The tram is late. It finally comes along Alcalá; it seems to be nodding. There's a slight, almost imperceptible movement from bow to stern. It's in a certain way acquiescent. It's somehow submissive to the trolley pole like a dog on a chain and, like the dog, used to its daily walk. That's the way it looks when you see it coming from some distance. Then, once inside, when you confirm that it is full, tired, injured and worn from the enormous amount of comings and goings which are its charge, its job or its orders, because it belongs to a district that comes from the East. You might call it Aurora's maidservant and not the attendant of the mournful or bloody crowds – mourning clothes and funeral flowers, or shawls and carnations – when you see it completely full, turned into a recipient for human heat that abates only briefly, thanks to a sudden benevolent gust of air when the tram starts up after a stop, and the nodding begins once again. One feels for the tram that sort of pity reserved for beasts of burden. The feeling that moves you to stroke their heads or their snouts, as though by doing so you might make them feel rewarded. Do you feel that? Who knows how much their muscles might relax thanks to the contact with a human hand – with a hand . . . or rather, with a human, a contact or current that can smooth their manes, penetrating their hides and making them tremble with the terrifying presence of what is impenetrable but, nonetheless, proximate. All this, the commonplace donkey – though very large, an ass by its inelegant caste – that can only be petted with a look when it brings us cotton-lined habituation, the soft eiderdown of hours abandoned to its automatic movement.

'Look at the newspaper that man's reading! They've killed some poor man in Sarajevo.'

'That's what they were talking about behind the *Lady of Elche*! I heard that name and it sounded atrocious. I couldn't understand a thing they were saying. Everything was mixed up. The only thing I heard clearly was that name like a shred of torn cloth.'

We are beginning a chapter of History. This means things are going to be messed up for an indefinite period of time. The dilemma is rather irritating. Are we beginning or are we ending? And what? Because even if we come to a conclusion about beginning or ending, we'll still be left with a puzzle, the thing itself. What thing? Those trumpet blasts reaching our ears from the house of that girl. What does the poor little creature know! For many those trumpet blasts are a promise, a dawn, a reveille.

They jump up, reach for their weapons and push through like an army of the future. For others they mean the end, the finish; those closest have said it. A new dilemma. Who sees more clearly – the closest or the most distant? And another enigma! What does it mean to be far or to be distant? Because here we are in this corner of the world called Spain and on top of it all we're backed into the most remote corner of this corner and we don't want to come out. And we don't want people coming and bothering us, because anything that happens – our dauntless aversion to anything happening! – might break or tear our proximity to what is not happening. That's the atrocious thing: that things should happen to what doesn't happen, to what we don't want to happen. Immobilism? No, no. It's unavoidable that things should happen and we're certain that, no matter how many things happen, what doesn't happen is nothing happening. The irritating thing is not being able to see clearly. Because it's horrible for a train to get derailed, but it's even worse if the derailment takes place in a tunnel, in the middle of the night. Of course: if you die you're dead, be it night or day, but a person who hears shouts for help and can't see where to go . . . And we're going to hear shouts for help very soon now. To go there . . . I don't know if going to help would do any good. Even if I did know, it wouldn't accomplish anything because the decision to go or not to go will be made by the most dull-witted forces and who knows where they'll end up taking us. But that's really not the question. If there's a question I could pose for myself – that I couldn't help posing for myself – it's the question of proximity. Extremely serious things are going to happen: they're already happening. The news in the papers is increasing. The headlines are becoming larger and blacker, more insistent. First it was insinuations, like diplomatic gossip: now we have news about facts and events. And the events, when they touch us – because they touch us all – is when they seem far off to us.

Because we'd like a close-up view of the seeds, the embryos, the newly-hatched chicks, the puppies – all the barely pubescent fauna of the beasts pulling the present into being. We'd like to see them, to know what they were like when the whole thing still wasn't inevitable. And so what? What about those who did see? Did their proximity do any good? Proximity bears impurities. The best things, passions, the most genuine intimacies, bear theoretical impurities. The anathemas, the judgments passed on this music – that never-ending trumpet playing seems to be coming from around the corner, but it echoes off the house across the street and focuses here with a rattling of windowpanes impossible to forget – these judgments were impure in theory. They were filled with passions, and these passions left their germs in them, but theoretically – practically because what we'd like is for the theoretical to be practical, practicable, and it wasn't. So, what was the result of all that? A ferocious dispute that will be stored away in archives, in the library stacks, in rare book collections. And in the meantime – what? In the meantime the events occur, and the others, the ones that stayed on the margin of the theoretical, who are the ones for whom the theoretical was theorized, carried on without hearing it – which is not the same as turning deaf ears to something, denying something or driving it back – they went on without hearing it because they were involved in things with a lower sound level. They were living their lives, absorbed in them. Absorbed in their own passions without taking on premonitory passions. They were dragged along by their trivial but real passions . . . Real because, powerful and peremptory, they are capable of being. That's it: *being* is what it's all about. And these people so deeply immersed in the present, *are* to such an extent, so very truly *are* that half of them are going to stop *being* before the battle is over. Only those of us who see from far off are the ones who see it purely, inconsolably. And it's not that we deplore our remoteness, no. We recognize that our position is the better one. Do we deplore the fact that our position is better? No, what we deplore is that from this better vantage point we don't do . . . But what is it that we ought to do? It's a stupid question because if there were something to do we wouldn't be filled with such anguish – even if we knew it was not possible to do anything – we wouldn't be in such a tunnel. Of course, the tunnel is nothing more than impossibility, human impotence, by day or by night. And when one has gone through it, when one has passed through the tunnel, there are only two ways out: toward bitterness – not Amargura Street, that's inside the tunnel – the bitter way out, systematic pessimism, theorized and packaged in seductive theoretical containers . . . or the way out which is not a way out. The exit taken by the person who comes out stripped of himself, which is to say that he does not come out. He has left his self inside and he comes out, not like a ghost, no, he merely comes out. What emerges is something that appears to be liberated – How ridiculous this craze for liberation is! What emerges is what is chained forever. The person who emerges is practically unconscious. Without forgetting – absolutely never! – anything except forgetting. He is no longer himself, but feels powerfully and fatally – one might say triumphantly as long as the triumph corresponds to the chain, not to the fatally enchained self, because he belongs to the least free and most liberating caste, to a caste destined fatally to theorize about and package liberation, the species . . . They're shouting the latest headlines . . . An old lame man weighed down by his burden of newspapers still has a powerful voice, that's for sure: he's silenced the trumpet blasts. Or could it be that the record has ended? Perhaps there was already silence and I didn't realize it because the trumpet blasts exceed all reality. Sometimes the simple form of something material, a geometrical form, has a voice, a meaning that is immense, immeasurable. The record turns, and the trumpet blasts, the meaning, the spirit of the trumpet blasts, shouts out with centrifugal force and fills the world. But the lame old man with the newspapers passes by and we listen to his insistent voice fading in the distance. I won't go running downstairs; they'll bring it up. His cries have told me the only thing that matters: the thing, the detestable thing is moving ahead, not falling back. No Angel of Balaam appears in its path. What magnificent tales that people has created! 'When it was a people,' someone said – any old guy, maybe like the lame newspaper vendor, he came because he was called – 'Come and damn them for me.' This was a commission! Now we'd like to stand in their path. We'd like to make someone bray like an ass to put some fear into them, to stop them in their stupid, despicable, useless, vain, humanly empty undertaking. But who can make himself heard? The tanks do not bray. They don't rear up on their hind legs in the face of a shining vision . . . We, the liberators, have excluded shining visions from the program. We've eliminated them. And we've created – I do not exclude myself, we who work only with pen and paper are not free of blame, *we* includes all those who make something, tanks, among other things – we've created everything that's happening and everything that will happen. And are we sorry? Yes. Do we detest it? No, we can't detest it. And even detesting it, we can't deny it, we can't deny ourselves to it. We hear the horrible reveille and we jump to attention, we emerge from our stupor . . . and we just cross our arms. Is this because we think it doesn't concern us? No: if we belong to the caste of liberators everything concerns us. But from the mere fact of feeling this . . . what? This drama, disorder, crime against humanity, a consequence, sediment, well-analyzed dross of humanity? Feeling it so near takes our breath away. And that's precisely why we end up feeling so far off, provincial, peninsular, that it's like being citizens of a little nest, of a geographical rag . . . The geographical notion emerges as a confinement. That is, feeling foreign because you're on the sidelines and wanting to see your alienation and to hear what the masses are saying . . . Because the crux of it is how evident geography has become. The hyperbolic expanse where the sun never set disappeared, and they brought out the broom . . . Several of them, from the above-mentioned caste. Others of us, still more provincial – unredeemed provincials – drag our little nook along with us, carry our modest burrow on our backs. We go out for a stroll and we look at the gondolas, the cathedrals, the boulevards with their cenacles, the nuclei of the present. And we don't go in, we don't enroll: we carry on with our attachment to our . . . I don't dare say, much less think 'our loves': this is too sacred a topic to be subjected to analysis. To subject it: would it be to profane it or to offer up to it the holocaust of our immortal, living reason? There you go! We can tear it to pieces: its blood – and it really does bleed – does not stain. Our loves relegated the world to second place: it was all background, dull, ornamental background, providing ambiance for the only form life really took. And we came back to our little dens as provincial as when we had ventured out, and we opted with obstinacy – or perhaps cowardice, walling ourselves inside our castles: castles are so beautiful and it's so easy to live in their shadow. Was that it? Who's to say? Maybe it was something that seemed to be modesty, simplicity. The provinces, the easily acquired professorship, the even more easily beautifiable house, since beauty is natural in a prepubescent being, since beauty flows from beauty. Everything was beautifully natural for those of us living off in a corner, savoring our memories because lived experience – things we thought we hadn't experienced – did we only think so? Maybe we were exactly right. – Lived experiences presented themselves with their own rights, established credibility, and we didn't feel like deserters, we didn't feel idle. We thought we had labored along with the four or five who had put their shoulders to the wheel – four or five names, four or five men shaken by geographic truth, assisting at the birth of the new century. Giving birth to it themselves – some of them are still kicking. And the rest, those of us who followed them, though we're no longer lads . . . Those of us who belong to the caste, to the zoological species – maybe the logical species, of our didactic logos – those of us who were born teachers: vocationally and irremissibly teachers because outside of the element we were born in, we're like fish out of water. And we twist and turn and gasp and cry for help, but we don't ask it from anyone: the only *someone* who might help us is within ourselves, but we don't know where it is, we don't know where we've left it. We're sure we haven't forgotten it or abandoned it, but, where did it end up? It's so difficult to make it out exactly that we begin to doubt its preterit existence and that thing we seek – which was unperceivable when it was actually existing – appears to our eyes like ectoplasm: it has the hardness, the materiality of the present, and it challenges us with this. It reproaches us with pitiless insults for having let it pass – it went by – when we passed through it, when we passed by – and, now that it is our past, it appears before us in clear forms, as clear and open as a polyhedron under a strong light – a polyhedron that talks, saying, 'Wake up, rouse yourself, you can grasp me now, you can manufacture something from my positive residue.' But we musn't delude ourselves. This is not the result of any effort or decision on our part: it's a kind of shame, a feeling of guilt. Not a feeling of having disobeyed or transgressed a law . . . No, it's a kind of shame about our suspicions concerning the abandoned faith . . . The embarrassment rises to consciousness at the sound of those voices on the stairway . . . The girls have come and they're going cheeping into my sister's room – the caste, the biological species thrives endlessly. The present, like a flock of hungry chicks, mouths wide open with the impudence of adolescence, stating,

'This is what we like. This is what is wonderful. This is our chosen path.' And here, far from the professor's chair – the professorship is nothing if one has not used it to give pasturage to a generation – I'm far from it here because I've changed it the way you change a job in a bank and I'm reduced to this children's school, a little girls' school – what herds will graze here? To what sucklings will they give birth? – Because the only certain thing is that they will give birth . . . And the sucklings will be nursed by the visions I saw sprout up some time back like the green seedlings of the fields. And, indeed, they sprout like vegetables in these easily fertilized fields. And what can I tell them? You can see it in their eyes, in the way they blink in admiration before an image, before a name. You can see they're in heat, in rut, because they've reached the season of genesis. They swallow everything – I don't know what elemental creature is fecundated via the mouth, as the mind is: fertile in direct proportion to hunger – but they would reject any theoretical drug that counteracted their appetite. And their appetite inspires respect. Does a teacher have the right to respect? They say it's our duty, . . . that's what they say. And what if respect is timidity or cowardice speaking with a silver tongue? What if it's indecision or confusion – not mental or sentimental: passional is the word here because confusion is the effect of struggle, of being overwhelmed – what if the indecision is inhibition, paralysis in the face of these too-tender shoots, as capricious as a weathercock, as rain with sunshine – their very nature, their vulnerability, their femininity in the final analysis. And, in any case, their youth, a remnant or sample of youth . . . But inhibition occurs – also! – in more serious cases . . . Much more serious because they affect or become part of the pedagogical or vocational environment. Because they occur like a heart palpitation – an extra beat that causes terror, is the presence of terror – that beat, though brief, is strong enough to stop what is permanent, to cut off the rhythm of what was flowing along the daily course of cooperative discussion, because it affects discourse with the student . . . It's not a question here of obscurity or confusion, but only of apprehension, fear of touching the delicate membrane of an embryo, so fragile, its formula so mysterious! If in the course of daily communication one were to suggest – hiding nothing and without misrepresentation or attenuation – the existence of another eucharist swallowed with total avidity . . . and it's discussed and not rejected because there are connections – the womb of human endeavor admits, takes in and shelters all semen, it preserves all tracks, like the zebra mare that Darwin mentions – and its products are not rejected because the paternal instinct . . . The paternal instinct is not benevolence or condescendence or accomodation: it is simply the clear evidence of paternity. The paternal instinct sees itself in everything, feels itself responsible for everything – even the first word uttered on the face of the earth . . . And with the security of an instinct, with the desire to be eternal that characterizes its shots at what it wants to be, it wants to go on overseeing, guiding or directing the words still to be pronounced and will not accept controversies that are never settled . . . because it's not clear: nothing is clear . . . We really don't know what there is we see in the embryolike thing, this outline or skeleton, or root or mass of branches that is going to grow. It must grow because it has all the ingredients, but we don't know what would happen if we pruned it . . . In the first place, who could think he had a right to prune anything? The act of sowing the seed is much more solid, more credible . . . solider than the work of those who think they're pulling weeds. Those who think that don't hesitate. The worst part is being afraid, wanting to walk on solid ground and not because of cautiousness. No, but because you long for the palpable reality you find in children of your flesh and blood. In that case, there is no question of more or less: they are, they exist. The veracity of their formulae, as far as blood goes, is evident . . . But it's the other progeny, those we all engender together from the beginning of time. Those we cannot cast aside, even though their physiognomies, their gestures, their signs might be dreadful: even though they turn out to be obscure and don't show their faces the way we might wish . . . the jawbone, perhaps. But we cannot cast them aside, although we might fear that their sign or shadow will fall upon the children of our flesh . . . No, no, no!, above all, because we're afraid that these, the undeniable ones, might one day . . . The lame news vendor is going past, shouting . . .

GERMANY DECLARES WAR ON RUSSIA

ALL-OUT MOBILIZATION IN FRANCE

The voice of human pain . . . The human voice narrating – not screaming as if in pain: informing, imposing itself as an echo of reality. But it's an impassive echo, like the wall that sends back the ball in jai alai: There's no reason to give it the name of the love-struck nymph who has been singing for centuries and has taught us to love without reward – to love Glory, for example. Glory: what does it give of love for a pawned life? Values rise and fall. There was a time when Glory's stock ran very high: its price was quoted in student songs and musical comedies – 'To surrender life eternal for vile existence now.' Yes, yes, that was its value; but the economy isn't stable: now it's another tune. The echo of reality does not sing: it informs. You know immediately, exactly and with no idealization what is happening. Without idealization, but not without ideas or ideals, quite the contrary! Distillations of secular wisdom, condensations of the mind, rush to battle with one another with the violence of ocean currents. Who can say where the maelstrom will strike? But in the meantime there is the inharmonious echo of reality modulating news, and dispatches – this is the atrocious thing: reality's voices are always dispatches, always partial, almost always partisan. They never offer the total picture in breadth, or more important, vitally important, in depth. Reality's echo arrives and informs: some understand it, others think they understand, others pay no attention, but they live it. And among these latter are created, if not myths – they are too weak in love to give shape to the conjectures they intuit – then climates, areas of darkness where the light seems to become a conspirator and takes the whole blame. These people live in the light of what they hear, passively. But not indifferently: subdued, suffering bad weather beneath a radiant sun, they experience the August solstice as though it were a cloudy day. The sky is pure indigo, but they live with darkness, under a shadow that is threatening because, since it's something far off, you can't really judge its dimensions. The only thing certain is that it could grow, but – how large? This question is the shape the shadow takes in the mind of Antonia, the cloudiness under the small skylight fried by the sun. There's a murmuring on the third floor like in the old times when the *tricoteuse* fitted out gaiters . . . The passing years have not stopped the movement of the needles that kiss affectionately like doves, beak to beak. In ages past, women without machines clothed bodies upon bodies. It would be interesting to calculate just how many stitches it took to cover with breeches and stockings masculine legs marching off to fight the Turk or to conquer the American Indian, how many it took to cover the exceptional thighs of the Italians of the Renaissance with multicolored hose, or to make the sad stockings of Don Quixote or those of 'The Count Don Peranzules with his hose of blue.' The stocking-makers knitted millions of stockings with the finest of needles and then when machines took over their production and stockings became socks or nylons, the images of the stocking-maker and the spinstress were no longer linked. Only the *tricoteuse* remained, working with a friend or a neighbor – but neighbor here is a word we use for those who remain close, dwelling under the same roof. There wouldn't have been a *tricoteuse* among the hetaerae of Sappho: there they wove a many-leveled theory known as Music. There was weaving as well in pastoral Judea, and the loom produced taut threads. Later came the interweaving of tiny loops that link with one another in chains of hooks and eyes that go from right to left and from left to right and go on hooking up with each other until they cover whole spaces to form elastic textiles that warm and protect bodies . . . This is what the women always did, while the men . . . It's in the critical moments, in the crises of human history – and this is not redundant – crises in which the human aspect of History wounds us, when we tremble for History and want to take its pulse and check its forehead for fever. These are the times when we see its real age and all its mishaps and misdemeanors come to mind, all its beauties and crimes: everything we wish had not happened, but since it did happen, compels us to try to discover *why*. The *tricoteuses* do not meditate, they chat and gossip, that's their mission. In Eulalia's room, where the green blinds are lowered to protect the potted plants – only the geranium is immune to the dry spell – the elderly neighbors are weaving from left to right and from right to left. Manolita, perhaps tending toward the right in her news. The man of science who preserved the cult of the Germany he had known: Romanticism, Idealism . . . Eulalia going along with *the poet* – a nickname, the way she said it – going along because she had no choice, because that had also been the position of the *maestro*. In that house the sacred deity had always been Liberty, the counterpoint of the Marseillaise had always been heard beneath the melody of Art . . . Among them, the cloudiness consisted of indecision, almost a suspicion, but not of themselves – defenseless, marginal. Instead, it was a scarcely articulated suspicion about how much credit to give the values stressed by the great old man, the elders . . . The green blinds did nothing to abate the clouds. And on the second floor, the one we've normally overlooked because we considered it foreign, with that dry foreignness that doesn't arouse curiosity, what is called foreign even when all its commonplaces and ins and outs are known, as well as its strict rules and regulations, which don't often cross the paths that run parallel. That is, the path of the intellectuals, the teachers, the artists, the creative scientists . . . the ones who don't follow a narrow trail, for their road spreads through the whole world. They're the ones – the people of the sword, speaking poetically – who unsheathe their arms to face the words that others have declaimed, created and enthroned . . . On that floor the clouds were extremely stormy. There were some who admired the Prussian helmet, some who hated the French invader, who had been fought and conquered not so long ago. There were some, however, who loved the lovely liberty of pleasure that came from France, and besides, it was known that Alfonso XIII was not altogether hostile to the Allies . . . On the first floor everything was harmonious, and therefore a mixture of melancholy, fear, pity and the odd vague hope. The cloudbank preserved the transparency of siesta time with the shutters half-closed and the usual persistent fly bent on breaking the luxury of silence with its buzz . . . The girls went up and down the stairs. Their cloudbank was hidden; no arguments brought it into the open. The cloud lived like a parasite in their most intimate zones, altering the tone of their behavior – the tone, not the behavior itself – giving a different tone to the very same acts. The cloud was a kind of apprehension, an antipathy to abrupt movements that could hurt . . . A fear of hurting and even a desire – like the weight of a gentle obligation – to go with some light, secret balm to heal some distant and secret wound.

'You're still mad?'

'I'm not mad.'

'No? Well, what are you, then?'

'Nothing, nothing at all.'

'What you are is a complete fool. Do you understand? A fool. You're a fool and you always were. A first-class fool!'

And the minor insult causes the eyes of Luis to look up into those other cold, hard, crystalline blue eyes. And he finds in the expression something trying to repeat the mocking grimace; but he sees in those blue eyes a very slight indication of cordiality – tenderness would be too strong a word. There's a sort of renewal, something indicating life might continue. And the banal, popular, playful insult is a word that is more than sweet: it's a deep personal contact . . . The street has its clouds, which grow darker every time the lame vendor goes by. There's an accumulation of news which is still too much of a prologue or an ntroduction to what cannot be turned back. The clouds persist at the intersection of the two streets, and Wagner thunders on vhile Schubert is hushed: the violinist went away when reveille ounded . . . On the first floor the storm gets worse because emote developments suddenly affect what is near. There's a ending which was foreseen, known to be inevitable; but its pproach provokes a useless conflict and, in the end, what had o happen carries the day. It's not a good-bye; it's a conclusion. 'he person who is true to himself goes by himself. The proessor stays, defeated not by ideas, but by events. The disciple eparts, emerging from the clouds, leaving them behind as iough the only way to challenge the storm were to take it upon imself: to become a storm, to fill himself with storm. For the rst time, his gaze was not empty: the decision that filled it ıade it seem blind, blind with decision. And after the argument, the leave-taking had to come, like a concession that is ırd to accept, but . . . Laura was looking for something deep side her soul to replace her overwhelming desire to bless him. ıe looked, but couldn't find it, and so she kissed him once on ch cheek as though he were going on a short trip to the country, apparently as if he were taking a short trip. He ran upstairs, and Antonia hugged him as well, looking for nothing. 'Good luck, my boy! God bless you!' The four went running to the entrance. A friend was waiting in a car. He threw his arms around the janitor. Then very abruptly he clutched the girls one in each arm and pulled them together in a tight hug: 'Goodbye, comrades!' Ramón embraced him effusively as he was getting into the car. The car started, and they were off. The three were left in the entrance wondering what else they could do bu go back upstairs: and in fact there was nothing else to do. Ramón had an ambiguous expression, like a man who has tossed coin without betting. Who knows what side will come up! Wh knows if some day he'll call heads or tails! Who knows? T know something, to really know it, is harder than doing tw academic years in one.

'Why would he call us comrades, when he used to wear him self out calling us decadent?'

'That's exactly why: to erase it so you don't remember him i a bad way.'

'Yes, you're right. That's the way I felt and it passed throug my head to ask him if there could be decadent comrades, but bit my tongue.'

'You were right; it would have been out of place. Decadent not, he's treated you like comrades. He's guided you towa your artistic careers.'

'You can laugh if you want, but it's really true that he's taug us a lot. More than the school where all the kids go for th high school degree. Real artists, the ones who take it serious go to the Academy.'

'No, I'm not laughing. I know very well what he thinks of yc He knows you! That's why he's held back from initiating you this business of the comrades, if you want to call it that. H never even brought the matter up, right?'

'No, absolutely never.'

'It would have been hard for him to leave you virgins, at least in regard to politics. I don't know if you still are in the other sense.'

'And what do you care!'

'I didn't say I cared. I just stated it as an assumption.'

'So, what does he think of us, if it's okay to ask?'

'Oh, that's not an easy question. It would take hours, but I might be able to synthesize.'

'Do it, do it! Let's hear the synthetic version. Sit right down on that step.'

'All right, he says – or we both say, because the two of us agree completely on this. I don't really know who came up with the dea first.'

'Out with it! Even if the two of you rated all our talents as the owest of the low.'

'It has nothing to do with talent. I said synthetic because it's otal and definitive. Consequently, we have concluded that you wo are *aesthetes*, *teats*, *teats* . . .'

'Cretin!'

'Idiot!'

'What do you mean, cretin? Do you think it's a dirty joke? There's nothing cretinous here! You haven't figured out the ncredible formula I've just handed you?'

'My lord! It was a gift? And how can we use it?'

'I could explain, but no, you wouldn't understand. To under-and something you have to have guessed it beforehand, and nce the two of you live your lives immersed in this business of sthetics, like *aes – teatlets*. Do you understand or are you com-ete idiots?'

'Well, it must be because on the whole . . . Did you under-and?'

'Not completely . . . no.'

'You don't understand because words make you afraid. You don't know how to play with them. You don't know how to play with serious things. All right, maybe you understand those serious games they play with etymologies and things like that but this is something else. It's like when you say a word and you wink a little or make a certain gesture . . . Then you see what the thing looks like when it's not all dressed up.'

'Okay, so you mean you make it vulgar.'

'No! No, I don't. I get up close to it and look at it from all sides. Do you think I'm getting too close? Do you think getting close is indecent, naughty or something dirty? That's something I can't get out of your heads. I've been silly enough to talk to you as if it were man to man.'

'Oh, my God! You're impossible to understand. You don't want us to think it's indecent, and then you say you're talking to us man to man.'

'But everything men talk about isn't indecent. First we'd have to know what is really indecent. What's vulgar is easier to understand. And my intention here was to joke about the matter, to bring out its . . . that's it: its *contours*, its *charms* . . .'

'Frankly!'

'Frankly? If you would think about it frankly you'd understand. For example, if I had said, "We've come to the conclusion that the two of you are women," you'd have found it disagreeable but not wrong. On the other hand, this other way of saying it is much more suggestive . . . You're useless! You're useless as comrades and as the other thing. That's why he didn't call you that up to the last moment, so he wouldn't have time to see that it was true.'

'He left you in charge of that, no?'

'Well, I'm the one who should be. I don't treat you with any special consideration because we're all about the same age and we're going to have to play the same games. That's how it came up.'

'What exactly came up?'

'The definition. We talked so much about what lies ahead for all of us. About what lies ahead for all of us in general and also what each one of us is going to do . . . It's not that he ever tried to bring me over to his side. He's never, ever tried it, although I can't swear that he might not have wanted to. But if somebody tells another person about a love affair he's involved in it's not so the other will get involved too. It's not a good comparison, I know. But it's the impression I always had.'

'Always? Since when? You've known him since you were five.'

'Of course, but nobody talks about their loves to a little boy of five. And it's probable that when I was five he didn't feel this particular commitment yet. No, of course, now it's all coming back. I didn't find out because he took me into his confidence. I ust began to sense that there was something going on that my ather didn't like. The same, exactly the same, as when they atch a boy with a girlfriend who's not appropriate. And then ince I was always hanging on their every word and began to nderstand what they were talking about – even before I was ive I understood them – he began to offer explanations so I vouldn't criticize his choice.'

'And you, what did you think of it?'

'Well, it didn't seem so bad to me. But the strangest part is hat I didn't find it odd that, being so close to my father and aving been trained by him since he was a boy, he would end up ith this.'

'Yes, it's odd.'

'But it's not that I didn't see the differences. I saw they were compatible, and nonetheless I wasn't surprised he ended up here he did . . . Just recently we were talking about where e're all going to end up. It came out in one of those prediction ssions we used to have. Sometimes we would talk about the o of you, and we would suppose one thing or the other. If such and such a thing were to happen, what part would the aesthetes play? What decisions would they make? What good are those *aes-teatlets*? Do you get it? Those *aes-teatlets* . . . Isn't it a cute word? Then we went on elaborating and the theories we came up with were endless.'

'Oh, how sweet!'

'We didn't think we were of so much interest.'

'You interest us because you exist. We're not the kind of people who skip a page and keep on reading. We amplified our theories one day when we came upon you drawing the Amazon It was the very day when he had decided to go off there. The news was shocking. They had invaded Belgium. The defense o Liège was the seventh. The two of you weren't aware of a thing Can you understand? What must it be like in a city, the women who must have had to shoulder rifles, without cutting anythin off like the Amazons. And the newspapers assuring us all tha Spain would remain neutral . . . Yes, yes, we'll see. You'll se whether or not you can go on not giving a damn . . .'

'But to stop not giving a damn, do we have to cut off some thing?'

'Of course! Naturally! Or don't you understand that you hav to cut off *inside your heads* whatever hinders your freedom movement? Don't you understand that this means submittir to necessity: being different people, thinking in another wa talking in another way?'

'All right, the theory has crushed us. We've got no way ou unless you give us a hand. But as smart as you are, you're stupid that . . .'

'Hush! Someone's shouting down the stairs . . .'

The cloud is hovering over all of Madrid. The sun has devour everything green, burnt everything to a crisp. The leaves clin ing to the trees turn a dusty white. The trams have a mo scratchy sound, as though they were munching sand with their wheels. One must go on, nonetheless. September has come and the entrance exam must be confronted. But the distance between the Plaza de la Independencia and El Casón has grown. There's just no way to walk it! You can't protect yourself along the right-hand sidewalk: there's not a bit of shade. You're left with no strength to walk or really talk: just enough, finally, to comment.

'I'm incredibly thirsty. How about you?'

'Yes, of course. Let's have some water. The kind you get in the earthenware jar from that Egyptian fountain is really good.'

The idea of drinking water doesn't satisfy thirst, but appeases it. It lightens the weight of the discouragement thirst can cause when you don't know how you'll ever slake it. Now the idea of water brings the memory of the spout placed down low with water gushing out like a little glass column that starts out straight and then bends, in the perfect curve dictated by its own weight, the force that conquers its consistency. It doesn't come splashing out over the edge of the spout. It comes out straight, whole in itself and falling by itself in a curve to the ground. The idea of approaching that glasslike column with your lips and feeling its drops splash over your face provides the energy to walk across the garden toward the pond which is now dominated by that horrible monument left by the rage for brickwork, marble sculptures, funereal but not solemn. The light reverberates, white, blinding, but there's a bit of shade around the fountain and the water is delicious, just cool enough to be savored indefinitely. To drink more than you need, to let it splash on your nose, slide over your eyelids. Now with your thirst slaked and your wet hair dripping down your shoulders, you can walk aimlessly through the Retiro, leaving the broad walkways and strolling through shady places filled with turtledoves and their calls or sobs. Their call is a loving, enveloping sound. The faithful turtledove holds her lover with a cooing like a spider's web. The captious moaning fills the air and spreads like a fog of sadness. Nearby there's the hint of a meadow. The lawn is green on a short incline going down toward the water. There's a small pond; or rather the broadening of a brook which gives a half-turn, forming a sort of peninsula. Something else there has stayed green, perhaps thanks to the care of some guard. The hose coiled next to the faucet works every day, you can see that. At the end of the peninsula, almost at the edge of the water, there's a statue.

'What could this be? There's nothing written and you can't see the signature of any sculptor.'

'You wouldn't be able to see the signature from here, but o the pedestal there must be some indication of what it's suppose to represent. What ancient figure could it be?'

'I don't think it's of anyone in real life or from mythology. It' the representation of something like a feeling, something big. think it represents Tragedy.'

'Exactly! Look at the right hand and the way it holds the robe Look how it holds it, with what energy.'

'And the other hand moving toward her brow. It's exactly th gesture of somebody *tearing her hair out*. That's the only way t say it. It couldn't be more clear.'

'The slight inclination of the head, as though she were look ing at something that fell in the pond: she's crying for some thing fallen, something lost.'

'And what about the fact that the robe is tied at the waist a the torso is naked? I don't know exactly what sort of dress tha meant to represent.'

'It's not a question of dress. She's like that with her brea bared so you can see her suffering more than just in her fac She's weeping with her whole body. It looks as though her titti will fall off from all that weeping.'

'Ah, you've picked it up! So Ramón won't accuse you of being prudish. What we're going to have to listen to! That's a comrade who doesn't mince words. What a difference between him nd Montero!'

'But Montero is kind of prissy. Remember the day I decided ɔ call him Máximo? And he got furious, saying he couldn't ɔlerate his first name because it was an exaggeration. And then Don Manuel chimed in, adding, "It doesn't suit an anchorite aint like you." He was miffed!'

'Because it's true. You can tell that, more than being a wellrought-up young man, he's a boy who went to church with his .om. It's just that later on he took it into his head to . . . It all has do with books; but in him it seems to be a passion. Ramón is the right track.'

'That guy doesn't let books go to his head. With him everying is mathematical, even though he doesn't deal with numrs.'

'All right, and how do you feel about what they think of us?'

'And how do *you* feel about what we think of ourselves?'

It seems to me that we have to settle down and think about eir theory that we're going to have to cut off quite a few ngs . . . That was what he meant when he told us. As they say out slander: "Slander, there must be something to it." Bease slander passes from one person to the next and you never ɔw to what extent it's true. With this famous theory of theirs 're left with the same question: how much of it is true?'

Γhat's it – that's what we've got to figure out.'

ey thought and thought, but didn't figure it out as the aftern waned. They spent a long time in silence – but not time ugh, not years enough to get any answers. When nothing ained visible except the statue in its violent pose, its hand in air as if wanting to tear its hair out, they went home.

Other volumes in the European Women Writers Series include:

Artemisia
By Anna Banti
Translated by Shirley D'Ardia Caracciolo

Bitter Healing: German Women Writers from 1700 to 1830
An Anthology
Edited by Jeannine Blackwell and Susanne Zantop

The Book of Promethea
By Hélène Cixous
Translated by Betsy Wing

Maria Zef
By Paola Drigo
Translated by Blossom Steinberg Kirschenbaum

Woman to Woman
By Marguerite Duras and Xavière Gauthier
Translated by Katherine A. Jensen

Hitchhiking
Twelve German Tales
By Gabriele Eckart
Translated by Wayne Kvam

The Tongue Snatchers
By Claudine Herrmann
Translated by Nancy Kline

Mother Death
By Jeanne Hyvrard
Translated by Laurie Edson

The House of Childhood
By Marie Luise Kaschnitz
Translated by Anni Whissen

The Panther Woman: Five Tales from the Cassette Recorder
By Sarah Kirsch
Translated by Marion Faber

On Our Own Behalf
Women's Tales from Catalonia
Edited by Kathleen McNerney

Absent Love: A Chronicle
By Rosa Montero
Translated by Cristina de la Torre and Diana Glad

The Delta Function
By Rosa Montero
Translated by Kari A. Easton and Yolanda Molina Gavilan

Music from a Blue Well
By Torborg Nedreaas
Translated by Bibbi Lee

Nothing Grows by Moonlight
By Torborg Nedreaas
Translated by Bibbi Lee

Why Is There Salt in the Sea?
By Brigitte Schwaiger
Translated by Sieglinde Lug

The Same Sea As Every Summer
By Esther Tusquets
Translated by Margaret E. W. Jones